Avila Beach, California, mid '60s.

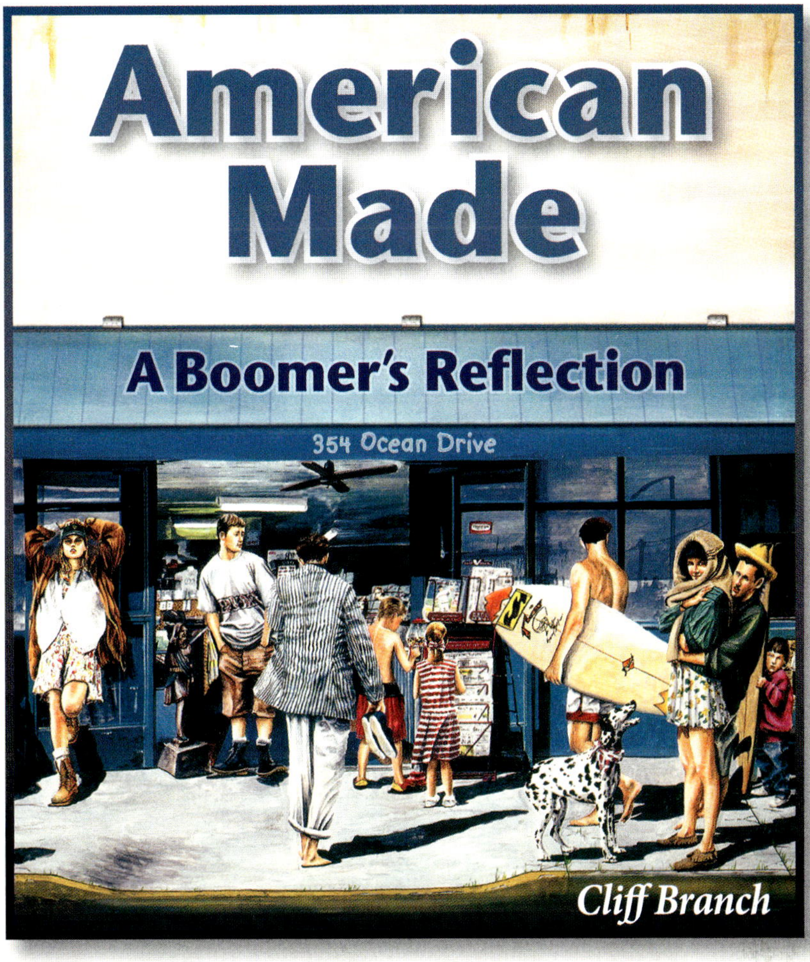

Annie's Publishing
Berne, Indiana
AmericanMadeStory.com

Published by Annie's
Berne, Indiana
AmericanMadeStory.com

ISBN: 978-1-57367-734-9

Design and Production
Ashala Lawler and Brian P. Lawler

Editing
Nels and Vicki Hanson

Image Acquisition and Assembly
Terry J. San Filippo

Production and Editorial Assistance
Tyler Jenkins

Cover Illustration
Gene Francis

Photo and Art Credits... page 378

Wine Country, San Luis Obispo County, California

Author's Note

For the better part of a year, I made it a practice to sneak out of bed in the middle of the night. I'd head upstairs to my study and work on this book. When morning came, I'd hear a sweet voice calling me from downstairs:

"Where's my husband?"

I spent nearly all my spare time at the keyboard, so I need to thank Lynette, my wife, for her patience and support. Many other people helped – and I owe them much gratitude. It's a long list and their names are included on page 378.

The original version of this book was printed and sent to my family, friends and longtime business associates. Subsequently, an offer was made to publish the book, so I made some minor updates to my original version and added a few pages.

The title *American Made* simply reflects who I am: born and raised in the U.S.A.

As the author, I am solely responsible for the contents of this book. You will find no solutions or guarantees offered herein, except a promise from me that I've danced my chubby fingers across the keyboard in good faith. I am not an "author" by trade, and I plan on keeping my day job.

Manufactured in the United States of America

California

I grew up on the Central Coast of California, and most of the stories in this book take place in this area.

Outside the Palm Theater, downtown San Luis Obispo

Contents

The author at work in his study

A Boomer's Reflection

In my mind's eye, the memory was remarkably clear.

It was my first deal and it was fun.

Easy money.

It was 1965. I was 16, cocky, and on a mission. I sat at a polished wood table in a secure room at Santa Barbara Bank.

A 12-year-old kid from my neighborhood, who could be described as my "first employee," sat at the other end of the table. He was busy with a machine that repacked coins into green paper rolls. I had a sizable pile of pure silver half-dollars to my right, and to my left a smaller heap with traces of copper at the coins' milled edges. I took the razor blade and carefully slit the length of a fresh roll. I pried back the paper and scanned the four-inch column of stacked coins. The all-silver ones were still running about two-thirds to the roll. Cool.

My young accomplice looked up from his work at the coin machine. "Man," he said with a grin, "you're going to be rich!" I remembered laughing at the kid's naïve remark, but in a way he was right. I had just discovered "the art of the deal" and had more than doubled my money in two months. Pure silver coins were running 13% over face value. I had the sense that I was running full throttle and *going places.*

My eyes snapped open as I was jerked back to the present. It was 2014 and I was seated in a medical clinic waiting room, surrounded by old people.

The receptionist was calling another patient's name. The silver coin deal had happened nearly 50 years ago, in a more innocent time when I believed the world was my oyster.

I was minutes away from a consultation with my doctor to discuss the results of a recent biopsy, and was awash with melancholy. I sensed that life, as I knew it, might be about to take a serious turn. Previous worries and triumphs were of little consequence.

I was nervous about my appointment, but at 65 I had developed a modicum of patience and waited quietly for my summons to the examining room. The table in front of me was piled with magazines, but all the best ones were in the hands of other patients. I picked up a copy of *AARP* magazine and read an article about the various medical tests recommended for people over 60, skimming past the full-page advertisements showing attractive older men and women.

Another senior magazine featured an article titled: "*Sex in the Golden Years.*"

I tossed it back on the table.

It was not an accident that I was positioned right next to my teacher, Mrs. Peterson. She had her hand held tight to the back of my shirt to keep me from moving.

Stories From My Youth

1955

When I started school in the mid-1950s, educators labeled a kid like me "a problem child."

Throughout my early years, the school authorities said I was hyperactive, incessantly inquisitive, yet easily bored. In the early '60s, my mother was counseled to put me on daily doses of a new drug called Ritalin, but she declined to medicate her growing boy with a relatively unknown psychoactive drug.

The principal of my first school urged my mother to transfer me to another school – *before* I had even finished first grade. My mother, bless her heart, found another school more suitable for my feisty personality, and I fared much better. But I would never call any of my youngest years smooth sailing.

My First Trip to New York

WHEN I was 5 years old, our family took an airplane to the East Coast to visit my grandparents. My middle brother, Greg, was 8, and my oldest brother, Tony, was 13.

The trip to our grandparents' house was to celebrate our great-grandmother's 100th birthday. My grandfather, a serious and conservative man, was the president of a large engineering firm. We stayed at his elegant home on Long Island during our visit.

In later years, my mother told me that the experience of my first airplane flight, coupled with the sights and sounds of New York City, lit me up like a sparkler on the Fourth of July. She said that all five of my senses seemed to be on overload, and she felt as if she were trying to contain a baby chimp that had consumed a big cup of coffee. My dad agreed with my mom's description – by the end of the visit my grandfather was so taken aback by my level of energy and brazen behavior that he had come to the conclusion that my parents were raising a little West Coast hooligan.

The first night on Long Island, when it was my bedtime, I refused to leave the living room where the adults were gathered. I would not comply with any coaxing, so my mother finally grabbed me tightly around the waist to haul me upstairs. At the first or second step,

Circa 1954

My grandparents' new Chris Craft, *Vagary III*, with my grandfather wearing his commodore's cap

A photo from my granddad's biography, taken during his younger days at Stone & Webster Engineering

My grandparents, Russell and Leila Branch in later years, at their home on Long Island

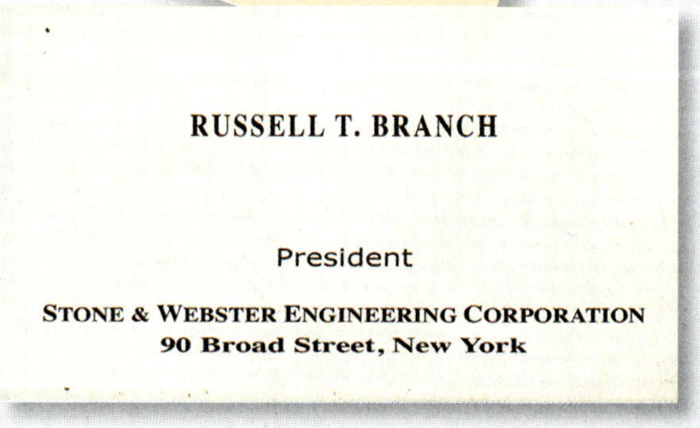
RUSSELL T. BRANCH

President

STONE & WEBSTER ENGINEERING CORPORATION
90 Broad Street, New York

I latched onto one of the rails, and when she tried to pull me loose the heavy end-post gave way and the banister cracked and tumbled down. I jumped from her arms and ran through the crowd of seated adults into the dining room.

When my dad caught me, I threw a tantrum and screamed bloody murder all the way up the stairs – passing my grandfather, who was inspecting the ruined banister in disbelief.

With older brother Greg during our first visit to New York City (1954), at the top of the Empire State Building

The second night my parents took us boys out to dinner to give my grandparents a break, and my dad drove my grandfather's new Cadillac. I fell asleep in the back seat on the way home and left a sizable puddle of urine in the cloth upholstery. My dad stayed up half the night trying to clean and dry the scene of my accident, but the next morning when my grandfather got behind the wheel his first comment was, "Which one of the grandchildren pissed in my car?"

On the third day, the entire gathered family went out on my grandfather's boat. During the cruise, while my grandfather was piloting the vessel, I snatched his Manhasset Bay Yacht Club commodore's cap off his head. I placed his cherished hat on my head and made my escape, but the cap immediately blew overboard into Long Island Sound. It was not recovered.

A few days later I sneaked down into the basement (which was off limits) and managed to knock over a large bottle containing a wooden model ship that was sitting on my grandfather's workbench.

My mother reminisced about how well Greg and Tony had behaved, and how she felt that they had been her saving grace. She had known that my grandfather was extremely perplexed by my behavior, so she took him aside before we left and explained that my hyperactivity was just a phase I would soon outgrow. She promised that on the next visit I would be settled down, more like my older brothers.

My mom, mid-1940s

She was relieved to find my grandfather understanding – he gave her a hug and told her not to worry. ■

Note: Some story details for *The Early Years* came from my parents and older brothers.

1953

Parents Russell and Betty and the boys

Opposite: Our prized record player played a stack of 45s. We liked Elvis, my parents liked Frank Sinatra.

put me on high alert. Frightened, I stood on tiptoes and made out a faint twinkle of headlights off in the distance. I hurried in that direction, determined to save myself.

I finally made it to a dirt road and waited. A car approached and I hailed it by jumping up and down and waving my arms. The big white Chrysler convertible pulled to a stop and I explained to the middle-aged couple inside what had happened. They told me to get in and soon I was riding in the back seat next to an ice chest. As we drove back to the trailer camp, the woman gave me a cold Coca-Cola. I gulped it down and asked if I could have another. She said yes and when I reached into the chest I spied a Baby Ruth bar. I looked up at the lady for approval – she nodded that it was all mine.

I was standing tall in the back seat, feeling like some sort of hero on my way home. I had no idea that my parents and the local police had already formed a sizable search party. There were flashing red lights, dogs barking, and a large group of people milling around as we pulled into the campground. Then I spotted my mom and shouted to her. She heard my voice, screamed hysterically, and with outstretched arms ran toward my rescuers' car.

Everything got quiet for a moment, until everyone realized that I had been found and was safe, and then the crowd cheered. What I remember most was the terrified look on my mom's face, which was a bright red color. She couldn't stop crying. My dad was overjoyed to see me and kept hugging my mom, hugging me and thanking everyone.

The next day my parents sat me down for a conversation, but I don't recall what they said. My mother's face was still very sunburned from her search for me, but she was calm. I understood that my parents had suffered by my actions, and for the rest of the trip I hugged them often and reveled in their embrace. ■

Las Vegas, mid-1950s

Las Vegas Strip, 1950s

I took this class photo in 1962 – Larry Leslie is circled.

The Vice Principal Comes Calling Again

THE Carmel School District had just completed a brand-new junior high school, not far from Highway 1 and Carmel Valley Road. It featured a new Pepsi machine outside the cafeteria. You put a dime in the chrome slot and a paper cup dropped down onto an open shelf and filled with Pepsi. The soda was always ice cold and it was fun to watch the machine operate, pouring Pepsi into the empty cup and then stopping just before it overflowed.

The Pepsi machine was a popular gathering place for a clique of fashionably dressed girls to gather – sort of like a "cool girls' club."

One day, Larry and I saw a man in a Pepsi uniform open up the machine and we got a brainy idea.

In shop class we made a curved, bendable rod with a sharp tip that we could angle up inside the Pepsi machine, under and then through the bottoms of the stacked paper cups.

We waited until the vending machine was deserted. The homemade rod worked perfectly and I could feel its sharpened point pierce all

Carmel Junior High School, 1963

This story includes photos from the old Sunset School in Carmel and from the brand-new Carmel Jr. High, which was constructed at the mouth of Carmel Valley in 1963.

Typing classes on new machines: My handwriting was so poor that my mother insisted I take the class. The yearbook caption read: "Students learned to type correctly and efficiently."

The yearbook read: "Cooking and sewing were important for young homemakers in Home Economics. The girls made cakes and pies and aprons and skirts, and were graded on their sewing."

the waxy cups. We stood back to wait for the machine's favorite thirsty customers.

Two girls screamed when they saw Pepsi dribbling onto their cute outfits and perfect tennis shoes. They hurried away in a huff to the restroom to repair the damage. We stuck around, anticipating our next victim, but when a woman teacher walked up to buy a cold drink we made ourselves scarce.

Cliff and Larry, 1963

The next day the vice principal came into my English class and motioned for me to follow him. I figured someone had seen us fiddling with the machine and squealed.

The Pepsi incident caused my *second* suspension from ninth grade.

My first suspension also stemmed from the misuse of a vending machine. Larry and I had stolen dead mice from biology class and stuck them into the slots where ice cream sandwiches were dispensed. Each sandwich had its own compartment and like freight cars they moved on a track to a sliding door you lifted to get your ice cream. Larry and I put in our coins and quickly removed our sandwiches, replacing them with dead mice before the track moved on.

The mice were already dead and we didn't see that we'd done any real harm – we'd only intended to leave a surprise for the vending machine man.

The dead little rodents spent a frozen night inside the machine, but appeared again the next day when a girl put in her dime, lifted the door, and pulled out a frozen mouse instead of an ice cream sandwich.

The girl screamed. Her parents called the school.

I had made the mistake of bragging about our prank to some of my friends. Larry had stayed quiet and so when the investigation started I took the rap. Again, we hadn't meant to hurt anyone, but the practical joke turned into a big deal.

I didn't know it at the time, but I was falling into a pattern, and it would be several years before I finally managed to accumulate a reasonable dose of common sense. ■

Life With Motorcycles and My First Time in Court

AT 14 my life revolved around motorcycles. I'd started out on mini-bikes at 11, but quickly worked my way up to a BSA 250 dirt bike with a shiny chrome gas tank. My brother Greg rode an Ariel 500 Red Hunter.

When I saw *The Great Escape* in 1963 and watched Steve McQueen trying to get away from those Nazis – roaring up steep hills and trying to jump his Triumph T6 over several barbed-wire barricades at the Swiss/German border – that was it. Motorcycles became my passion.

My dad had owned motorcycles in his younger years. We'd heard his interesting stories about his Vincent motorcycle and his Ariel Square Four. But he also told us how dangerous they were, and that he finally stopped riding after his first son was born, when his father bribed him with a new typewriter to keep him from buying another motorcycle.

When Greg turned 15 he wanted a street motorcycle but Dad said no. Greg went off for his second season working at Tassajara Hot Springs. By the end of the summer when he returned home, I had somehow convinced my dad to buy two dirt bikes so he and I could trail ride together. Greg was incredulous, but Dad offered to buy him a dirt bike too, and soon the whole family got into motorcycles – even my mom had a Honda 50.

DUCATI, 1964

We kept the bikes in a separate garage and workshop, because we ended up buying several more: a BSA, a JAWA, a Harley-Davidson and a BMW. We lived near Farm Center at that time (mid-Carmel Valley), and a neighbor with a tractor scraped a small dirt track for me in the open field next to our house, where I practiced every day.

I had heard there was a motocross race track not far from Salinas, run by the Salinas Ramblers Motorcycle Club, so I joined. I regularly attended the meetings at the Harley dealer showroom in Salinas. The club had two defined groups: the Harley road guys and the dirt bike riders.

By then, I had a new Ducati 250 Scrambler, which I thought was "totally bitchin'" – except it had a weirdly shaped gas tank that smashed my privates every time I crashed. I spent some time motocross racing at the club track in Prunedale, but in later years I stuck with enduro events – timed motorcycle contests held outdoors – because I knew that I wasn't brave enough to win at motocross. The fearless riders from Salinas raced by a perverse mantra: "If you're not crashing, you ain't going fast."

At some point I came to the not-so-bright conclusion that it would be cool to show up on my dirt bike at a Rambler Club meeting in Salinas. I took off on Carmel Valley Road, heading toward the Las Laureles Grade, but just a few miles from my house a CHP pulled up behind me and turned on the red light.

Mom didn't leave any photos of Greg, Dad or me on any of our motorcycles from the early years, but there was this photo of Mom on her Honda 50 taken around 1963.

The officer had probably noticed that my dirt bike had no stoplight and no license plate. I told him that I was "just testing the bike," and confessed that I was too young to have a driver's license. I explained that I lived just down the road. He was not impressed. I received the first of my many tickets and the officer escorted me home.

I had to go to court in Monterey with my dad. My father explained to the judge that I was mature for my age and a good rider, and assured him that I wouldn't ride on a public road again until I was older and had my license. Dad made the mistake of downplaying the incident in terms of "Boys will be boys," implying that the whole thing was not that big a deal.

HARLEY, 1963

The judge was neither swayed nor sympathetic and gave my dad a loud and stern lecture. It was the first and only time that I heard someone dress down my father, and I felt awful for putting him in that position.

But the embarrassment of court wore off soon enough. Greg and I managed to convince my dad to let us ride street motorcycles when we were old enough to ride them legally.

At 15½, I began riding a Harley Sportster to Carmel High School, often hitting 85 miles per hour on Walter's Straight. The only reason I didn't go faster was that the bike had questionable suspension and lousy brakes, and over 85 it never felt safe. *[See page 329]* ■

Grand Central Station and Times Square, mid-'60s

1964: Missing the Midnight Train

I blame it all on my cousin, Christopher Nichols.

In an excited long-distance phone call, Chris had promised that together we would "check out the City."

It was l964 and I was a California teenage boy headed to the East Coast, where I'd be playing on my cousin's home turf of Huntington, Long Island. Chris said we'd take a 30-mile train ride to the legendary Big Apple, where it was all happening – where we might even see a "real hooker" walking down the street.

The week before my family boarded the airplane, I overheard my mother discussing New York City and saying that "after dark, Times Square turns into a seedy place full of weirdos." Of course her comment only increased my interest.

And just days before we left, when I told my best friend, Larry Leslie, about the trip, his eyes lit up. "I've read there're strip clubs all over New York City!" he said. Larry suggested that maybe my cousin and I could "sneak our way in" – and report back all the details of what we saw.

After I'd been staying at the Nichols house for a couple of days, Chris suggested we should make our break and explore Times Square. He promised it would be totally cool. We even joked about the possibility of trying to buy a beer with fake IDs at some cheap bar.

I was curious, eager and unafraid.

• • •

On my third day on Long Island, everything was set. We told Chris' father (my uncle) we were headed off to watch a double-feature movie and would be home late.

It was a Saturday night, without adult supervision. Two gleeful cousins caught a 7 p.m. ride on the Long Island Railroad.

Of course our secret destination was Grand Central Station, and when we got there we headed straight for Times Square.

The place was buzzing – taxies everywhere, honking, and giant flashing neon signs. Times Square was overflowing with strange and interesting people, including long-haired hippies banging on bongos or playing guitars, and many older men in ragged clothes who Chris referred to as "winos."

One block smelled of fresh popcorn, but there were plenty of sidewalks that reeked of urine. Hustlers tried to sell us drugs and other stuff, some of it legal. We were two cool cats looking for adventure.

We wandered for hours, looking at a thousand passing faces and into every store window. We didn't have the guts to walk into a bar, and we got stared down by a bouncer outside a strip club before we were within 10 feet of the entrance.

Chris and I did manage to spend a lot of money on hamburgers, milk shakes and souvenirs. I also bought a "nudie magazine" from a guy on the street.

We discovered a pawn shop with a switchblade knife, and a magic store where I scored a magic eight ball that answered any question you asked.

Before we knew it, it was near midnight, and it began to get *weird* on the streets.

We ran the half-mile back to Grand Central Station to catch the last train home and arrived out of breath, just in time to see the final car leaving the station. We were exhausted and out of money. And – reality sank in – *we were screwed.*

The station was deserted, except for a couple of janitors sweeping up the trash and a few bums who had parked on benches. So the two cousins from opposite ends of the country claimed their own bench inside the cavernous place, lamenting their bad luck.

We did not *dare* call Chris' parents collect. The only thing we figured we could do was stay put, our adolescent brains calculating: *Well, we'll just stay here all night and catch the 6 a.m. train home, sneak in, and they'll never know anything happened.*

As some point, we nodded off on the bench, leaning on each other dead asleep.

And then we were suddenly awake.

A police officer was tapping us on the shoulders with his baton.

"Boys, there is no sleeping in Grand Central Station," he said.

"Yes, sir!" we said and sat up straight, eyes wide open.

But we fell asleep again around 2 a.m.

There were more baton taps on our shoulders – same policeman, same baton.

"What are you boys still doing here?"

At this point we felt desperate, so we told him our true story.

He listened carefully, then asked us our names and ages – then *our parents' names*, and *their telephone numbers.*

1964

Next thing we know, he's on his radio talking to another policeman and a minute after that we're following him like scared puppies to the station.

It was now around 3 a.m. and Chris and I sat on another bench, this time in the station house. An older police officer informed us that Chris' father had been called and he would be driving into the city to pick us up – it probably would be an hour before he arrived.

Uncle Nick, circa 1964

Chris and I looked at each other with the understanding that our world, as we knew it, might soon come to an end. We had *lied* to his father, who had now been awakened in the middle of the night with the news that his son and his nephew were in "police custody," in a city and place that we knew were strictly *off limits.*

We imagined that the call from the police was not exactly well received, and we also knew that the long drive into New York City would give his father plenty of time to plan our demise.

When Uncle Nick arrived at the police station, he thanked the officers for taking us under their wing. Chris and I did not say much on the drive home.

Uncle Nick broke the silence. "You boys really crossed the line," he said, "and there will be consequences. We will talk about your punishment in the morning."

There was a long pause, and then Uncle Nick went on, in a friendlier tone: "Well, tell me about Times Square – what did you boys see, and what did you do?"

"Not much," Chris mumbled. "We just walked around and ate a hamburger. We tried to make the train on time, but we think it left the station early."

After all these years, I'm not sure exactly what punishment Chris received, but I know that I escaped back to California with my magic eight ball safely tucked in my pocket. I had ditched the nudie magazine earlier.

My parents never mentioned a word about the incident, so I assume Uncle Nick decided that (*considering I was their guest)* it was best to let my role in the Times Square adventure slide under the radar. ■

Huntington, Long Island

1967: Serious Trouble

IN THE summer of 1967 my family traveled to the East Coast again for an important celebration – my grandparents' 50th wedding anniversary.

Unfortunately, I didn't know my grandparents very well. They came out occasionally to visit us in California, and we'd visited them on Long Island from time to time, but that was it. There was not much contact and I never grew close to either of them, although my grandfather made quite an impression on me.

My grandfather was always larger than life, the president and then chairman of Stone & Webster, which at that time was the largest engineering and construction company in the world. Its headquarters were in New York City.

Stone & Webster built projects around the nation, including many facilities at Oakridge, Tennessee, as part of the top-secret Manhattan Project. At one point during World War II, there were 800 engineers, draftsmen and technical workers on the Stone & Webster payroll.

My dad told us that after the war my grandfather confided that he had known about the construction of the atomic bomb long before it was public knowledge, but of course he never said anything.

I once heard my grandmother say to my mom, "My husband was always gone during the war and I had no idea what he was actually doing. I only knew that the company had construction projects in other states for the war department, which he said he had to oversee. I found out about the atomic bomb like everyone else, when the news about Hiroshima came on the radio." [See page 367]

My grandparents' golden anniversary was a formal affair, and was held at my Uncle Nick's impressive house in Huntington, on the north shore of Long Island. Uncle Nick commuted on weekdays into Manhattan, where he worked as a vice president for Mobil Oil.

My grandmother's brother, Foster McGaw, also attended the anniversary party. Like my grandfather and my uncle, he was a bigwig, the founder and chairman of the American Hospital Supply Corporation. Foster had no children, but he had two wonderful sisters: Aunt Frances and Aunt Agatha, who both lived on Martha's Vineyard. Neither Aunt Fran nor Aunt Aggie ever married. I was particularly fond of Aunt Aggie, who was a schoolteacher. She was funny, warm and smart and had stayed with us several times in California. It was great to see her again at the party.

In fact, the entire extended Branch family clan had traveled to Long Island from all over the country, as had many of my grandparents' friends and my grandfather's business associates. I remember being impressed by a couple of black limousines parked behind the house.

From joy ride to jail

My cousins and I were all dressed up for the anniversary party and bored stiff. Cousin Chris had just turned 16. Chris' buddy, who lived across the street from Chris, suggested that we take the Nicholses' Buick convertible for a ride.

Chris got behind the wheel. I don't think anyone at the party realized we were leaving.

We drove down to the beach and stood on the shore, picking up stones and skipping them across the water. For some reason, we began filling a bucket with some nice smooth rocks and put the bucket on the convertible's back seat. We started to drive around again, and next thing I knew everyone was throwing rocks.

We tried to hit the mailboxes along the road as we zoomed by, and suddenly rock throwing seemed like a great new sport.

Soon we entered downtown Huntington, an affluent community that reminded me of an East Coast Carmel. We were cruising the main street when things turned weird.

We were throwing rocks at a street sign, when one stone sailed too high and smashed the plate-glass window of the Huntington Bank. Alarms went off. We panicked and sped off, racing several blocks before pulling off the main street to wait out of sight. Then one of us shouted, "Let's put the top up, so no one will recognize us!"

We all jumped out of the car and started lifting the Buick's canvas roof when all hell broke loose. Only five minutes ago the bank window had shattered, but now cop cars were all over us, lights flashing. It seemed like they just appeared out of nowhere.

The cops jumped out, guns drawn, and shouted, "Get down on the ground!"

We were searched and then loaded into police cars and taken to the local jail, where we were locked into a single cell, except for Chris. Chris was taken down the hall. We were told not to talk in the cell and so we waited and none of us said a word. Then I saw my Uncle Nick heading up the hallway with a police officer. They walked by, glancing at us through the bars.

My uncle disappeared for about 15 minutes, then returned and told us we were being released and to get into his car. He was furious. I don't remember his exact words, but in the car he expressed his bewilderment and anger. He used a few cuss words, none of us made a peep, and then came this growl, spitting through his teeth: "We are all going back to your grandparents' party. You are not to speak a word about this to anyone tonight, or tomorrow. If any of you nitwits spoils your grandparents' anniversary, he'll regret it. Tomorrow I'll speak to each of you individually. When we get back to the party, you'll split up and stay with your own family. I expect you to act like gentlemen."

As the new kid at a big school, I was more subdued in my behavior and my classmates perceived me as a very different person than my Carmel friends had known. I had no history with anyone in Santa Barbara. It was as if I had secretly red-shirted 10th grade and got to play a second season as a sophomore. I quickly discovered that the other students and even my teachers thought I was one of the smarter kids in my class.

Varsity baseball, 1968

I was also the oldest boy on the sophomore baseball team (a big advantage) and by doing my homework I was now getting A's and B's. I also became one of the class leaders.

After my successful year at San Marcos, we moved into a new home closer to UCSB and I enrolled at Dos Pueblos High, which had just been constructed – a freshly built high school where I continued to excel.

New roles at the new school

At Dos Pueblos, I was elected student body president, played first string on the varsity baseball team, made the honor roll and drove a late-model Chevy Malibu coupe. My hyperactive nature also allowed me to take up acting as one of the leads in our school play, *You Can't Take It With You.*

All things considered, my mom's guidance worked out pretty well, but that's not to say it was all easy going. I still managed to irritate Mr. Nordenson, the vice principal in charge of student government – twice.

The first problem came during my campaign for student body president.

All of the students in the school were in attendance to hear the candidates' pre-election speeches. On the stage the other would-be presidents stood like statues behind the podium as they addressed the audience. When my turn came, I grabbed the microphone and walked to the very edge of the stage, then back and forth past my rivals as I made my points. I even asked the audience for questions and a couple of friends lobbed pre-arranged softballs, which I answered with witty, pre-planned responses. Later, Mr. Nordenson informed me that my antics had been a no-no.

The second transgression involved buttons.

My brother Tony had been helping me with my election strategy, and he suggested that I needed a bunch of campaign buttons for students to wear to enhance my name recognition.

At a sports banquet at a local restaurant, I'd seen some nifty name-tag buttons, each with the Budweiser logo emblazoned across the top. Instinctively I knew the buttons were perfect. I told the restaurant owner my story, and asked if he could sell me the same buttons printed with *Branch for President*. The owner was a sports booster of our high school, and he knew I was a member of the varsity baseball team. He liked the idea. A week later, he gave me 100 campaign buttons!

The next day at lunch, my friends passed out all the buttons. Instantly, 100 kids were walking around campus with my Budweiser-sponsored campaign badges – a really hot item.

A couple of parents called the school, and I was summoned to the office. Mr. Nordenson instructed me to reclaim every button we'd handed out.

I promised to try my best, and I got a few back, but the buttons had already done their job. The next day, when Mr. Nordenson informed all the teachers that no Budweiser buttons were allowed on campus, my victory was clinched. Every teacher told his class: "No Branch Budweiser buttons."

The fight

The day of my election as president, I was feeling like Mr. Big Shot, dressed in a new shirt and pants and looking forward to sharing the good news with my parents when I got home. But one kid had other plans for me.

I was strolling through the parking lot when a skinny boy, about six feet tall, wearing a tattered jacket, walked right up, shoved me hard and barked: "Hey, asshole – you think you're tough shit? Not to me!"

Then the jerk punched me in the face. I was stunned, like I'd been beaned with a fastball, and my books went flying.

The kid swung again but this time landed only a glancing blow. I charged the numbskull, grabbed him, got some leverage and slammed him to the ground.

Mr. Nordenson, vice principal, 1967

Next thing I knew I had the skinny kid in a half-nelson and saw that he was hurting. I locked him tight in the wrestling hold while students began to gather. A few minutes later two coaches pulled us apart and took us to the administration building.

Mr. Nordenson was not happy to see me again. I told him the other kid had attacked me and there were witnesses. I demanded that the school call my parents and the kid's parents so we could get to the bottom of the matter. The coaches took the other kid into one office and Mr. Nordenson took me into his office.

"Shut up, Mr. Branch," was the only thing that Mr. Nordenson said as he grabbed me by the shirt and sat me down. He shut the door as he left his office.

I waited.

About 40 minutes later, the door opened and I had the full attention of the vice principal and my mother. Without saying a word, she motioned me to follow her.

In the car, my mom asked "Are you okay?" I nodded yes. On the ride home she was quiet and I knew she was upset. I started to feel sorry for myself. My jaw ached and my new clothes were ruined with asphalt stains. To gain sympathy, I begin whining about the aggressive kid and the vice principal, and how unfair it all was.

"Enough!" my mom blurted as she pulled off the road to stop. She turned off the engine. She looked me in the eye and went on, in an emotional voice:

"I talked at length with Mr. Nordenson. He actually likes you. If he were really against you, he'd have caused a major problem over your Budweiser buttons stunt. He didn't. The boy who attacked you has been abused for years by his alcoholic father, who was arrested yesterday for beating his mother. The boy is now on his way to the Santa Barbara Juvenile Detention Center, because he has nowhere else to go. Now, do you want to know more or is that enough?"

Silence. I shook my head no. We drove home, but when we got out of the car, she gave me a long, tight embrace. She was crying, but I knew the tears weren't for me.

I didn't sleep much that night, thinking about the boy I'd wrestled to the parking-lot ground. It was my first real fight and nothing like the fights in the movies.

It was humiliating and painful – and both fighters lost.

My first deal

Life at school went on, and for me it improved. After a week, Mr. Nordenson told me that he'd had it confirmed that the other boy had started the fight, and he had passed the information on to my mother.

I never saw the kid again and I always wondered what happened to him.

During my years in high school, I volunteered at the Santa Barbara YMCA as a student counselor for boys 9 to 12. We played volleyball and basketball and went on hikes and ate a lot of ice cream bars.

Young Men's Christian Association
Certificate of Award
This Certifies that
Cliff Branch
of
Summer Adventures
High Point Group Older Boys
has been awarded this Certificate for
Outstanding Leadership
Date
Summer Adventures
Director
Activity Director

I loved the kids and the YMCA was fun, but there wasn't any paycheck. In my free time I took odd jobs. I was 16 when I received my first entrepreneurial brainstorm and managed to make some serious cash.

I was leafing through my dad's *Wall Street Journal* when I discovered that the government was starting to call in all pure silver coins. (They weren't completely pure, but before 1965 America had real money: The silver content in U.S. coins was 90%.) The value of the raw silver was now worth more than the face value of the dimes, quarters and half-dollars. The government had decided to take back the old metal currency and replace it with silver-coated coins.

A few days later, I noticed a coin shop's ad in the local newspaper. The dealer was offering 13.5% over face value for pure silver coins. The idea of receiving more than face value for exchanging money was very appealing and I quickly figured out a simple, no-risk plan.

Earlier that year my dad had released a gift from my grandparents of $850. I pulled the money out of my account, asking the teller to convert the cash to coins. I told her I was in search of rare coins – it was my hobby. She appeared puzzled but agreed to my request, and I carried the money home in a box.

I separated approximately $600 in silver coins from the rolls, took them to the coin dealer and received about $680. I took the $680 in cash and the $250 in non-silver coins to another bank and asked for $930, all in coins.

I repeated the process a couple more times, and it worked. But I needed some help. I hired a 12-year-old boy from my neighborhood to sort coins, with the promise of $20 when we completed the job. I exchanged paper dollars and silver-coated coins for fresh coins at other banks, and the manager of my dad's bank let me use the secure merchant room, which was equipped with a coin-rolling machine.

For the first time in my life, *I was in business.*

The gig ran out in a couple of months, after the government had called in about 90% of the pure silver coins. But my "investment" had paid off. In a short span of time I had more than doubled my money without incurring any risk or retribution.

Of course, my dad had kept a skeptical eye on my scheme. He was proud of my initiative, but he suggested that I might want to put my energy into a more productive effort.

In the years that followed, I never said much about my silver story. Even though I knew what I'd done was legal, I always felt a bit slimy about it: I'd scammed the system and paid low wages to a kid. I obtained the coins under false pretenses as a student searching for rare coins. Even as I'd gone from bank to bank and the kid and I sat around sorting coins, I'd begun to feel that it all served no purpose, except to satisfy my own greed.

After the whole thing was over, I shared my misgivings with my father, who nodded and answered:

"Good. It's nice to hear that you see the other side. I was worried you might be headed toward a career on Wall Street."

Max Rafferty, California superintendent of schools

At the end of my junior year in 1967, I was elected president of the Associated Student Leaders (ASL) for our area of the state, a sizable district that included 13 high schools. I traveled around Central California to meet with other student body presidents and was a student advisor to the state board of education.

On two occasions, I traveled to Sacramento to meet with Max Rafferty, who was then the California superintendent of schools.

The first meeting was supposed to be my chance to sit down and "discuss high school education" but Rafferty cut it short, citing his tight schedule.

I was taken aback, and in front of his staff I asked for a new meeting. Rafferty promised to give me a couple of hours if I would return to Sacramento another day. I told him I'd be back, and prepared for our next meeting.

Dos Pueblos Youth New ASL President

The retiring student body president of the newest high school in this area, Cliff Branch of Dos Pueblos, is the new president of Associated Student Leaders, District 17B, William (Mike) Martin, adviser, said yesterday.

A junior, he is the son of Mr. and Mrs. Russell T. Branch of Santa Barbara Shores, in the Ellwood area. He won out over Al Riemenschneider of Santa Barbara High School in an election held at Nordhoff High School, Ojai, and succeeds Ernest Stern, also of SBHS.

Beccy Cole of SBHS, recently elected ASB secretary, who has served as Forge editor this year and a school writer for the News-Press, was elected vice president.

Phil Irwin, currently yearbook editor at Cate School, is the new treasurer.

Secretaries will be appointed by the officers.

Associated Student Leaders is an organization sponsored by the California Association of Secondary Principals and embraces 13 schools in this district. Each school is allowed four voting delegates and a quota of other students from each school may attend meetings. About 200 were on hand for the election and dinner Wednesday at Ojai.

The new officers will plan for the annual ASL leadership conference at Rancho Oso Sept. 8-9, when members will take part in workshop sessions on parliamentary procedure, leadership and project planning, and meet as officers of their own schools, Martin said. He is co-ordinator of instructional services for the county schools.

CLIFF BRANCH
New ASL Head

1967

I was not a fan of Rafferty, who was politically to the right of Attila the Hun, though evidently not much of a military man. During his later campaign for U.S. senator from California, his former wife had informed the press that her ex-husband had celebrated V-J Day by throwing away the canes he'd started using after Pearl Harbor.

My parents warned me to be careful. In the early '60s Rafferty's bestselling book, *Suffer Little Children*, had established him as a staunch anti-progressive educator. He railed against the very idea of any school teaching anything about sex education or psychology. Rafferty wanted classrooms to focus on fundamentals, memorization and drills.

When we finally met again, he put his arm around me and his staff photographer snapped a couple of shots of us. Then, just as before, Rafferty went into his "Something has come up" routine. He only gave me five minutes after beginning our conversation with a disingenuous "Tell me what's on your mind, son."

I was nonplussed and pissed. As Rafferty started to leave the room, I reminded him of his earlier promise of an extended dialogue. I emphasized that as state superintendent of schools he might actually want to hear what student body presidents thought of their high school education.

He stopped near the door and instructed his assistant to contact me for a new date.

Weeks passed and I never heard from the assistant or anyone else in Rafferty's office.

In my eyes, he was just another uptight adult who failed to keep his word. ■

1968: A Long Summer at 18

NEAR THE END of my senior year at Dos Pueblos, I was growing restless and made the decision to leave high school early.

I was bored with student government because it was a joke. Our faculty advisor had warned me twice about discussing any kind of real politics at any student government meeting or with the local newspaper.

The first warning came after I wrote a letter that appeared on the editorial page of the *Santa Barbara News Press*. The advisor considered my message controversial, especially because I signed *ASL President* after my name.

Next, he got wind that I was talking to other ASB presidents about setting up a forum for student leaders to discuss the Vietnam War. He made it clear that the only power that student government had, essentially, was to select the theme for the senior prom. There was to be no discussion of any other non-school issues.

I pointed out that many of us would soon face the draft – if we were old enough to go to war, why shouldn't we talk about Vietnam with other students in public meetings? The advisor dismissed my argument and informed me that the principal had told him I was "treading on thin ice" and any future incident might affect my graduation.

I didn't care. I'd had enough of high school and was eager for more freedom, a chance to spread my wings before going to college. My parents acquiesced to my leaving school early after only minor pleading with me that I graduate with my class.

I informed my baseball coach that I was leaving early and he told me it would be the biggest mistake of my life. He warned that I'd never play college ball because "No coach wants a quitter." I told a few of the guys on the team and they understood, as did Debbie Windsor and Cheryl Higgen, two of my closest friends. *[See page 368]*

The other person I told was Kay Montgomery. I'd spent considerable time pining over Kay, who wouldn't give me the time of day, at least not romantically. We'd become good friends, but her side of our conversations were mostly about her adoration of a guy named Steve Moore. Steve just happened to be the star quarterback, as well as the best player on the basketball and baseball teams. I didn't stand a chance. Kay also had two knock-out older sisters, so I hung around the Montgomery household as much as I could, but I lost track of Kay after high school.

I passed the required civics test at the school superintendent's office, and his secretary promised to send me my diploma.

The truth was that my decision to leave high school early was only partly due to my hassles with the school administration. I'd been in touch with an old friend from my Carmel Valley days. He had great expectations for the summer, which we had discussed on the phone.

Joining Larry

My escape from high school involved my childhood friend, Larry Leslie. After he had finished up at Carmel High, he rented a small house by the wharf in Monterey.

Wharf at Monterey Bay

Larry promised that if we roomed together for the summer we would be free from adults and I could work with him on a boat that took tourists deep-sea fishing. Larry's boss needed another deckhand and said I could have the job if I arrived within two weeks.

In our telephone conversations, Larry had bragged about some big tips he'd garnered from happy sportsmen when they caught a big fish or after he cleaned their catch. Larry added that we might occasionally borrow a sports car off his dad's dealership lot.

I was in.

After my civics exam, I loaded up my car and left for Monterey. On arrival I discovered that Larry's glowing description of the neat digs he had found for us was overstated: What he had rented was basically a dirty shack, although it did have power and running water. I was a little stunned to go from a nice house to a shanty, but at least it was ours, and we were free from adults, except at work.

My experiment in freedom turned out to be bittersweet. My summer in Monterey stretched to nearly four months, during which time I was fired from three jobs in a row and suffered a serious injury. When I returned to Santa Barbara, I lost my fourth job because of an explosion.

Job 1

Working on the fishing boat every day was an adventure. There were always interesting people to meet, and they always seemed to be in a good mood and talked openly about their lives while we bounced around Monterey Bay. Larry and I liked helping the customers, especially the young ladies. But it wasn't long before we ran afoul of the captain.

On our final afternoon, we'd returned to port, tied up at the dock and had just disembarked when the captain spotted Larry locking lips with a girl who had been on the boat – she was the daughter of one of his best customers.

Before he fired us, the captain noted that Larry's indiscretion wasn't the first time that he and I had entered into inappropriate behavior with female clients. He had warned us several times about paying too much attention to teenage girls that came on board with their parents or friends.

There was no way we could complain: On at least one other occasion, we'd both been busted for breaking his non-fraternizing rule.

The captain said our dismissal wasn't about the kissing – we were being canned for disobeying his orders. It was like a court martial – and we were stripped of our jobs. Larry and I walked home to figure out our next move.

Job 2

After our fishing career went south, I snagged a job at the Pacheco Club – a private men's club near downtown Monterey, not far from our shack. The club wasn't fancy – I think it was just a converted residential property. The manager needed a part-time dishwasher who could work odd hours and occasionally help serve food to the diners.

No women were allowed in the club. The men played cards, drank and told stories. Good stories. Every so often, one of them would get so drunk that he had to sleep over on the couch in the family room. I knew a few of the men. They were the fathers of some of my friends in Carmel, but I wasn't sure any of them remembered me.

Pachecho Club, Monterey, California

A few weeks into the job, I was serving food and eavesdropping on a conversation among several men at a table. I was offended by a remark about a boy I knew, and I responded as if I were an adult, a club member and a party to the conversation.

An old geezer who'd been drinking made a derogatory observation about Ronny Parsons, a boy I had grown up with. Ronny lived in Mission Fields, near the mouth of Carmel Valley, and his mother drank too much. I knew Ronny to be a great kid in a tough situation, and we were good friends. The old geezer told another member that Ronny was "a little shithead with a bad attitude" and I said, "That's not the Ronny Parsons I know, and he was always one of the best guys on our baseball team." The member was taken aback, and changed the subject.

A few hours later the manager let me go for mouthing off to a club member. I think he realized I knew too many people the members knew, and they didn't want me overhearing their conversations.

It was the beginning of a bad week.

A couple of days after my firing, I slipped and fell while running up the wood stairs to our shack. I put my hand through a small window in the front door and severed an artery. I was bleeding profusely. Larry wrapped my arm tight in an old towel and used black electrician's tape to bind the makeshift bandage over the wound.

Blood was still flowing out of the bandage, so we hopped in Larry's loud Ford hot rod. My injury gave Larry an excuse to be a hero and drive like a maniac up the hill to the Monterey hospital. We nearly spun out at a busy intersection before Larry corrected just in time and raced on.

Within a few blocks, Larry's crazy driving attracted the attention of police. A cruiser started chasing us with red lights flashing and a siren blasting. Larry wasn't fazed – he was all jacked up trying to save my life, so he kept the car flying while the cop chased us to the hospital.

I jumped out and ran in while Larry handled the officer. Larry told him that I was bleeding to death and the patrolman entered the hospital to investigate. He saw instantly that I was badly cut. The officer spoke to me and to the doctor, who had to call my parents for permission to sew me up.

My parents wanted to drive the four hours up from Santa Barbara to be with me, but I told them that there was nothing for them to do and that I was fine.

It was true. I was stitched up, and hung around the shack for a spell.

Job 3

A few weeks later, I read in the local paper that long-distance operators at the Monterey phone company had gone on strike. Replacements were needed immediately. I went to apply and easily landed a temporary job as a scab. The pay was excellent.

After a brief training session, and one week on the switchboard, I had the job down and worked every hour I could get. I was motivated by the magic of overtime pay, plus the job was very interesting. I could listen in on conversations from all over the country, and the callers had no idea they weren't speaking in privacy.

Long distance operator, 1968

Long distance was a big deal in those days – it was expensive. Talk had to be condensed, just the awful or intimate facts. The caller had to deliver the message quickly or feed the pay phone more coins.

The switchboard dialogues covered every topic, including sex. It was especially intriguing when soldiers from Fort Ord lit up the lines each Friday to call home.

One afternoon I was listening to a soldier talk to his girlfriend in New Jersey, and she just kept yelling at the poor guy because she hadn't wanted him to join the army. I quickly concluded that the girlfriend was a total bitch. I could only endure so much of her abuse.

At a pause in the one-sided conversation, I pushed the special operator lever and cut into the call:

"You know what, buddy? I'd break up with any girlfriend who yelled at me like that. If I were you, I'd find a new girlfriend!"

The girl shrieked, then demanded, "*Who's on the phone?*"

I panicked and disconnected the line. Cutting off his girlfriend probably didn't help the soldier's situation, and certainly it didn't help my own.

A woman supervisor walked up and down along the switchboards, behind our operator stools, watching us connect calls. I found out later that day she had observed my intrusion into the lovers' long-distance spat. The office manager called me in to tell me I was through.

On the way back to our shack I realized that apparently I hadn't learned much of anything from my two previous firings.

Job 4

Living with Larry did not go so well. I had been hired and then fired from three consecutive jobs and had severed an artery in my arm. I decided it was time to return to Santa Barbara before I became a student again: Prior to leaving high school, I'd applied to college and been accepted at Cal Poly. In the meantime, I got two new jobs: at a junkyard and at a Union 76 gas station.

The owner of both operations was a good friend of my parents. At his junkyard he let me build a beach buggy from an old Chevy. I cut most of the body off the car and welded rims together to make wide rear wheels. My actual job – when I wasn't working on the buggy – was removing good mufflers off wrecked, newer-model cars. My main tool was a cutting torch.

The boss said I was doing a good job, I was having fun and I was proud to be a member of his crew.

Everything was going fine – until I blew the lid off a 50-gallon steel drum. Unwisely, I'd been using the barrel for a sawhorse. I didn't know the empty drum had once contained paint thinner.

As the blast knocked me to the ground, I instinctively put up both hands to guard my face. Lying flat on the ground, I dropped my hands and saw that they were covered in blood.

My first thought was that I had blown off my face.

I ran screaming through the shop, palms pressed to my cheeks. In the bathroom I washed the blood from my face.

In the mirror I saw that I had only split my chin wide open – in the explosion the cutting torch had flown up and its control knob had cut me.

I started laughing – my whole face was red with burns and my eyebrows were singed, but I'd expected far worse and felt giddy with relief.

The narrow welding goggles had saved my eyes and for the most part I was okay. Two men in the shop ran over to bandage my chin and gave me a cold wet towel to put over my face and some Vaseline to soothe the flash burn.

Luckily, the owner was not in the shop at the time of the accident. He did hear about it when he later arrived at the junkyard, and asked me to come into his office. He asked me if I was all right and then reminded me that I hadn't followed his safety instructions, which was true.

It came as no surprise when he told me I was fired. It was a fair punishment. He handed me my final check and told me I could take the beach buggy home.

I left with one other valuable item.

Losing the last of my first four jobs, I had finally learned a lesson about how the real world worked in 1968:

If you screwed up, you got fired. ■

The Later Years

Cal Poly, San Luis Obispo

Home to 20,000 undergraduate students

Cal Poly Administration Building, 1969
Inset: President McFee and his cabinet

Totally Inappropriate Subject Matter

AFTER I returned to Santa Barbara from my summer in Monterey, my father received an unexpected phone call that changed the course of our lives. His former employer, the Stanford Research Institute (SRI), asked him to take a choice assignment in Bangkok, Thailand. The offer required a quick decision – my parents discussed it for a day before they accepted and began preparing to live in Southeast Asia for several years.

Cliff, 18

My dad returned to the SRI as the senior editor on a top-secret project under the joint direction of the U.S. Army and the U.S. State Department. My mom took a job at Chulalongkorn University, where she taught courses in English to Thai women.

It was 1968, and after my parents left America for Thailand I was alone. I drove north from Santa Barbara to San Luis Obispo for my freshman year at Cal Poly. There was a bureaucratic snag with my admissions paperwork, but I got it untangled and rented a studio apartment downtown. I started school two days later, with no sense of any academic direction. English was my favorite subject in high school, so I chose it as my major.

My first attempt to write something substantial started that year when my

English professor announced that any student who wrote a sizable piece of fiction – a short story collection or a novel – would receive credit for two creative writing courses.

I began writing my novel in San Luis Obispo before I received approval from Cal Poly to attend the University of Maryland's overseas extension program for a semester in Bangkok, where I continued work on my book.

Travels in Asia

In Bangkok, I stayed with my parents in a luxurious house in a compound not far from the SRI offices. During the semester, I traveled alone in and around the city. My dad's driver, Phueng, would gladly take me anywhere I wanted to go, but more often I took a taxi so no one would know where I traveled. Throughout my three-month visit I found the Thai people to be friendly and soft-spoken and eager to ask me questions about America.

My parents took me for several trips up country, where we skirted dense jungles and passed by ancient Buddhist temples, traveling along wide rivers and through vast rice paddies where women and men worked knee deep and wore their traditional pointed straw hats.

Later we flew for a vacation on the island of Penang off the coast of Malaysia. Penang was spectacular, one of the most beautiful places I'd ever seen, with flowering jungle plants and pristine white-sand beaches.

When I left Thailand to head back to San Luis Obispo, I went solo. That's when I made my secret and scary trip to Saigon, South Vietnam, to gather material for my novel. I'll describe my narrow escape from danger in Part Four: The Vietnam War.

Although I hadn't planned it, I ended up in Hong Kong for a few days after I left Saigon, where I bought several cases of Sony headphones from a wholesaler, as well as other Sony stereo components, and had them shipped to me in the United States.

Then I flew to Osaka, Japan, staying on for several days while planning to travel by land to Tokyo. Along the way, I had a few experiences that made stark impressions on my 19-year-old psyche.

In Osaka, I bathed a few times in the public baths and found it very interesting to watch entire families bathing together. There were boys, girls, men and women of all ages: different families from the immediate neighborhood, all chatting, laughing, completely unself-conscious and comfortable with their nudity. I was a foreigner and over six feet tall and received some stares from the children, but otherwise no one paid me any special attention. Everyone was very cordial, though they spoke no English and I spoke no Japanese.

I remember thinking, *I'm not in Kansas anymore.* I was touched at how the Japanese seemed so much more comfortable with nudity than Americans back home.

My mom (circled) with Thai children at a small village in up-country, Thailand

The view from our home in the Bangkok compound where we lived

My parents with their friend from Chulalongkorn University

Cliff looking over a beach on the island of Penang, Malaysia

Touring up-country on one of the numerous canals

Below: Elephants, prior to a race, lining up at the track outside of Bangkok

When it came time to choose a place to sleep, I wanted to stay in one of the small family inns in a residential section of Osaka, but it didn't work out. Each time I inquired at the front door of an inn, I was told there were no vacancies. After several turndowns, I had a weird feeling that for some reason no one wanted me as a guest.

I happened to see another American buying food from a street vendor and asked him where I could find a place to stay. He quickly filled me in: "Well, you'll have to go over to the business district of the city. None of these neighborhood inns will rent to you." I asked why not, and he answered, "Americans eat meat. The Japanese don't like the smell you'll leave in their tiny rooms." I felt a bit insulted, a victim of prejudice – the "no meat-eaters" bias. I found my way over to a Westernized motel in Osaka's business section.

From Osaka, I boarded one of the very first bullet trains and traveled cross country into Tokyo. The streamlined train was quiet and very fast – the ultra-modern engine and cars made the trains in the States seem like antiques. The Japanese were ingenious and practical, and heading swiftly for the future. I had a feeling the bullet train was a sign of things to come.

Tokyo, one of the five or six great cities of the world, was much more modern than Osaka. The public baths were newer and more Westernized – the beautiful large baths had two separate sections, divided by a privacy screen, one side for males and one for females. The boys and girls spent most of their time giggling, running to the edge of the screen to peek at the other side.

Japan was a strange mix of the very new and the very old. I saw myriads of strange three-wheel motorcycle-cars, and in the crush of constant traffic I started noticing a lot of cute new mini-pickup trucks and one cool little red sports car – all bearing a chrome decal: Honda. It hit me that Honda was a much bigger company than I had realized.

I had no way of knowing that, before long, Honda would begin making a huge impact on America, or that McDonald's would soon introduce the ubiquitous Big Mac to Japan.

The sights and sounds of Tokyo, especially at night, were exhilarating, and it was obvious that the huge city was continuing to modernize itself at full speed. The world appeared to be changing at an accelerating pace, and Japan was at the forefront of a global cultural transformation. As a teenage American alone in Tokyo, I never imagined that in less that two decades I'd return to make a presentation to a boardroom of Japanese businessmen about an odd new device called a "personal computer."

Judgment Day for My Novel

When I returned to Cal Poly in 1969, I handed in a 138-page manuscript to my professor. It was my youthful attempt to write a serious novel and I'd used a pen name, Justin Miles. The story was a thinly veiled autobiography, a tale of initiation overflowing with a 19-year-old's angst and rebellious spirit.

My 1969 book began like this:

> Preface
>
> In deference to all that's Right--including my parents and girlfriend's parents, agencies of the U.S.A, and Thailand, and particularly local draft board #78--the author disclaims any possible resemblance to the narrator of this tale. The persons and events depicted are obviously the product of a disordered imagination and are not intended to represent real life. So turn on, read on, and enjoy the trip.

The preface was probably enough for my conservative professor to drop a silent penalty flag. He'd been born around 1920 and proudly related to our class many of his combat experiences from World War II. I wasn't born until 1949 and didn't know much about the war that began for Americans with Pearl Harbor in 1941 – except what I'd heard from my dad, who'd been in the Merchant Marine, or what I'd learned from John Wayne movies.

I knew my prof was pro-Vietnam War and that he had no patience with anyone who displayed the least symptom of what he called "Hippie Peace Movement Disease," which he warned was spreading like a plague across our beloved country.

I was aware, beforehand, that my sentiments and opinions boldly set forth in my manuscript ran counter to my very traditional professor's personal and political beliefs. Yet I was still young and idealistic, and I thought that he might be open-minded enough to be moved by my story.

The first chapter of my 1969 book began:

Two weeks ago the whole damn world was a pain in the ass. Justin reflected on all the baloney he had to take from the dean of the English department about how privileged he was to leave school early. It seemed like his life now involved having to kiss ass to a bunch of old fogies. But the whole summer was in the balance as was his adventure to the other side of the world. He'd won.

Now he was eager to return home from campus. Late that night, as he was lying in bed, he pondered the underbelly of the higher educational system that produced graduates so bent on scratching their way up the corporate ladder. He wondered how he could stay cool and not let the pursuit of money become too big a part of him. Sure, money could buy many possessions that were meaningful. He loved his beach buggy and how it flew down the beach and because it was bitching-cool and it seemed to excite the girls who went for rides into a mood to get naked and wild. He loved playing his drums and his four-hundred-dollar stereo because the speakers pounded out the bass notes, and he dug music and how it made him feel. Was his life the American Dream? Where would it lead? All the adults he knew seemed so uptight and stressed-out. Justin sensed inside that all this stress and the Vietnam War was somehow sucking the American Being into madness, and it had come clear in a nightmarish dream that was hard to shake:

Justin saw this giant grotesque robot that turned its own key so tight that inner springs busted bloody with ulcers, coming forth from a porcine stomach like infections far beneath the skin. He saw men sacrificing their bodies in reverence to another similar robot who was consuming vast quantities of gin, tonic, and tranquilizers. There were huge plastic barrels full of sleeping pills, and gigantic drums of Coca-Cola. The giant Robot consumed it all until his fat hung so sweaty that it polluted the air with smoke. Everyone who was watching could not breathe without hacking up horrible black scum. Then he saw other men dressed in shiny polyester suits, who were selling everyone diet pills, and face cream to clean the goop off their faces. It worked for a while, but suddenly the Giant Robot made a horrible sound, vomited, and destroyed them all.

Justin awoke from his dream just in time to avoid the vomit, but the dream still left a bad taste in his mouth. He left for Bangkok that morning, wondering what it all meant.

High hopes

To my credit, I had banged out nearly 140 pages on a portable typewriter, trying to capture the zeitgeist of my generation. I was serious about charging the windmill, so I'd had the first draft professionally typed, finished the chapters about Saigon after coming home from Thailand, paid again to have the novel re-typed, and then with great anticipation submitted the work to my English professor.

I waited day after day for his response, or at least some kind acknowledgment of all the work I'd put in. I fantasized that he might soften his views about Vietnam and congratulate me on my compelling story.

Two weeks later, at the end of class, the professor approached and plunked down the manuscript on my desk without comment. He turned on his heel as I read the terse notations scribbled across the first few pages. The first brief criticism simply said: Ambiguous and sloppily written.

There was also a handwritten note attached to my book:

Mr. Branch,
The subject matter covered in your novel is totally inappropriate for a college-level writing course and therefore it is not acceptable for credit.

I was crushed.

Forty-five years later, as I reread my novel, I have to wince at much of the writing, mostly the spontaneous ramblings of a cocky adolescent full of himself.

But the scope of the work, and the sincerity of the political message that I'd tried to get across, still seem a notable effort. What had I expected from a 50-year-old conservative English teacher at a polytechnic college? My novel questioned the validity of the Vietnam War – just as the war was beginning to unravel into a disaster.

I should have known better – and yet in 1969 I'd intuitively sensed that the professor was doing me a favor. His abrupt and angry response to my novel was a stark reminder that the world was not always fair, and that there were plenty of other people who didn't share my beliefs. The professor squelched any desire to continue writing at that point, but I did receive some encouraging words from my parents in the weeks that followed.

A letter from my father

While I was living with my parents in Bangkok, my dad had commented on how hard I was working on my novel. Many nights he watched me type away into the late hours before he went to bed. I never showed him my work in progress and he didn't ask to read my opus, which was fine with me – I feared being busted for certain aspects of my behavior depicted in the book.

My parents had no idea that I had discovered Bangkok nightlife, including massage parlors and sex shows frequented by thousands of American soldiers on R&R from the war in South Vietnam.

SRI

RUSSELL T. BRANCH, JR.
STANFORD RESEARCH INSTITUTE

EDITOR/PROJECT ADMINISTRATOR
SIRINEE BLDG. FLOOR 6
518/4 PLOENCHIT ROAD
BANGKOK, THAILAND

TELEPHONE: 57939

Neither my mom nor dad had a clue that I had traveled to Saigon in the midst of the war to interview soldiers for background material for my novel, or the trouble I'd gotten into there.

Nor did they have any inkling that I had invested childhood savings and part of my college fund in sapphire gemstone rings while in Thailand, and in the stereo components during my solo travels to Tokyo and Hong Kong. I had shipped the jewelry and stereo equipment to the States, duty free, using my dad's special security clearance.

Obviously, I was not a model citizen at 19. My parents didn't know how off the rails I'd strayed, and I wasn't that anxious for them to find out.

It was easier to send them a copy of my novel once I was thousands of miles away, safely back in San Luis Obispo. I was curious to see what my dad thought of my writing, despite the questionable disclosures I'd made in the book. I respected his judgment and knew he could help me improve the novel that my English professor had summarily dismissed.

After all, Dad was a professional editor.

Here is my dad's first-page summary of the 12-page letter that arrived in the mail after I returned home in 1969, about a month after I'd sent my book to my parents' home in Thailand:

My dad, at his office in Bangkok

SRI

December 1969

Dear Cliff:

Before I start in with the nitpicking, let me reassure you that I think your novel is a very sizable accomplishment--and has enough to it so that it would be a shame not to go through the tedious work of revision that my comments may suggest. Furthermore, these are only my own suggestions. Even though I may state them in impolite and blunt language, you can consider them, accept them, or reject them as you see fit. You are the writer. Let me begin with some general comments:

Every piece of creative work has to have a central theme to hold it together. The writer's job is to find that central theme through the characters and then develop it: that's one way in which a work of art differs from life itself--which as you know, is a rather diffuse series of events. I think you would help yourself if you would boil down your central theme into a simple statement and then measure your plot development as to whether it illustrates and carries out that theme.

The theme that your story carries, for me, is simply that the Draft and the Vietnam War is the Big Stick that the Establishment holds over its young people today, and none of your characters can escape--neither a clever pragmatist like your Justin nor an idealist like Richard. In fact, they both end up in the same circumstances in order to deal with their dilemma. Richard bugs out because he finds the young activists foolish; Justin begs out in the end, because the System was too much for him to cope with--not because he develops any convictions about the Vietnam War, but simply because he finds he can't lick 'em and he'd rather cop-out than deal with the situation. At least that's the way your story reads to me now. If you want it to convey more than that, perhaps you should sharpen up Justin's decision by having him ponder it more or discuss it more; perhaps he should tell Barbara explicitly about his feelings, rather than playing it cool and smart as he has always done before. Your reader should know that Justin finally draws the line and takes the hard way out, rather than the easy way that his character would suggest.

Unless you're a Thomas Hardy trying to show that Life Screws Everybody, no matter how worthy, your hero must be master of his own fate; he must arrive at a decision and take action because of that decision, not just because that's the way the ball bounces. Certainly, up to the climax your hero has been anything but a patsy - but then, as far as the reader can judge, he is just being forced into an unhappy course of action by Big Brother, not because he himself has arrived at his own decision. Maybe you could set out the basic conflict between Justin and Richard in that initial scene (with Barbara) at the beginning of the story. Mull it over.

I have reserved any comment about the "fictional adventures" of your hero, Justin Miles. We can discuss that subject at a later date. The rest of my comments are arranged in a chapter by chapter fashion, over the following pages.

Good luck and with much love, Pop

Moving on

In 1969, I did not fully appreciate my father's letter. I did revise and rewrite some parts of my book, but I'd already made up my mind to move on, and ended up placing his letter in a box with the manuscript. The box sat on a shelf in numerous closets for the next 45 years. When I recently reread my dad's letter, it brought tears to my eyes. His thoughtfulness permeated every page – his words honest, measured and knowledgeable.

My father was also calm in his response, in spite of the fact that both of my parents must have been taken aback by some of the subject matter. He was willing to treat my novel as a serious attempt at art and social commentary, carefully separating the work from my carefree and careless personal behavior.

In short, his reply was a 12-page love letter from a father to his son.

There was also a note from my mother – always the counselor – folded inside my dad's letter:

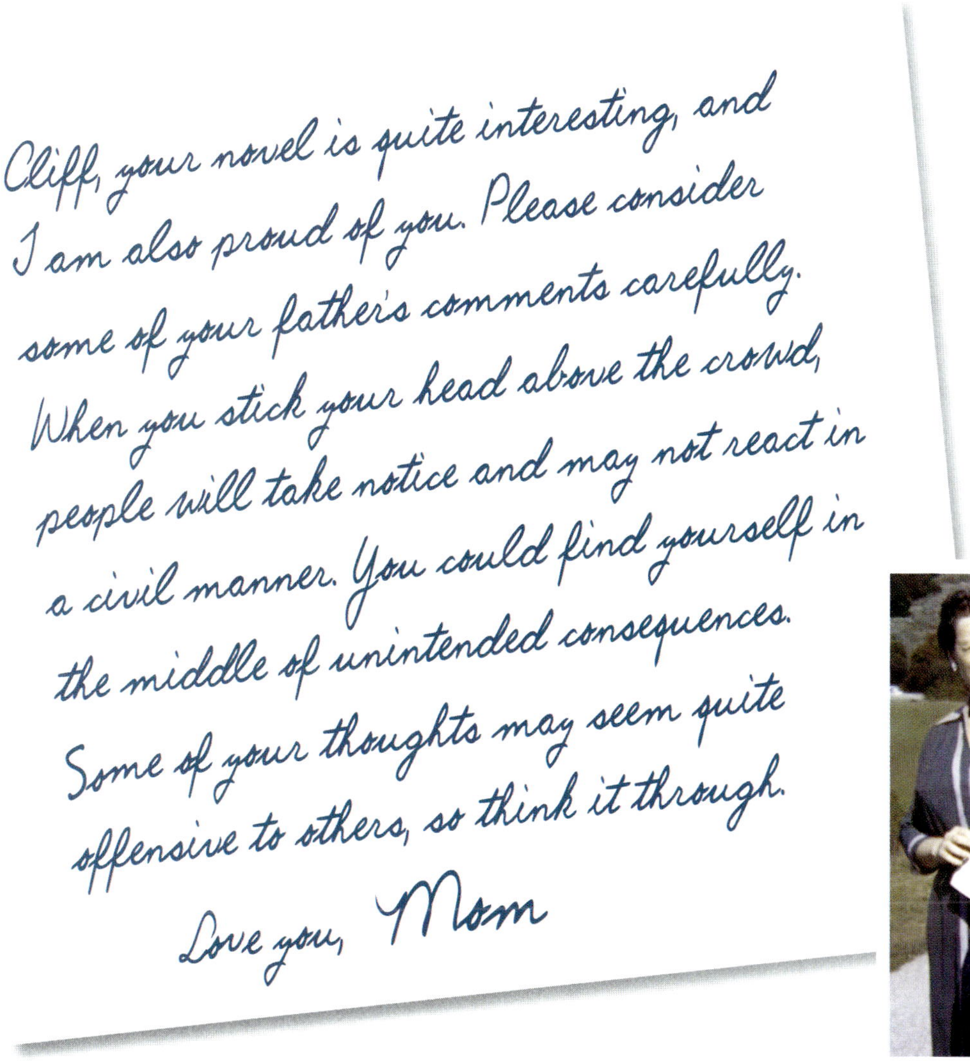
Cliff, your novel is quite interesting, and
I am also proud of you. Please consider
some of your father's comments carefully.
When you stick your head above the crowd,
people will take notice and may not react in
a civil manner. You could find yourself in
the middle of unintended consequences.
Some of your thoughts may seem quite
offensive to others, so think it through.
Love you, Mom

No Fear of Failure

NOT LONG after returning from Thailand to San Luis Obispo, I was off and running with exciting new plans. My novel was just a memory, and Richard Nixon's draft lottery gave my birth date a lucky high number. Suddenly, like so many other students, I no longer had the draft hanging over my head.

Since high school, I had been philosophically against the Vietnam War, but I'd also grown disenchanted with the anti-war movement. I was disgusted by the behavior of many of my fellow college students toward returning soldiers, many of whom were friends. These young men had been subjected to hell on behalf of our country and deserved respect and better treatment from their fellow citizens and our government.

In the winter of 1969, I was again attending classes at Cal Poly, but at the same time I'd started a small business, selling the sapphire rings and stereo components I'd sent back from Asia. I'd become good friends with a classmate, Tom Spalding, who was seriously smart, and we became business partners. We were making the transition from students to – that '60s dirty word – *capitalists.*

Tom and I were in the right place at the right time with the right merchandise – we sold our goods like hotcakes to the people we knew best: college kids who'd joined the counterculture.

The Flower Children, the long-haired students with their unconventional, anti-establishment tastes, were the springboard to our first success.

Good Times and Good Tunes

Tom and I rented a small commercial space and started a hippie retail store, more accurately described as a head shop. We named it Super Sonic, a tiny establishment just off campus on Foothill Boulevard, the main artery for students on their way to and from Cal Poly. Initially, a fellow student, Roger Rohrs, was a partner, but he was in ROTC and he left to serve in Vietnam before we got rolling.

The commercial space was a shambles, but Tom and I fixed it up, and crammed the new shelves with record albums, eight-track tapes, car stereos, black lights, psychedelic posters, Indian incense, and dorm room accessories. We also sold all the stuff that law enforcement referred to as "paraphernalia" – papers, roach clips, and pipes, as well as Trojans, the most popular condom.

Tom and I offered at reasonable prices everything the college-age consumer required in the late 1960s.

Cliff and Tom, inside their first store – called Super Sonic. The store was located on Foothill Boulevard, near Cal Poly.

All of my Thai sapphire rings and the stereo equipment from Tokyo and Hong Kong sold quickly, and I tripled my investment. Soon we needed more capital to restock our inventory. I had no interest in the jewelry business, but like most boys my age I loved and was fascinated by the latest stereo gear.

We quickly obtained lines of credit from two big electronics companies, Sony and Pioneer, and concentrated on selling component music systems. Ironically, even though Tom and I ran a head shop and had a firm handle on what our customers wanted and needed, we had no interest in pot or alcohol ourselves, or anything that might slow us down.

We started pushing the stereo equipment and quickly hit around $30,000 per month in sales.

I was 19 and Tom was 20. ■

A typical Warehouse Sound Company advertisement, early '70s. We placed ads nationally in *Rolling Stone* and *National Lampoon*. Bellbottoms were the rage.

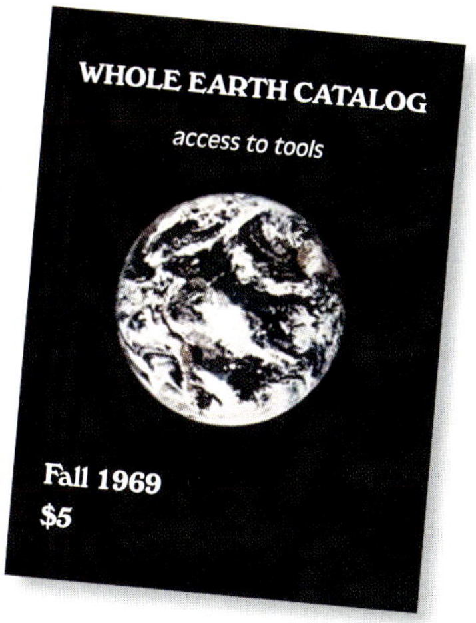

Not long after we published our first catalog, we received a positive write-up in the *Whole Earth Catalog*, a huge, bestselling catalog of counterculture tools and services.

Tom and I already had college reps distributing our catalogs on campuses across the nation, in return for a credit toward one of our music systems. Among American college students, we had become the most trusted source for stereo equipment.

Warehouse Sound Company Expands

Warehouse Sound grew quickly and in our second year in business, Tom and I began looking for a larger building. Our friend and investor John King suggested an ancient three-story brick warehouse on Santa Barbara Street as a new home for our mail-order business. It was on the railroad tracks, had loading docks and it was cheap. There was only one drawback: The building had been condemned and was about to be torn down.

John felt that the late19th century building was structurally sound and worth saving. I thought that was a grand idea and our real estate partnership (which included Johm, Tom and me) bought the 25,000-square-foot facility that no one could legally inhabit for $88,000. We had a tough time convincing the city planning department that our refurbishing plan was feasible but they finally agreed. John King's construction company finished the remodeling to meet building codes, and Warehouse Sound Company moved in.

Administrative offices were on the top floor, which left two floors for storing our products. We also had space for an advertising agency and a recording studio. We loved our new home. Ironically, when I wanted to make a few minor changes, the city council turned me down. By then, a host of new regulations prohibited any alterations to our building, which was considered an historical site – a cherished landmark.

After leaving school to pursue my business career with Tom, I'd been in regular communication with my parents, who were still in Thailand.

The *Whole Earth Catalog* was published by Stewart and Brand between 1968 and 1972. It was the first hip "database" and sold 2.5 million copies. Our write-up was a major boost for Warehouse Sound Co.

Tom and I decided to throw a concert in an effort to properly test a PA sound system we had put together for a Christian touring group called "Up with People." The $55,000 sound system was to be used at their 1976 Super Bowl halftime performance, so it was a good idea to make sure everything worked before we sent it off.

Recording artists Tim Weisberg (A&M Records) and David Riordan (Capitol Records) performed at Railroad Square. It was a great day of music, and the airplane banner advertisements in the sky went off without a hitch.

A second reason for staging the concert was to create a poster I wanted to send out with each stereo music system, to show that our mail-order business truly existed. The inset photos give an idea of the '70s crowd – particularly the guy smoking a joint.

The concert was perhaps one of the first "flash mob" events. I was later called down to the police station because we did not have a permit – but everyone had a good time and no one fell off the roof.

[See page 335]

Pro-Products Catalog

WAREHOUSE SOUND COMPANY
WAREHOUSE SOUND CO.
LOADING ZONE
NO PARKING
WAREHOUSE SOUND CO.
Send for our 96-page color catalog packed with the latest in component music systems and professional sound gear: Amps, tuners, turntables, tapedecks, speakers, accessories, microphones, mixers, PA equipment—everything in the world of sound at huge discounts.
WRITE: PO Box S, San Luis Obispo, CA 93405
CALL: 805/544-9700 for catalog, or prices.

A packaged music system offered by Warehouse Sound Company. Most systems were shipped to college students across America. This is a typical page taken from the catalog, circa 1978.

I kept assuring them, "Things are going really well," but they had no real idea of what Tom and I were up to – until Warren Groshong, a local journalist, wrote a feature that ran in the *Telegram Tribune*, the San Luis Obispo and countywide newspaper. The article headline read:

LOCAL BOYS MAKE GOOD AND $5.5 MILLION

I think my parents were a little shocked when they read the story. It appeared with a photograph of Tom and me, and informed the reader that Warehouse Sound employed more than 100 people whose average age was 23.

My dad knew that I had gone into business, but I think he was surprised by its scope. I'd told my dad that I was writing most of the copy for our catalogs and sent him our latest edition. My dad read it and called to say:

"Good job! I'd buy a music system from you guys! I knew you would put your writing skills to work." There was fatherly pride in the tone of his voice. We were both proud.

Catching a Ride on *Rolling Stone*

The size of our Warehouse Sound staff and the reach of our catalog rapidly expanded. By 1978, when *Rolling Stone* magazine ran a feature on our company, our annual sales were exceeding $10 million – about $35 million in 2015 money.

It was an exciting time for Tom and me, our investors and our employees, and the article in the world's foremost rock-and-roll publication further boosted our sales and credibility. Shortly after we were highlighted in *Rolling Stone,* I was invited to give the keynote speech at the Consumer Electronics Show in Madrid, and headed for Spain.

I didn't know what to expect, and found myself on a stage in a huge ballroom, at a podium under a spotlight. I gave a speech to several hundred company executives, most of them twice my age. My presentation was titled "Understanding the Pepsi Generation" and was well received.

Tom and I had been keeping our eyes open for other business opportunities beyond our stereo enterprise. Now we had some money of our own to invest and had begun selling redwood hot tubs.

Later that year, I got a call from *Good Morning America*. Someone there had written for information on our new product line. They were intrigued with the idea of California hot tubbing. The caller from the ABC network wanted me to sit with the Midwest show hosts in one of our hot tubs in the winter snow so I could explain to viewers across America "the allure of the new California craze."

Of course, I was more than happy to oblige.

Some months after the *Rolling Stone* article was published, I was invited to return to Cal Poly, not as a student but to teach a course to graduate students in business. The offering would be called "Youth Marketing in America" and I gladly accepted the invitation. I even offered to teach the class for free, but the head of the business department insisted that I accept payment, as it was required by some sort of regulation. For a short time, I was on the state's payroll.

I even had a Cal Poly faculty ID card.

So many students enrolled that the venue was quickly moved from a classroom to a lecture hall. In addition to my lectures, I brought in guest speakers from around the country, the vice presidents of Sony, Capitol

Rolling Stone

September 1977 Issue No. 247

How to get hi-fied a hundred miles from nowhere

Tom Spalding (left) and Cliff Branch, the mail order wizards of San Luis Obispo

By Merrill Shindler

CONSIDER FOR A moment the difficulties of buying stereo components if you happen to be a resident of the quiet rural hamlets of, say, Duck Hill, Mississippi; Shallow Water, Kansas, or even Purgatory, Alaska, below the Philip Smith Mountains. Obviously you don't have a hi-fi shop down the block desperately slashing prices to compete with the Pacific Stereo store nearby. Indeed, you probably don't even have a stereo store acting as a monopoly. Obviously, you have only two alternatives: to continue listening to your vintage Victor with the worn-out needle or to buy a stereo system via mail order.

Mail-order stereo sounds at first like a legalized form of the old traveling medicine show; I mean, for many people a sound system is going to be the third most expensive item they'll purchase in their lifetimes (after a house and a car) and is not the sort of purchase to be made sight unseen (or more to the point, hearing unheard). Still, if your alternatives are severely limited by geography, mail order is all that's left to you, and the unquestioned leader in mail order is Warehouse Sound of San Luis Obispo, California.

Warehouse Sound grew out of a record and poster shop opened in 1969 by a pair of sophomores at the local Cal Poly State University – Cliff Branch, an English major, and Tom Spalding, an engineering student. Recognizing the lack of understanding for the stereo needs of the college community among San Luis Obispo's few hi-fi shops, Branch and Spalding began stocking stereo components. After ten months, they grossed $100,000, moved to larger quarters and reopened as Stereo West.

"We realized the role music was playing in young people's lives," says Branch, Warehouse Sound's president, as he sits in his office surrounded by bare brick walls and unfinished redwood siding. In his Warehouse Sound T-shirt, Branch exudes a boyish enthusiasm, which pervades much of the Warehouse operation. "The old fogies who were in the business at the time, they didn't understand kids wanted to get ripped and listen to Jimi Hendrix. Kids knew there was a whole log of hypocrisy in that long cabinet with nothing in it, and that these little components were functional and you got good sound for your money. We just exploited that."

Stereo West quickly grew to five stores along the central California coast and probably would have continued to grow had not Branch and Spalding taken to traveling about the country. What they found was that the situation in San Luis Obispo existed almost everywhere. "We'd go to a town like Columbus, Ohio," says Branch, "and there's 50,000 kids there and one stereo shop where they sold Jesus with each stereo. Literally, it was run by a religious sect. This kept happening over and over again, and we finally said, 'Hey, we can put together some sort of catalog and relate to the market better than these guys face to face.' We ran an ad in ROLLING STONE and got like 5000 pieces of mail."

In 1974 Branch and Spalding sold Stereo West to CBS Corp., which also owns Pacific Stereo ("They made us an offer we couldn't refuse," Branch says), and moved completely into mail order, eventually employing more than 100 people who process some 4000 pieces of mail per day, which adds up to over $10 million a year in component sales, making Warehouse Sound one of the top ten component retailers in America.

To better relate to the kids who'd be buying equipment for the most part on faith, Branch started an advertising agency in San Luis Obispo (Different Circle), which produced the company's carefully wrought catalogs. Until recently, Branch wrote all the copy for the catalogs. That copy, Branch feels, was essential in developing the trust a mail-order stereo firm needed to survive.

"Kids buy stereo," explains Cliff, "because they emotionally identify with the music, and they want to hear it better and they want to hear it louder. Even though it's subconscious, if you can't have a fulfilling experience in buying the thing, you're bummed out to start with. So the thing we did was say, 'Hey, we understand where your head is.' You know, it's no different than the people who sell cologne in Cosmopolitan."

Today, the workings of the Warehouse Sound operation are a model of efficiency coupled with a personal touch. The day an order is received – by mail or phone – an acknowledgment is mailed to the sender. Normally, within another day the merchandise is shipped out, with a T-shirt and Frisbee on larger orders, and a letter under separate cover telling the customer how the equipment is being sent and, more importantly, the "Official Customer Care Kit," which includes a manual entitled "How to Hook Up Your System without Blowing It," a tiny red screwdriver, 30 feet of speaker wire, various logo stickers and forms about how to match up the boxes with the invoices and how to deal with warranties. In short, it's perfected stereo for the complete idiot.

With Warehouse Sound's business slowing down slightly in the more competitive, big-city markets as a result of the abolition of fair-trade laws, Branch has expanded his mail-order techniques into a new firm called California Cooperage, which sells hot tubs for $995 and up through the mail. After eight months, Cooperage is the largest seller of hot tubs in the world. "It's the same thing as the stereo systems," says Cliff. "The timing is just right, it's not even a marketing function, it's really a social phenomenon. We respond to the social needs more than anything else."

Cliff Branch and staff, in administrative offices.

Records, *National Lampoon* and *Playboy* – people Tom and I had met through our electronics and hot tub businesses.

Obviously, some of the business professors were not thrilled by my sudden appearance as a special, "expert" instructor. Two profs audited the course and showed up for the first few sessions. I think they were relieved that I taught in a fairly traditional manner and didn't urge any of their students to quit school and become renegade entrepreneurs.

Teaching the course was a blast.

David Riordan, circa 1976

Tom and I simply had no fear of failure. We were too naïve to realize that our stereo sales company was seriously undercapitalized for the speed of its growth – we just knew that we had to keep growing to succeed. When capital was short, we always came up with new promotions, and/or found additional investors.

We were lucky. In the early stages, a mere string of six months of poor sales could have put us under.

In the late 1970s, our stereo company had become a big account for Pioneer and JBL. We'd also started our professional products division, which brought us into contact with rock bands from L.A. We sold Fender and Vox guitar amps and other equipment from Teac and Altec Lansing, as well as custom mixing boards.

It was during this time that I connected with David Riordan, a former Poly student who became a professional musician and songwriter. David had co-written "Green-Eyed Lady," a hit song that garnered national attention.

David and I managed to sign a deal with Capitol Records for David to record a solo album, and we also produced other albums, independently, for Warehouse Sound Company. *[See page 353]*

Tom was in charge of our rock-and-roll products, but I often traveled south to the Troubadour in L.A., where I took in shows that featured some of the best performers of the time, including a young Jackson Browne, James Taylor and The Eagles, among many others. The Troubadour was a small club, but the JBL sound engineers used it to field test their equipment. I was admitted *gratis*, had a great seat and learned about sound equipment. It was a terrific time. ■

Friends Near and Far

Susan Branch

My life revolved around our company, and I often interviewed applicants when we increased our staff. One day I interviewed a young woman named Susan Stewart, who would eventually become Susan Branch. We became friends, and our relationship soon stepped beyond the workplace.

Susan Branch, circa 1978

Susan and I were together 10 years before we divorced and she moved to an island off the Massachusetts coast. On our visits with my relatives back East, Susan had become captivated by a hamlet called Vineyard Haven on Martha's Vineyard. She was always a great artist and wonderful cook, and over the years she became a bestselling author for Little Brown. Sue has published 14 bestselling "Heart of the Home" lifestyle books, which include eight cookbooks. Her various products can be seen at most Barnes & Noble bookstores or at susanbranch.com.

Susan was, and still is, a great friend. For the past 30 years, she has spent most of her time at her home on Martha's Vineyard with the love of her life, Joe Hall. They also have a home on our Central Coast. When they come to town, it's always a pleasure to catch up over dinner.

All I can say about our break-up is that we were young, and the matrimonial portion of my brain had not fully developed. *[See page 345]*

Chris Whittle

In the 1970s I became inspired by Chris Whittle, a very confident young man who walked into my office one morning to sell advertising aimed directly at college students. Like Tom and me, Chris had started a business while in college. His venture was a magazine called *Nutshell,* which was distributed to nearly every college student on campuses in several large areas of the country.

Chris Whittle, circa 1975

Chris and I hit it off immediately, and during our conversation I boasted, a little sarcastically, "You know, I'm the leading youth marketer in the nation." Chris instantly replied, "No, Mr. Branch – that can't be true, because I am."

He was right. He convinced me to advertise in his magazine, and over the years we became close friends. Chris would stay at my home when he came to town. When I traveled to the East Coast, I was a guest at his Manhattan apartment at The Dakota, and a few times I traveled for visits at his farm in Vermont. Within a decade, Whittle Communications grew into a conglomerate, owned *Esquire* magazine, and later sold to Time-Warner. *[See page 356]*

Emmons and Richard Blake

In Tom's and my early years, Emmons Blake was another figure who helped and inspired us. Emmons owned Blake Printery and was my father's age. He gave us a long line of credit for printing catalogs, and a lot of good advice to a pair of green kids, one a college dropout and the other still a student.

Emmons was a civic leader in San Luis Obispo and I always could go to him for thoughtful guidance. He even corrected the errors in my copy. When Richard Blake, Emmons' son, graduated from UC Berkeley and joined his dad in the family printing operation, he was skeptical about the large line of credit that Emmons had extended to our company. But Dick and I became friends, and he quickly learned that Tom and I always paid our bills – a trait I learned from my father and a practice that has served me well to this day.

Emmons and Richard Blake, circa 1975

A few years after I first met him, Richard purchased a 10-acre parcel in a 140-acre residential subdivision that Tom and I developed in the hills above the San Luis Obispo Country Club. Tom and I called the new development Alta Mira (High View). You could see Morro Rock – *The Gibraltar of the Pacific* – in Morro Bay, 13 miles west. It was our first major real estate venture.

Tom, Dick and I all built homes up on Alta Mira and were neighbors. Through the years I built and lived in three different homes within the development.

We all hung out together. Dick and I often raced our dirt bikes in the Pozo wilderness. Dick was always smoother and faster on his Husqvarna, but it didn't matter because we often ended up in the hospital. After one bad crash, I had to give Dick a ride to the pickup on the back of my bike. He was in a cast for weeks. Another time, I took a bad spill on a motocross track up behind Cal Poly. It was near dusk, and like a fool I was riding alone. I had to walk down to Sierra Vista Hospital's ER.

I rang the emergency bell and when the nurse opened the door her first words were, "Oh, you again." That night I had surgery for a separated shoulder.

Dick and I had many adventures exploring the back country on dirt bikes, ATVs and later in the air when he bought his first helicopter. *[See page 354]*

Never a dull moment with Richard.

Closing Doors and Opening New Ones

Johnson Design Associates

The success of our retail stores and mail-order company depended on constant advertising and I worked closely with many designers and photographers. Through our stereo business I developed a close relationship with manufacturers (Sony, JBL, Pioneer), and they would allocate a portion of their national budget for *youth marketing* – dollars that were often funneled through our company.

Doug Johnson, circa 1977

For a relatively small operation, we had a big budget for advertising aimed at the Baby Boom Generation across America.

I began to work with Doug and Carol Johnson, who were very talented, and we formed an advertising agency, Johnson Design Associates, or JDA. Doug, Carol and their staff handled the promotion for our company, as well as ad work for outside clients. Doug was an excellent graphic designer and Carol oversaw the production of the catalog art and other projects.

Frank Bez, a famous photographer from Los Angeles (who moved to San Luis Obispo) worked for JDA for several years. Another photographer, Forrest Doud, a young man who was just beginning his photographic career, began working for the agency and still has his studio in SLO – dozens of his photos appear in this book.

The new agency gave me a chance to work on marketing and advertising outside my and Tom's immediate company.

Selling to CBS Corporation – from Hi-Fi to Hot Tubs

Tom and I discovered that the mail-order portion of our company was more fun and less hassle than the retail end, so we sold our stores along the Central Coast to the CBS Corporation, which owned the vast Pacific Stereo chain. Then we also sold the mail-order business, to focus on our start-up hot tub company that needed our full attention.

Tom and I were branching out, and together and singly we became involved in a variety of businesses as the decades unfolded. ■

Hot Tubs and Boomers Make Warm Friends

WE CALLED our hot tub venture California Cooperage. It was the first and only national distributor to mass produce redwood hot tubs. We also offered the more traditional vacuum-formed plastic spas, as well as redwood saunas.

The idea first germinated in my early 20s, while I attended hot tub parties in Santa Barbara. At each of these gatherings, it seemed that people felt comfortable relaxing in the warm water without their swimsuits. I wondered if this phenomenon was something unique to Santa Barbara, and how people outside of California might view hot tubbing. Intuitively, I thought that there might be a wider market.

I ordered a redwood hot tub for my house in San Luis Obispo. Dick Blake, who lived in Pismo Beach, was one of my first friends to also install a tub in his back yard. At my house or his, we quickly found that the hot tub experience was the same as in Santa Barbara. Our friends would soak together *au naturale*, chatting, sipping wine and having fun. It was magic. One day, sitting in Dick's tub, it hit me: *These puppies will sell nationwide.*

I had a prototype engineered and took out a full-page ad in *Playboy* magazine. The response was immediate and overwhelming. We began buying tubs from redwood tank manufacturers in Oregon. But they could fabricate only limited quantities, and by the end of the first year we knew it would just be a matter of time before we outstripped our tank suppliers' ability to produce.

However, before I tackled the manufacturing/supply issue, I wanted to ensure our distribution. In 1979, we took a booth at the annual Swimming Pool and Spa Convention in hopes of signing up retail dealers across the country.

Big Brother Comes Through

That year the convention was held in San Francisco. For our booth, I figured we needed more than a simple sales counter and an empty tub. Our company hatched an ambitious plan – we would construct a large, custom trailer to serve as our display and booth. We'd outfit the trailer with redwood decks and a working redwood hot tub.

The challenge: The whole thing had to look sharp and be self-contained.

As luck would have it, my brother Greg had become chief engineer at Johnson Machinery, a Salinas company that manufactured special trailers and other

The advertisement shown at right ran in *Playboy, Rolling Stone, Esquire* and other national publications, and is a good example of our 1970s ad campaign. The fellow with the grin is an old friend, Tim Haley, who worked at California Cooperage and was more than happy to model for the shot. I'm uncertain who the women are, although I remember writing the copy and thinking the ad might be "too provocative." By today's standards, it's tame, but in the '70s the picture and text confirmed many Americans' fantasies about "Californians and their hot tubs." The ad hit a nerve – we received thousands of inquiries and began shipping hot tubs to customers in all 50 states.

Hot tub systems were delivered directly to the consumer (with do-it-yourself instructions), or purchased from and installed by 300 dealers nationwide.

Playboy **magazine, June 1979**

"Life hasn't been the same since I bought my California Cooperage Hot Tub."

"Just take a look at my neighbors, Susan and Donna . . . they've never been so . . . well, neighborly before!

"You see, it all started about a year ago when I was visiting friends on the West Coast. There I was, a normal guy from Cleveland when my date casually asked me to go hot tubbing. I wasn't even sure what a hot tub was, but I decided to go for it. . . .

"Next thing I knew, I was sitting in this huge redwood tub, submerged in bubbling hot water and loving it! An old California custom, she told me, and I thought . . . 'Why not Cleveland?'

"So I called California Cooperage and they had all the answers. I received their brochure and book describing several do-it-yourself packages, complete with hot tub, heater, filter, plumbing, the works — all for about $1,600. I did it!

"When the boxes arrived in Cleveland, I tried to explain the physical, spiritual and social benefits to Susan and Donna. But they just stood there, amused. Well, an office buddy helped me put it together over a weekend and the system worked fine, right from the start.

"That was a year ago. As you can see, Susan, Donna and I have added a new dimension to our lives. Regardless of sun, rain or snow, my back yard simply has never been so healthy, fun or sexy — and the same goes for me too!"

Find out what a hot tub can do for your life. Call California Cooperage at (805) 544-9300, or write P.O. Box E, San Luis Obispo, CA 93406.

PB-2A

☐ Rush me your 20-page color brochure on hot tubs, and your 64-page book on hot tubbing, via First Class Priority mail. I've enclosed $2 for postage and handling.

☐ Just send me your free brochure, via Third Class mail.

Name ______________________

Address ______________________

City ____________ State ______ Zip ______

P.O. Box E, San Luis Obispo, CA 93406 J6

CALIFORNIA COOPERAGE

California Cooperage catalogs for Hot Tubs, Spas, Saunas and Accessories

complex machinery for the agricultural industry. I had a couple of sketches drawn up, and Greg drove down to San Luis Obispo to assess the project.

Greg designed a hot tub trailer that incorporated an air-bag suspension system – the trailer would lower all the way to the ground when shifted to "show" mode. It featured all sorts of equipment compartments, folding contraptions and
a striped canvas awning. Every bit of the operational gear was built in. The whole thing looked completely natural, as if it had been lifted whole from a boomer's suburban backyard. Our real-life display wouldn't bear any resemblance to a trailer when it was set up at the convention.

The first time I watched the trailer transform itself to an exhibition booth I was thrilled. Greg's creation had surpassed my expectations. The hot tub trailer was both elegant and functional. It stole the show – with the help of two beautiful women.

Making redwood hot tubs irresistible

In the mid-'70s, the swimming pool and spa industry was run by conservative businessmen, most of them in construction trades. Our hot tubs were catching on in California, but most of the would-be corporate buyers at the National Pool and Spa convention – better known as the NSPI convention – were from the Midwest or East Coast. I figured we needed to shake things up a bit to bring nationwide attention to California redwood hot tubs.

I called Bruce James, a good friend and business associate in San Francisco. (He would become the 24th U.S. public printer.) I'd known him for several years and he'd become both a friend and mentor. Bruce was one of the few guys I knew who could get *anything* done. *[See page 357]*

I asked Bruce if he could find two attractive professional actresses to take part in a publicity event. I explained that hiring and paying the women had to be handled through his firm. California Cooperage couldn't be associated with what I had in mind. Everything had to be confidential. I outlined my entire plan, which would require finesse on Bruce's part. I was a little apprehensive as I outlined the details, but his response was immediate: "Absolutely. No problem. I'll get it done." He also assured me that he'd provide a professional photographer, and that photos would make it to the media covering the convention.

Frankly, I was nervous. After all, it was the first time our company had a booth at the national convention.

A big splash at the convention

The day the convention opened, two dazzling women in provocative attire arrived at the crowded Cow Palace. The head-turning pair made a slow circuit of the convention floor, cruising up and down the aisles and mingling among the conventioneers. Ninety percent of the attendees were men between the ages of 30 and 55, and the actresses Bruce had hired quickly began catching their attention.

The two finally completed their casual inspection of all the different booths, then made their way toward our California Cooperage exhibit, pausing beside our trailer with its redwood tub and bubbling warm water. Both women looked on with sudden interest. They put their hands in the inviting water and splashed each other. Without much fanfare – as if it were the most logical, most natural response in the world – the women began shedding their clothes, dropping them on the redwood deck.

Then they eased themselves with obvious pleasure into our waiting hot tub.

The naked actress plan hits the mark

My plan turned out to be fun – and almost became a riot. At first the women sat quietly in the moving water, content to chat with men as they approached. But a growing buzz had traveled rapidly across the convention floor when the actresses disrobed and entered the tub. Within minutes, the word had spread and now men were packed 10 deep at our booth.

A security guard came over to see what the commotion was about. He got a quick eyeful and informed the women that they needed to leave. He tried to grab one actress by the arm, but she retreated to the middle of the large tub, out of reach. Both women began laughing and splashing the guard as the crowd broke into cheers. Several men started yelling at him to leave the friendly bathers alone.

Outnumbered, the soaked security guard left the scene – I suppose for reinforcements – and the actresses promptly emerged from the tub, drying off on the trailer's deck before the admiring crowd. The all-male audience broke into applause as the hot tub models left our booth to slip out through the hall's rear entrance.

By late evening, the next day's convention newspaper was printed and the story appeared on the front page. Before morning, I made sure that the newsletter was delivered to every local hotel room occupied by conventioneers.

The article quoted the actresses as if they'd spoken in tandem: "Who could resist a California redwood hot tub? We're sorry if we offended anyone, but the tub felt so good against our skin."

All day, conventioneers walked by our trailer, most of them pointing out our hot tub as they passed. We didn't need to be lip readers to make out the common remark: "That's where those girls were."

My effective but fairly chauvinist marketing ploy – a sales pitch I wouldn't repeat today – was the talk of that year's pool and spa show.

We sold hot tubs like hotcakes. John King, Jim Smith and Dr. Brendan McAdams – all previous investors in our stereo business – helped us bring in new investors. John King and I were already business associates and now we became close friends – we lived next to each other in Monterey Heights and I'd take John's son, JG, to wrestling matches at Cal Poly. When John entered the restaurant business, Jim, Brendan and I invested in his first two locations.

California Cooperage continued to grow, and, John's construction company built a 60,000-square-foot manufacturing complex with offices and warehouse in the middle of a cow pasture on Industrial Way, on the outskirts of San Luis Obispo. Within a few years, California Cooperage was supplying a nationwide network of approximately 300 retailers.

John King also helped by remodeling seven of our own hot tub stores. Our outlets were located from San Rafael in Northern California to Sherman Oaks in Southern California. We had extra capacity at our new mill facility, so we formed a second company, American Tank and Mill, which offered a separate line of redwood tubs to our competitors.

Other key people (all still residents of the Central Coast today) had a significant hand in the hot tub ventures: Bob Silva, John Doyle, Elaine Sullivan, Sandy Johnson, Gary Gatel, Tim Haley and Beth Hamel. *[See page 358]*

As the company continued to attract new customers, we realized that the solid redwood tubs had three inherent flaws.

The main problem had to do with ecology: The watertight tubs required all-heart kiln-dried redwood (with zero knots), which came from old-growth redwood trees. Not a good thing – and not a renewable source.

Secondly, the solid redwood provided only moderate heat retention. We quickly designed a hybrid, the Spa Tub, made from cedar and other renewable woods. From the outside, our new model looked like a traditional wood tub, but on the inside the walls were lined with dense foam, which provided excellent insulation.

Finally, a redwood hot tub had a bench and used more water than the Spa Tub. The Spa Tub's molded interior seat design was more comfortable, and the tub's lower water capacity reduced both heat-up time and the power bill. Our handy, insulated roll-up cover worked like a big thermos to keep the water warm. And the tub's lined walls made it easy to clean. The spa Tub becaue our biggest seller. ■

In 1981, *Time* published one of the first major cover stories detailing the rise in cocaine use among baby boomers. The story documented how the drug had gained popularity for recreational use among white-collar professionals, moving from the music and film industries to include a cross section of the more traditional business community. Similar articles covering the cocaine epidemic appeared in *Newsweek, The Wall Street Journal, Rolling Stone, Esquire,* and several other national magazines. For a time in the late '70s and early '80s, cocaine became the drug of choice for boomers. By 1983, *Time* ran yet another cover story as the problems resulting from cocaine addiction continued to mount.

The All-American Cocaine Story

LIFE WAS GOOD in hot tub land. On one of my birthdays, late on a Friday afternoon, two of my best friends came into my office to offer me a small vial full of white powder.

I had no idea (at that time) that cocaine was highly addictive. My buddies seemed to be in a great mood. One of them rolled up a dollar bill. They showed me how to snort a line, and after a couple of sniffs I felt terrific! We sat around my office, talked about sports, and then we went to a bar and met some friends. We all sneaked trips to the bathroom to snort more lines.

At 9 p.m., when I realized I had skipped dinner and was looking for another snort of cocaine, I should have had a clue.

For a time in the late '70s, "doing cocaine" seemed just fine, especially with Jackson Browne's "Running on Empty" blasting in the background. I had been slowly and secretly seduced by the drug. It was self-inflicted agony, and it did not take long for addiction to mess up my life. I finally wised up enough to get some help, and quit. Not long after, I felt motivated to write a book about my experience with the insidious drug. I decided to compose a self-help guide about cocaine addiction under the pen name of David Britt.

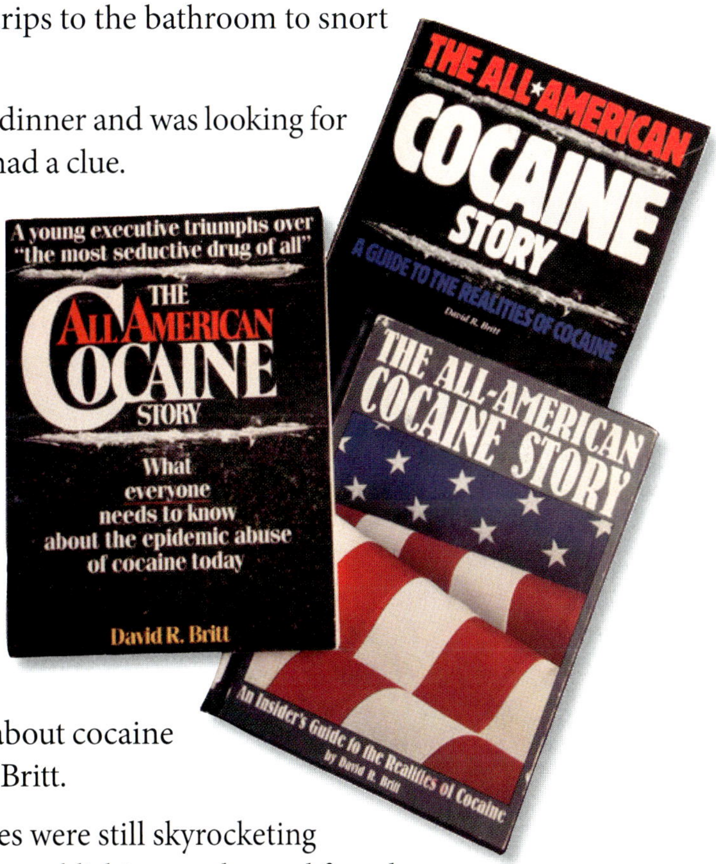

Self-help best seller, first edition, 1983

By 1984, cocaine sales in the United States were still skyrocketing and so was addiction. I had researched the publishing market and found no books on the dangers of the drug or how to kick a cocaine dependency. I self-published the first edition and ran ads in *Rolling Stone* to promote *The All American Cocaine Story.* After it received favorable reviews, a national publisher purchased the rights.

My personal story and tips for recovery hit the mark, and suddenly my book was on the self-help bestseller list. The book was published about the time that users and/or their worried friends and families had learned that cocaine was bad news.

My book was also used by a national chain of stop-smoking clinics that quickly added a cocaine addiction program to complement their treatment for nicotine dependency. Three editions of *The All-American Cocaine Story* were commercially printed.

I wrote under a pen name because it would have caused havoc, both personally and professionally, if my real name been connected to the book. My addiction and counseling occurred long before "going to rehab" was in vogue. I am thankful that 1984 was pre-internet. Today, I would have been outed within a few days. Because my real name was never used, I did not suffer any public fallout, but it was a painful learning experience and a contributing factor to the break-up of my marriage.

The 1983 *All-American Cocaine Story* began:

Preface

The first thing I should tell you is that David Britt is my pen name. I copped out to a pen name simply because my affair with cocaine is behind me, my future is bright, and I'd like to keep it that way. You'll find that my real name is unimportant, as are the few other minor details I've changed. In spirit, and in all essential facts, my story is true.

Odds are that you've already tried cocaine, or have considered it, or have a friend who uses it. I know this because cocaine is flowing around our country like teenage hormones at a Saturday night drive-in. It's everywhere, affecting you, me, and the guy next door.

In 1982, upwards of thirty billion dollars were spent on cocaine in this country, and that's more than our movie and recording industry grossed worldwide. Conservatively, in fact, it's three times as much. An estimated twenty-five million people in this country have purchased cocaine, and five thousand new prospects try it every day. Slowly, perhaps, but surely, many are turning into addicts – while those who understand cocaine use and abuse remain few and far between.

Drug treatment clinics won't be able to cope when the full impact of today's cocaine use hits the fan. Government officials are only beginning to get a glimpse of the situation – let alone solve it. According to Jean Miller, director of public information at the 800-COCAINE hot line, at the time of this writing they have received an average of one thousand calls each day since opening. That's over forty thousand callers in the first six weeks!

While alcoholism has long been labeled as a "disease" and thus gained some measure of respectability, cocaine addiction is still in the closet. There's a plethora of public information about alcoholism; there's virtually nothing available about the everyday reality of cocaine abuse and what to do about it.

July 11, 1983

In short, that's why I wrote this: not as a scholar, but simply as a rehabilitated cocaine addict who feels an obligation to help.

To simplify things, I have divided this book into two sections. The first deals with my own cocaine experience. The second section combines a lot of information I absorbed from fellow users, drug counselors, and various written material. The facts and figures I use in these pages were taken from the sources listed in the bibliography.

I have no illusion that this book will free a heavy user of cocaine from addiction. My intent was to get out some basic information to the recreational users and their families, and anyone who has used cocaine a few times, and now finds fascination with this new drug. I had to find out about the realities of cocaine use the hard way, so if you give some attention to the following pages, maybe you can avoid some of the hassles I experienced.

Essentially, I've gathered together the stuff I'd give my best friend.

Letters From Strangers

My cocaine book was short (133 pages) and told my own not-so-glamorous story: How I became addicted, how I stopped and what steps others could take to stop. There was also a reference list of clinics around the nation to contact for help.

After the book was published by Comp Care Publishers, good reviews appeared in *The New York Times*, the *New York Daily News* and the *West Coast Review of Books*. The positive write-ups further boosted sales.

The book hit a nerve, and I received hundreds of heartfelt letters (via my publisher) from strangers who wrote that the book had helped them quit using cocaine. Reading the letters was the best part of the whole experience. Writing the book helped end that unhappy chapter of my life. ■

Riding the Windjammer, Coleman and the Las Pilitas Fire

THE REMAINDER of my 30s and the 1980s passed quickly. With a new outlook and a healthier lifestyle, I charged forward. Recreational drugs no longer had any place in my life, but I remained a workaholic and always in the entrepreneurial mode. Patience was not my middle name. I was so busy "doing business" or building new houses that I had little free time for my marriage to Susan, for my family or for my friends. Looking back, I'm not sure exactly who I was, or where I was going.

Tom Spalding, my partner since college, had made the decision to go in a new direction. Tom took some of the proceeds from the sale of Warehouse Sound Company to become a professional race car driver, leaving California Cooperage very early in the game. As crazy as Tom's new career decision seemed, it wasn't. Tom had a previous background in racing, and became the pro top rookie driver in the 1977 Trans Am racing series. I had no clear idea about his driving talent until I watched him take third at a major racing event at the Riverside International Raceway in the Can-Am series, the top level of American racing. Frankly, I was in awe. *[See page 332]*

Double Duty

Tom's departure from our hot tub business coincided with an increasingly frenetic chapter of my life. I was running California Cooperage and also serving as director of marketing and advertising for the Vetter Corporation, a company that produced and marketed motorcycle fairings, streamlined fenders and other parts to reduce wind resistance. In the '80s, motorcycle fairings were generally a bolt-on after-market product. Vetter's "Windjammer" fairing kit included a windshield and bodywork that lowered drag and helped protect the rider from wind and rain.

In late 1977, I'd received a call from Craig Vetter, who had traveled from his company's headquarters near Champaign, Illinois to visit San Luis Obispo. He said he'd like to chat with me in person.

Craig was well-known in the motorcycle world as a gifted designer, and it turned out that he had also become enamored of hot tubs – and California. Craig seemed to know about my previous business background and was aware of the Warehouse Sound Company operation. We got to know each other by discussing motorcycles, hot tubs and marketing.

Craig was the majority shareholder of Vetter Fairing. The Vetter Corporation was the world's largest manufacturer of motorcycle fairings and accessories. The annual sales of the company were in excess of $30 million (equivalent to $80 million in 2014 dollars). Vetter-built fairings dominated the U.S. market.

It didn't take long for Craig to lay out his plan: He was going to live in San Luis Obispo and open a second Windjammer facility here. He also wanted to buy California Cooperage. Craig made an excellent offer and I signed a convoluted contract that put the hot tub business under the Vetter corporate umbrella. As part of the deal, I was to take over responsibility for all advertising and marketing for the Vetter Corporation's motorcycle business as well as continue to oversee California Cooperage.

The new San Luis Obispo-based combined operation meant that Vetter Corporation became one of the largest employers in town. Craig, John King, Jim Smith and I also formed a real estate partnership to purchase the former General Fireproofing building on Laurel Lane, which included a 140,000-square-foot complex and five additional acres. (Today, this property is home to Crux Climbing Gym, the South Side Office Complex, warehouses and the Southwood residential project.)

For a brief period I worked directly for Craig, but most of my time with Vetter was spent with John Doyle, Craig's VP for operations. John oversaw manufacturing of the motorcycle fairings and we consulted closely on new products and machinery for California Cooperage. John was the backbone of the company's San Luis Obispo manufacturing operations and a pleasure to work with. I learned a lot by watching how he seemlessly managed the two very different businesses.

Above Whale Rock Reservoir, near Cayucos, California

My double role was demanding, but I had a dream job. With my background in motorcycles, it was no stretch for me to oversee the marketing of motorcycle fairings and cycle accessories. Another plus was that Vetter Corporation (as part of their R&D) kept a full stable of new motorcycles, so I was always able to try out the latest models.

During my work for Craig I made several trips to the main Vetter plant near Champaign, Illinois and was busy planning and implementing sales strategies for Windjammer products. I oversaw the production of the following year's advertising materials, and for a while things went smoothly.

A surprise phone call

The next year, out of the blue, Craig Vetter called me one day while he was away on a road trip. He said that he had sold the motorcycle portion of the company to an investment group from Chicago. Craig said the sale was final – the check was in the bank.

At that point, I regained control of California Cooperage, and my responsibilities to Vetter Corporation ended.

Craig's quick move took everyone by surprise, but his sudden firm decision was consistent with the way he conducted both his business and his private life. He was passionate about his beliefs. Once, in an interview, Craig stated for the record – and in no uncertain terms – that he was against the licensing of a proposed PG&E nuclear power plant on the Central Coast. The new plant was planned for construction right on the coastline between Los Osos and Avila, approximately 12 miles southwest of San Luis Obispo. Craig warned that if the nuclear facility ever started operation, he would move away, and his outspoken views were covered in the local press.

The PG&E plant finally obtained its license – and Craig, true to his word, moved with his wife to Carmel Valley. His new residence was just a couple of miles down the road from my family's former home, adjacent to the Saddle Mountain Ranch campground. My parents had been friends with the Frumpkin family, who owned the ranch, and my brother Greg and I used to swim there as kids.

Craig Vetter is still active in the motorcycle community, as both a designer and lecturer. He was inducted into the American Motorcycle Association (AMA) Hall of Fame in 1999 and continues to run his company from Carmel Valley.

The Coleman Company

It was the early 1980s and I was staying busy running California Cooperage and developing real estate, when one morning I noticed an intriguing article in *The Wall Street Journal*. The Coleman Company, famous for its outdoor lanterns and its large line of camping products, was planning to diversify into backyard recreation. At the time, Coleman was a $500 million company traded on the New York Stock Exchange.

I was interested in the burgeoning company and phoned the Coleman vice president named in the article I had read. He was familiar with our company and seemed interested, so I sent him a package detailing our operation. We began discussions and I completed the sale of California Cooperage and the Cooperage real estate to Coleman within eight months of our first contact.

During the due diligence process, I flew back to the Coleman headquarters in Wichita, Kansas, several times. On one visit, I met with the president and CEO of the company, the son of the founder, W.C. Coleman, who assured me the hot tub company would remain in San Luis Obispo. As part of the deal, I signed a contract to continue as president of California Cooperage and oversee the San Luis Obispo operation.

Does anybody want to move to Arizona?

It was my first time working as an executive for a large corporation and I soon found myself writing a constant stream of management reports to Wichita. As the months went by, I heard rumblings about a shake-up in Coleman's corporate management. I wasn't surprised, as Coleman had acquired 10 new companies over the previous 12 months as part of their diversification plan.

One day, without any warning, a Coleman corporate VP flew into San Luis Obispo. I'd never met him before. He informed me that Coleman planned to move the entire company to another state. He said they had acquired a spa-shell manufacturing company in Arizona, and nearly one half of the 160,000-square-foot facility was presently vacant.

This was the first I'd heard that Coleman wanted to combine the administrative, manufacturing and warehouse operations of their entire spa business under one roof, far away from the Central Coast.

The Coleman VP asked me to gather the department heads and senior staff to inform them of the new plan. He assured me that all California Cooperage personnel could keep their jobs – *if they moved to Arizona.*

As you might imagine, the VP and I had a heated discussion. I basically told him that the hot tub company was not going to relocate to Arizona or anywhere else. At one point, he pulled out his letter of authorization signed by Mr. Coleman and said I could confirm the details of his decision by calling corporate headquarters in Wichita.

I did make the call, but it was a *fait acompli.* I explained to the visiting VP that he would have to address the employees himself, tell them the move was Coleman's idea and that I had no part in the plan. He made a strong effort to convince me of the merits of transferring California Cooperage to Arizona, and promised me a bonus if I'd move there, but I wanted nothing to do with his offer. On that morning, any good will I had toward Coleman was wiped out. I considered their relocation scheme a personal betrayal, and I was furious.

As our confrontation unfolded, the VP realized that I was adamant, so he finally accepted my resignation: "Okay – I regret that you'll be leaving the company, but I'm still calling the employees together."

During the argument, I could feel a knot growing in the pit of my stomach. I knew what this man's sudden visit would mean for my staff and their families. It was an awful day.

Within an hour, everyone had gathered in the warehouse to hear the news. All of us were blindsided, and almost all the employees ended up losing their jobs – only a few moved to Arizona.

Coleman soon shipped the entire operation to Arizona. Our buildings on Industrial Way have since been used for a variety of other businesses.

The California Cooperage brand of hot tubs and spas are still sold today by the Coleman Corporation.

The sunset view from the Oakenshaw Resort site above San Luis Obispo

Oakenshaw

After the Coleman fiasco, I took a month off.

Cliff, with architect Paul Smith, who designed Oakenshaw Resort

John King and I had lunch one day, and he offered me office space at the Rossi-King Organization (RKO) offices on Higuera Street, in The Promontory, a new development John's company had built. The complex of contemporary shingled-sided buildings overlooks Santa Rosa Creek, near the intersection of Marsh Street and Highway 101.

I thought I'd been busy at California Cooperage, but as I began watching Rossi and King in action, I realized I'd been doing business at a semi-fast pace. RKO *always* had dozens of irons in the fire.

I went to work on my next project independently. For quite a while an idea had been kicking around in my head, and now I decided that the time was right to start planning a very special spa resort.

The new project was called Oakenshaw. The name seemed to conjure romantic images of ancient oaks, cool shade or maybe old wooden buckets that drew pure water from a well. I'd just made the word up – I thought it sounded solid and unique. (In later years, I learned that Oakenshaw had long been the name of a village in England's County Durham.)

My concept for the venture had taken shape slowly, over several years, while vacationing at a number of world-class resorts in California and other states. In the 1970s, luxury health retreats catered almost exclusively to women. I often found myself one of the few men in a spa's swimming pool or on its scenic hiking trails. I was supposed to be relaxing, but even on vacation I was working.

I stayed for Men's Week at the Golden Door, near San Diego, in consecutive years. During each visit, I was able to talk at length with the spa's owner, Debra Szekely, who was very helpful in answering all of my questions about resort operation. She also owned Rancho La Puerta in Tecate, California, and I spent a week there, both unwinding and observing.

The Canyon Ranch, in Tucson, Arizona, was another location I scouted during vacation, and again I sought the advice of the resort's owner, a kind man named Mel Zukerman. I did the same at The Houstonian, in Houston, owned by Tom Fatjo. He was a well-known Texas entrepreneur who had built several businesses, and was as gregarious as he was helpful. I also vacationed at the Sonoma Mission Inn, in Sonoma, California, and the Heartland Spa in Gilman, Illinois.

Aerobics at The Ashram with Dreyfuss

My favorite place was a modest low-key operation known as The Ashram retreat in Calabasas, California. On one visit I shared a portion of the main house with Richard Dreyfuss, who had had just won an Academy Award for his performance with Marsha Mason in the 1977 film *The Goodbye Girl.* He had come for a week, to get in better shape for an upcoming role.

We were the only men in residence and spent several afternoons hiking together. We were both about 30 and had some interesting chats as we went up and down the jeep trails near the spa. Dreyfuss confided that he'd been overindulging in various ways, so we had a lot to talk about. He was very smart, very hyper and very funny. One afternoon, while hiking in the Calabasas Hills, I mentioned that I was planning to open a new spa that would attract men as well as women, and he gave me a dissertation on what features a good men's spa should offer. He had great ideas, and was certainly the most interesting man I met in my various spa travels.

The acreage (seven miles north of San Luis Obispo) was spectacular, with breathtaking views of the coastline. The pastureland – classic Spanish California ranch country – was scattered with hundreds of old-growth oaks and tall pines. The elevation was perfect for conifers, and the 40-acre parcel looked more like the forest around Cambria than most of the Central Coast's dry and open landscape.

The Oakenshaw Resort would be the perfect place for corporate executives to spend healthy vacations, restoring themselves as they enjoyed the attractions of a back-country retreat in an unspoiled setting conveniently accessible from San Luis Obispo and its airport. Designed by Paul Smith, a gifted architect I'd worked with on several previous projects, Oakenshaw would be the "Golden Door" of the Central Coast.

My vision for the spa also included a pragmatic financial element. I was actively talking with a venture capitalist and with reps from two high tech corporations. The three parties were interested in establishing a corporate retreat for top-level executive staffs, within a three-hour driving radius of both San Jose and Los Angeles. My plan was to form a partnership or sign a long-term contract with at least one of the well-funded potential investors, to ensure the development's financial stability.

It was a solid business plan, and I secretly hoped that owning a resort would encourage me to follow a more consistent, healthier lifestyle.

A Return to Houston

Not long after meeting Tom Fatjo at his resort in Houston, I found myself back in the Lone Star State. The Santa Margarita Ranch where I wanted to build Oakenshaw was managed by Rob Rossi and John King of RKO, but was owned by a Texas family named Cullen, who were in the oil business and had ranches all across the nation. I flew to Houston with Rob to arrange the Oakenshaw land deal with Corbin Robinson, the Cullen family patriarch.

Mr. Robertson lived on a magnificent estate in River Oaks, the Beverly Hills of the city, and was very hospitable. His representative, Bob Bouchard, took Rob and me on a tour of a new skyscraper that the Cullen family had built on the outskirts of Houston. Mr. Bouchard told me that they'd done the project on spec, calculating that the location was directly in "the path of progress" for downtown Houston. The multi-story office building was a joint venture with a national insurance company and had just been completed.

Rob and I quickly noticed that the towering project was virtually empty, but Mr. Bouchard didn't seem concerned. He said the Cullens were long-term players and were confident that the project would pencil out over time, and the investment would return a nice profit.

We had an informal meeting in Mr. Robertson's home office, during which I presented the Oakenshaw Resort plan. Mr. Robertson apparently approved it on the spot, with a simple nod or gesture to Mr. Bouchard. I didn't realize it was a done deal until after Rob and I left Mr. Robertson's office with Mr. Bouchard, who congratulated me on the purchase.

I returned to San Luis Obispo, excited and eager to move forward with the 40-acre parcel located above the Santa Margarita Ranch.

Up in Smoke

The environmental feasibility studies were completed in early 1984, and I had the green light to proceed. I'd had a test well drilled that verified there was plenty of good water. The resort master plan comprised three large facilities, 20 individual guest cabins and a separate residence that I planned to make my home. At the beginning of 1985 I received approval on the project from the county board of supervisors. Everything was falling perfectly into line.

Until one morning in the first week of July.

It was another day of 90+ degree heat and dry winds. I was eating an early breakfast at McLintocks Saloon on Higuera Street when I overheard a gentleman at the next table. He was describing a monstrous range and forest fire burning out of control and told his companions that it was moving fast and headed for San Luis Obispo. I rushed to the office and turned on the TV to hear more.

The Las Pilitas Fire burned almost 75,000 acres and 12 homes during the course of one week. On the worst days the entire sky was a chocolate brown, the sun turned orange, and ash fell on San Luis Obispo. At first, the city seemed out of harm's way, but one night the prevailing winds shifted and fire swept south down the Cuesta Grade. For a while, the Cal Poly campus appeared to be in immediate danger from the advancing inferno. California fire officials closed 17 miles of Highway 101 to all traffic except firefighting vehicles, in an attempt to use the freeway as a firebreak.

Additional firefighters from other counties rushed in to help. Eighty fire engines and their crews came up from Los Angeles. Helicopters, bulldozers and army of 1,500 men and women tirelessly battled the week long blaze.

Thanks to the heroic efforts of firefighters, the city was spared. To my knowledge, there were no human casualties, although there must have been a considerable loss to wildlife.

The Las Pilitas Fire was the worst fire to ever threaten San Luis Obispo. Thirty-foot flames had risen at the eastern and southern edges of the city.

Los Angeles Times

Residents Flee Fire on Edge of San Luis Obispo

July 9, 1985

JOHN HURST and JACK JONES | Times Staff Writers

A wall of flames threatened the eastern edge of San Luis Obispo for a time on Monday, destroying several structures and forcing the evacuation of numerous residents when erratic winds abruptly pushed the week-old 58,000-acre Las Pilitas fire down out of the foothills.

San Luis Obispo County Airport on the south side of the city was closed. On the north side, California State Polytechnic University shut down for the day and thick black smoke prompted San Luis Obispo High School officials to send summer school students home. Three youth camps in the hills also were closed.

A 17-mile stretch of U.S. 101 was closed to traffic between the junction of California 1 and Atascadero. State forestry officials said continued backfiring efforts by fire crews probably would keep the highway closed throughout the night and much of today. Motorists were rerouted through Morro Bay and over California 41 to Atascadero.

City Considered Safe

Late in the day, according to California Department of Forestry spokesman Jack Dueck, officials concluded that San Luis Obispo was safe and that the fire was no longer a threat to any other heavily populated area. Residents were told they could return to their homes.

There was some confusion over how many people actually fled their homes. One fire official said the evacuation area was a strip three to four miles long and about a quarter of a mile wide along the eastern flank of San Luis Obispo where 500 to 600 people live.

Others, however, said 5,000 to 10,000 persons were evacuated. In any event, some chose to remain and water down their roofs to save their homes.

"It's the worst fire we've had in the history of the city and county," said Steven Seybold of the San Luis Obispo Police Department. He said police had to switch to emergency power, and the city was clogged with traffic as residents fled the flames and as sightseers crowded in to look.

Seybold, crime prevention coordinator for the department, then drove home on his motorbike to check his house, only to suffer a leg injury when struck by a car and to find himself forced to flee on his new crutches as a flare-up destroyed his barn and outbuildings containing several antique cars and television sets. His house was saved, however.

By early afternoon, the 30-foot-high flames along the eastern and southern edges of the city were pretty well knocked down with the help of helicopters and bulldozers. Emergency crews from other counties rushed in to help the 1,500 firefighters worn down by their weeklong battle.

City Fire Capt. Ed Marcom said only two structures within the city limits appeared to have been damaged. Cause of the blaze was under investigation.

Apparently the fire had been started accidentally, probably by sparks from a car on Las Pilitas Road, near the Salinas River.

A few days after the fire was finally out, I went to visit the Oakenshaw site. I knew what I would find, but I had to go.

I was stunned by the scene. Almost all the native trees, the stands of beautiful red manzanita, the pines – everything was charred to the ground. It was eerily quiet. No animals, no birds chirping, no signs of life. It was obvious that the land would take a decade or more to recover its former beauty.

Many people suffered from the fire. It was a tough personal blow for me, especially following the Coleman Company's surprise move to Arizona. I'd lost a year's worth of work and a sizable chunk of capital trying to make my vision of Oakenshaw a reality. I was bummed. My dream to build a world-class resort had disappeared – literally, up in smoke.

It was time to take a break. ■

After a year in Sausalito, it was time to come back home to Avila.

Cliff and Jim Smith, circa 1985

Above: View from the Avila Beach house on San Rafael Street. Below: Avila Beach and pier looking toward the house.

No Place Like Home

I WAS IN MY 30s and had been working non-stop since I was 19. I decided to take a year off.

My wife at that time was Randi Branch, and we leased a comfortable home in Sausalito, overlooking San Francisco Bay and Angel Island. We sold the house I'd built on Alta Mira in San Luis Obispo to my partner Jim Smith and his wife, Beverly, who have now lived there for the past three decades.

Our San Luis Obispo friends came often to visit in Sausalito, and Jim and I bought a 30-foot twin-V8 offshore boat to cruise the Bay and up the delta of the American River to Sacramento. Most days I bicycled down Alexander Avenue through Sausalito to the Nautilus gym, and afterward I'd eat at one of the cafés along the yacht harbor. I got my body back into decent shape and spent the year exploring San Francisco and Marin County to the north. I saw a number of great acts at the American Music Hall, went to Giants baseball games at Candlestick Park and hiked the hills around Mill Valley.

The view from the Spyglass Restaurant patio in Shell Beach, overlooking the San Luis Bay towards Avila Beach.

But what I discovered during my year off was that I really missed San Luis Obispo. San Francisco is one of the great cities of the world and the Bay Area was an exciting place to live, but it was full of *strangers*. I found out that I'm a small-town guy at heart.

Eventually Randi and I returned to San Luis Obispo County, where I oversaw construction of a new home in Avila Beach near the top of San Rafael Street. The house was a contemporary structure built on four levels with a panoramic ocean view. But as time went by, Randi and I came to understand that our marriage was, and had been, on shaky ground for quite a while.

Randi wanted her life to take a different direction and moved east to Aspen, Colorado, in the Rockies. She bought a new home and soon began a new life with someone else.

Ours was no more nor less than a failed marriage, and we both had to go our separate ways. It was a painful time and once again I found myself starting over. ■

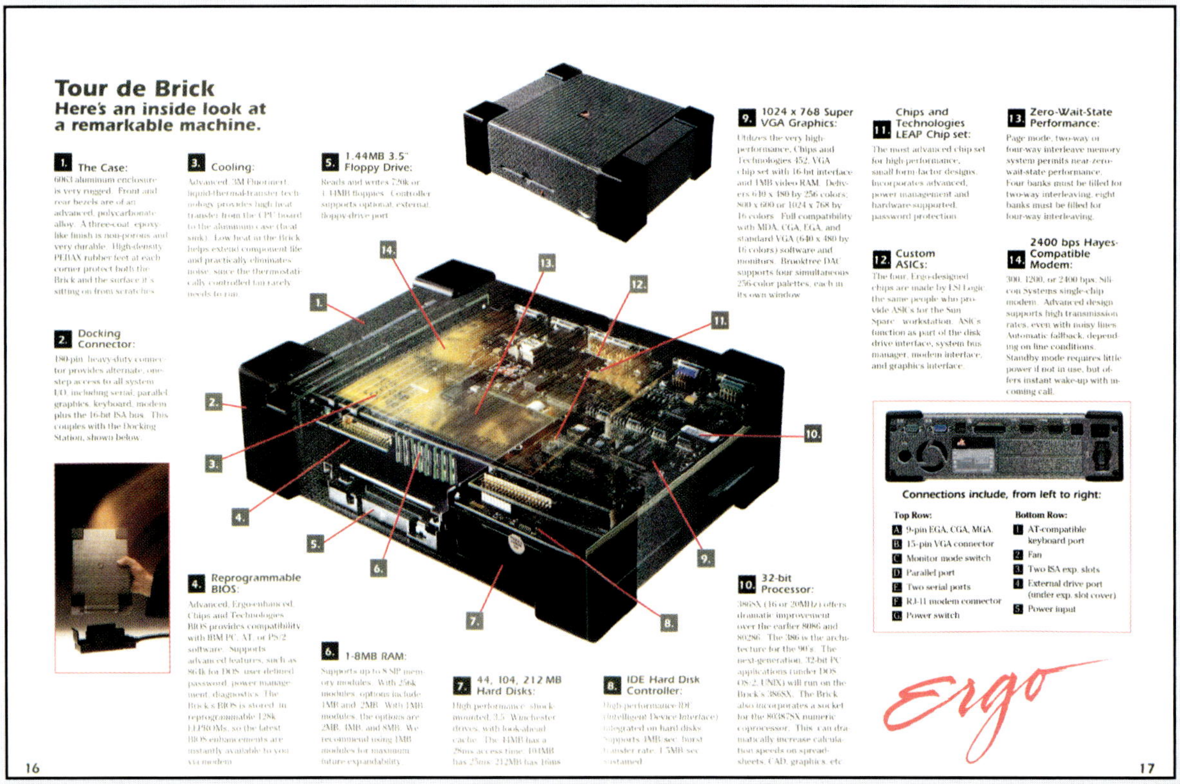

The Ergo "Brick" PC was highly innovative in its day. It was a small size (8"x11") and manufactured in a solid aluminum case with liquid heat sinks, which made it useful under rugged conditions. It also had a connector for use with an Ergo docking station, which allowed the entire PC to be snapped in and out as required for security.

Ergo Computers

Off to Asia and a Year in Boston

MY LIFE continued uneventfully in the new house above Avila Beach, until Tom Spalding phoned me one day. In the late '80s, my partner from college had ended his professional racing career and was calling to make a proposal.

He asked me to help him run a start-up computer company called Ergo, which he'd formed and was operating from the East Coast. The company had developed a new state-of-the-art personal computer that had a very small form factor and could also be used as a docking station. The PC was an elegant device about the size of a standard Webster's dictionary, with many unique features. It was Tom's version of a "PC race car," and it was seriously cool and *portable* for the time.

At first I resisted the idea, but eventually Tom convinced me to accept his offer, which included generous consulting fees and stock in his company, as well as a chance to live and work on the East Coast. At the end of the '80s and very early '90s I spent more than a year in and around Boston, where I lived in a townhouse outside of the city. I came home to Avila Beach for a few days every month to attend to my own business affairs.

Tom wanted to attract some additional capital prior to the product rollout, and I found myself on a flight to Tokyo with him within days of my arrival. We were going to make a pitch to ASCII, the leading software giant in Japan. Tom already had a relationship with Kazuhiko Nishi, who was both the founder and chairman of the company.

The plan was for me to make the basic sales pitch, and Tom would cover all the technical issues. So we made our presentation to the ASCII board of directors, in the boardroom on the top floor of the ASCII corporate headquarters.

Early in my presentation, I began to notice that not all the members of my audience were giving me their full attention. About a third of the ASCII directors gathered around the gleaming teak table had their eyes closed and seemed to be dozing, or barely awake. Occasionally, one of them would begin to nod off, until another board member would give a slight nudge to bring the sleeper back to consciousness.

Mr. Nishi, who was not much older than I was, had warned us about this possibility. He'd told me not to worry if some of his directors napped. Apparently, sleeping on and off through long meetings was a common occurrence in Japanese corporate life, since some of these men worked 16 hours per day. I found the lack of attention disconcerting, but I stayed focused, as if nothing was unusual. It was just a little strange to fly halfway around the world to talk to guys who were half asleep.

BusinessWeek

JUNE 25, 1990 A McGRAW-HILL PUBLICATION $2.00

Information Processing

ENTREPRENEURS

TOGETHER AGAIN: SPALDING AND BRANCH HAVE GONE FROM HI-FI TO HOT TUBS TO HIGH TECH

AIMING A POWERFUL 'BRICK' AT THE LAPTOP CROWD

Ergo's light 'portable office' can sit on a desk—or go to the beach

Tom Spalding and Cliff Branch have great timing. In the 1970s, when college-age baby boomers wanted a cooler place than Sears to buy a hi-fi, Spalding and Branch created Warehouse Sound Co., one of the first chains of stereo-component stores. With their hippie ambience, the company's outlets became a $10 million business for the two college students. Then, in the late 1980s, when the same consumers took down their Jimi Hendrix posters and began pursuing life in the fast lane, Spalding and Branch became overnight sensations by hustling hot tubs to the stressed-out.

Now, at fortysomething, the two drop-outs from California Polytechnic State University have a scheme for the 1990s. They have set up a company, Ergo Computing Inc. in Peabody, Mass., to sell their upscale audience a new kind of portable computer. Called the Brick, Ergo's machine is a $2,495 to $4,295 PC that weighs 8 pounds, fits in a briefcase, and is as high-tech sleek as a home espresso machine. Inside the black-flecked case is a powerful computer, based on Intel Corp.'s 80386SX microchip, with enough storage capacity to hold 200,000 pages of information, or about 10 times what the average laptop can handle. Ergo sees it as a traveling office that can hold all the data for a small company.

But there's a twist: The Brick includes everything but the monitor and the keyboard. Customers can make the Brick into a portable with Ergo's own keyboard and laptop-style display. Or, in the office, it can become a desktop PC by plugging it into a color screen, a full-size keyboard and connecting it to networks. And instead of lugging the laptop setup between office and home, the Ergo customer can just take the Brick.

TWO IN ONE. The idea behind Ergo is to carve a special niche in the U.S. portable-computer market, a business that market researcher Dataquest Inc. predicts will grow 32%, to $5.4 billion, this year. Spalding and Branch saw that laptops are good second computers—adequate for toying with a spreadsheet on the way to a meeting but too awkward for day-in, day-out work. The Brick, on the other hand, packs so much in a small package that it's two computers in one—a full-powered desktop for the office and a sturdy tote-along for the road.

The two entrepreneurs have already raised enough money to get things started. Backers include Singapore Technologies; software developer ASCII, which was Microsoft's Japanese sales agent until 1988; and DSC Ventures, an investment company owned by Novell Chairman Raymond J. Noorda. All told, they have to put up a total of $4 million to launch Ergo's first computer.

The Brick is plenty different, but that alone won't make it a hit. So instead of fighting laptop PC makers in computer stores, Spalding and Branch are relying on direct mail to attract high-tech nomads. Using slick mailers and targeting a select group of upwardly mobile types, the pair hope to sell $32 million worth of Bricks and accessories the first year.

Spalding, Ergo's 41-year-old president, promises something fancier than the typical computer mail-order piece. The first catalogue, which will be mailed to 150,000 consumers next month, mainly sings the praises of the on-the-go lifestyle. Instead of technobabble, it offers easy-to-digest suggestions for choosing software. Another twist: The Brick comes with a built-in speaker and software to talk novices through operations. Ergo has budgeted a lavish $6 million for sales and marketing in the first year.

LONGHAIRS. If computers can be sold with a soft-pedal approach, this is the pair to do it. Warehouse Sound blanketed campuses with catalogs, written by Branch, that profiled the company's long-haired staff instead of pushing tweeters and tuners. In two years, it was an $8 million business, and the entrepreneurs became dropouts. They sold the stores to CBS in 1974 and sold the mail-order business in 1977.

The pair perfected the catalog soft sell with California Cooperage, a hot tub maker they launched in1977. Spalding and Branch, now 40, split up after selling what was by then a $13 million hot tub company in 1984 to Coleman Co. Branch went into real estate and Spalding discovered computers. In 1986, Spalding landed in Cambridge, Mass., just when artificial intelligence hit. He launched A. I. Architects Inc. to supply software to AI developers. That company, the predecessor to Ergo, hit $4.6 million in sales two years ago, but shrank to $1.8 million in 1989 as interest in artificial intelligence faded. Nine months after hatching the Ergo idea, Spalding convinced Branch that he should come aboard as vice-president for marketing.

Are baby boomers ready for the Brick? Spalding is one, and he's convinced that the portable office really makes a difference. The night he pitched his first high-tech venture to ASCII President Kazuhiko Nishi, Spalding wound up running off a contract on his laptop computer over dinner. All in a day's work for a high-tech nomad.

By Gary McWilliams in Peabody, Mass.

DAMIEN STROHMEYER

Most importantly, Mr. Nishi liked the technology that Tom had incorporated into the Ergo computer, which Tom had nicknamed The Brick.

After our successful pitch in Japan, Tom and I felt confident as we flew on to Singapore to present Ergo to Singapore Technologies, a high-tech conglomerate. Just before the plane landed, the stewardesses came down the aisle, clipping the same message on the back of every seat. It was a short notice printed on a small yellow card: *Possession of drugs in Singapore is punishable by death.* Ouch.

Tom and I both knew that we had nothing to worry about, but it was just the first of many "signs" we saw in the island nation. In the restroom at the airport, a warning posted above the urinal caught my immediate attention: *Failure to flush results in a $500 fine.* The next morning, as I waited for Tom in the lobby of our four-star hotel, a man in a dark suit approached me. He wore sunglasses and an ear-bud with a wire running down into his jacket. Politely, but firmly, he informed me, "Sir, there is no loitering in the hotel lobby."

Singapore was our first visit to a *very serious* country. On the other hand, our assigned host was extremely cordial. We were taken on a tour of an immaculate portion of the city, and my presentation to Singapore Technologies was well received. Tom and I were interviewed by a woman who was the wife of one of the Singapore Technologies board members. She had been educated at Stanford University and she asked all the right questions. Both ASCII and Singapore Technologies invested in Ergo Computers, along with an American company, the investment arm of Novell, a Silicon Valley-based software firm. We gained over $4 million in additional working capital from our three new backers – capital that went a long way in 1990.

Ergo was our first venture-capital deal and it was an excellent learning experience. I stayed on with the company for only a little more than a year to oversee the marketing. It was fun, because I had a sizable budget, considerable freedom and I worked with a talented Boston advertising agency. My work for Ergo was challenging but very interesting, and my carefully tailored ad campaigns absorbed all of my time. Tom had given me a large office with picture windows looking out at a pine forest. The facilities were first rate, and the Ergo staff was kind and engaging.

But I found myself, once again, lonely.

I had no roots in Boston and I discovered that I was not an East Coast kind of guy. New England was freezing in the winter, and when spring finally came around there were bugs the size of your thumb in the air, and they loved to bite. I'd traveled from the East Coast to the Central Coast 14 times in a 15-month period, so I'd had enough.

After Ergo successfully launched its product line, I returned to mild and sunny Avila Beach nestled on San Luis Bay. ■

Avila Ad-Hoc Committee's
Proposed Mitigation Projects

A Response to the UNOCAL Avila Beach Clean-Up
Draft Environmental Impact Report

PREFACE

This document was prepared jointly by the Avila Ad-Hoc Committee, Uniplan Consulting, and Engineering Development Associates (EDA). The recommended mitigation projects described herein were developed at numerous Committee meetings, during which a wide range of issues was discussed.

Submitted by Uniplan Consulting on July 14th to Steve McMasters, Environmental Specialist with the County of San Luis Obispo, in response to the DEIR prepared for the Unocal Avila Beach Clean-Up Project. The short-term and long-term impacts to the community that will result from the proposed remediation activities require mitigation measures that go beyond removal of the contaminated soils. This document identified specific mitigation projects that can be implemented to reduce the magnitude of the impact.

Cliff Branch
Uniplan Consulting

Dan Lloyd
Engineering Development Associates (EDA).

A String of Projects

IT WAS NOW the early 1990s and I was into my 40s. Home again, I began work on several real estate projects, which included the construction of the Avila Bay Club and the development of Bassi Ranch, located in Avila Valley, not far from the club.

The Avila Bay Club is a fitness, swimming and tennis club adjacent to the Avila Beach Golf Course. I formed a new partnership that included Jim Smith and Neil Tardiff and we purchased the property from Rob Rossi in the late '80s and sold the completed development to an investment group from Santa Barbara in 2001. Neil Tardiff remained a partner in the new ownership.

The present owners have maintained the club beautifully to this day – it's a pleasure to have remained a club member.

Speaking Up for Avila Beach

I sold the Avila Beach house shortly after returning from Boston, but during the three years I'd lived in there I'd grown to love the town. During the late '80s and into the early '90s, Avila underwent extensive demolition for soil removal, as a result of pollution from Unocal Oil pipelines. I became involved in the process of determining how to rebuild the town, and took a public role in proposing options for the redevelopment.

Terry J. San Filippo, a third generation Avila native, co-wrote *Avila Beach, Images of America.* The book is filled with vintage photos and short narratives and is available at amazon.com

Avila was a very small town, and didn't have a traditional city council to represent the town's interests. I began a written response, on behalf of Avila Beach, to the Draft Environmental Impact Report (DEIR) that Unocal had produced for San Luis Obispo County. I asked one of the county's best known land-use consultants, Dan Lloyd, to assist me. I was confident that Dan would be of great help, because he was a good friend and also the savviest planning consultant I knew.

We volunteered our time and co-authored a 45-page document, complete with detailed exhibits and recommendations, which we submitted to the county and to Unocal. During the process, I worked with the Avila Beach Civic Association, Port San Luis Harbor District, the Avila Valley Advisory Committee (AVAC) and the Avila Beach Community Services District.

The report Dan and I drafted outlined various alternatives to facilitate the rebuilding of Avila Beach, hoping it would strengthen Avila's position with Unocal.

Not long after our report was sent in, I met with Roger Beach, the chairman of Unocal, at the San Luis Bay Inn. I was introduced as "the young man who co-authored the DEIR response," so I knew that someone at Unocal had obviously reviewed our document. Mr. Beach was gracious in his comments, and made it clear that Unocal "had always intended" to honor every aspect of its responsibility for rebuilding Avila Beach.

Avila Beach – *a jewel along the Central Coast.* Avila is home to the county's best weather, a protected beach, a wonderful golf course, an active port for fishing and three wharves.

During the review process there were many other local citizens who worked together on Avila's behalf, including Steve Puglisi, Russ Keissig, Leonard Cohen, Rob Rossi, Archie McLaren, Michael Kidd and several others.

In the following years, Unocal stepped up to the plate to fund the reconstruction of the town, and Avila Beach returned, better than ever, as a jewel of the Central Coast.

Fixing Autos and Planting Trees

After working with my old friend Tom Spalding on Ergo Computers, I never again had a *real job*, but I did continue to work as a consultant. Along the way, I become involved in several other enterprises, including auto body shops and a wholesale nursery.

The auto repair business

For the better part of a decade, I was a partner in two San Luis Obispo automotive repair shops: Otis Auto Body and Higuera Auto Body. Mike Hartwell and I had been very close friends for several years, and he was going through the break-up of his marriage. He asked if I would consider buying out his wife's 50% interest in his business and real estate holdings, and I accepted.

Otis Auto Body had operated since the 1950s, and Mike had taken over the business in the '70s, after graduating from Cal Poly. The operation was the largest body shop on the Central Coast, and the main part of the business was housed in a new facility Mike had constructed on Empresa Drive. I was a quiet partner in both the Otis and Higuera body shops, although I regularly helped as a consultant behind the scenes. We remained partners for nearly a decade, until Mike tragically died from cancer in his early 50s. I then sold the business to Simon Hunter, Mike's general manager.

Coast Growers Nursery

Sometimes businesses *don't work out,* and that was the case with Coast Growers. In the '90s, I invested in a nursery business that included a small farming operation. We planted 30 acres of Fuji apples – about 12,000 trees – on a parcel in Avila Valley. Our nursery also grew and sold a variety of native and ornamental trees, and I'm proud to say that most of them are still growing on the Central Coast. Planting trees has always been a hobby of mine, a tradition passed on from my father. As a business venture, however, both the orchard and nursery were failures. After several years, I sold the property to Rob Rossi and eventually the apple trees were pulled out and replaced by vineyards, which flourish today along San Luis Bay Drive, near Avila Beach.

Real Estate on the Gold Coast

During my high school years, I was constantly asking my father questions about the stock market and real estate. He took time to explain about business, and was open about how he managed the financial affairs of our family.

By the time I was 18, I'd managed to save $3,000 by stashing away money from odd jobs and the "big score" I'd made from the silver coin deal. In 1969, $3,150 was enough money for a down payment on my first house on Jaycee Drive in San Luis Obispo. (As a reference, a brand-new Ford Mustang that same year had a base price of $2,690). The house was a three-bedroom, two-bath tract house with a purchase price of $17,400. Today, that same house is probably worth about $500,000 – a testament to the wonders of inflation and the popularity of San Luis Obispo.

I fixed up the house and sold it in 1971 for $21,900. Before the escrow across town closed on Jaycee Drive, I had a new house in escrow. It was located in Monterey Heights on Santa Ynez Street, with a price of $23,500.

In the early years, I purchased and remodeled homes, but over the past several decades, I've been involved in building numerous custom homes, the last one in Bassi Ranch in Avila Valley.

During the last 50 years, real estate on the Central Coast of California has steadily increased in value. There were some slow periods and moderate dips, but overall, local properties have been a pretty safe bet. Beginning in 2007, on the cusp of the Great Recession, prices started falling, but sometime during 2012 the market stabilized and is now finally rebounding.

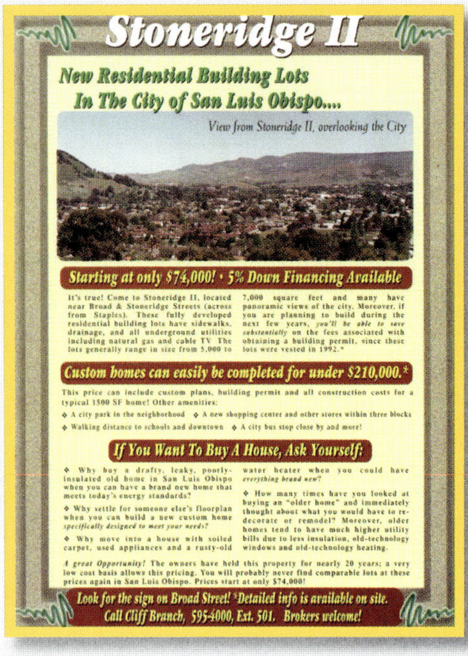

Flyers from various projects
in and around San Luis Obispo

Professional Office Building, 755 Santa Rosa Street
Designed by Steven Puglisi Architecture, 569 Higuera Street, San Luis Obispo

A Central Coast Developer

Between 1972 and 2012, I was involved in the planning, design and construction of commercial and residential building projects on the Central Coast. *[See page 370]* During the first 15 years of that period, I worked with Paul Smith, who designed several residences for me, and the Oakenshaw Resort before the devastating Las Pilitas Fire. When Paul retired, he told me that the best architect on the coast was a guy named Steven Puglisi, and suggested I contact him.

I'm glad I took Paul's advice, and I've been working with Steve ever since. His firm guided me through both the development and construction of many projects. We worked together on the Avila Bay Club and on projects in Cambria, Cayucos, Paso Robles, Arroyo Grande, Nipomo and Santa Maria.

Steve designed the art deco building in San Luis Obispo that was built by J. W. Construction in 2003 and has been home to my business offices for the past 10 years. Many of our other commercial properties can be seen on our website: CalCoastCommercial.com

Steve and I also worked together on residential tracts, including Stone Ridge II, Bassi Ranch and Cherry Creek.

Over the years, Steve and I have become dear friends – we often exchange thoughts and feelings about current events and compare notes on what we think we've learned over te span of several decades. We talk about some of the odd directions in which our country appears to be heading. And we discuss how our lives – and our independently minded wives – can quite often be challenging. These days we also console each other about our accumulating aches and pains.

Steve Puglisi

Watching From the Sidelines

When I reflect on the past 50 years, it's clear that I have learned to channel my youthful hyperactivity in a positive fashion, but for much of that time I was a workaholic, locked into the entrepreneurial mode – I was always looking for *the next project*.

That's changing now, as I'm much less intrigued with business and I just don't have the energy I once had. It's also a good time to take a breather – as it's a much tougher game for an entrepreneur these days.

Charging the windmill today is not so easy

For most businessmen, there is more wind in their faces from governmental regulations and from fierce competition in both national and global markets. It's a shame that we have entrenched bureaucratic agencies at nearly every turn that stifle the creative spirit.

Bureaucrats in our local and state government now spend much of their time finding some way to say "No" or demanding a sizable piece of the action through charging ever-increasing fees or by other convoluted accounting or regulatory echniques. Today, what government demands in *mitigation* often amounts to what some might call *extortion*. And if that doesn't kill initiative, government can slowly suffocate any idea or project with delays. Something the private sector can accomplish in months might take years in the spider web of the bureaucratic universe.

Government oversight of business activities is needed, but many of today's regulations have grown outdated, irrelevant or simply cost-prohibitive.

Obtaining credit is more difficult

It's also tougher now for entrepreneurs to obtain credit, because money-center banks (contrary to their advertisements) rarely lend to anyone who has a promising idea and a solid business plan but no ready cash.

Of course, if you already have money, everyone wants to lend.

Banks tend to bury potential borrowers with paperwork and complicated legal documents. The banks love to place all the blame on the government for the convoluted system, but we've all seen how well banks do on their own with less regulation.

In the past two decades, California has created a business environment in which would-be entrepreneurs have to spend a disproportionate amount of their time and resources navigating a rising tide of governmental officials, lawyers, tax accountants and bankers. I have nothing against the above–mentioned professions, but I have yet to see any of their practitioners actually design, build or produce anything.

Salman Khan, the creator of an online educational website called Khan Academy, was a featured speaker at the 2012 conference of Technology, Entertainment and Design (TED), where he made a comment about his new-found joy in building the academy:

"I was previously an analyst for a hedge fund, and so it was very strange for me to do something of social value."

Khan's statement must have hit a nerve, because his audience responded instantly with applause.

In contrast to the traditional, brick-and-mortar economic model, the Khan Academy approach exemplifies the potential of open-source internet-based services. Khan's creation is a good prototype in showing how new technology can level the playing field by increasing free access to learning, and by fostering a wave of other web-based educational enterprises.

The internet provides a new doorway for those who are short on capital but long on imagination. The opportunities offered by the Web are nearly endless and its evolving influence on how we live and work will be profound.

Frustrated but optimistic

Despite my grumblings about bureaucracy, I have every reason to be optimistic about the future of our country – resiliency is the central strand of America's DNA. Thomas Wolfe, one of our nation's greatest novelists and author of *You Can't Go Home Again*, once wrote:

"It's a place where miracles not only happen, but they happen all the time."

Like most people in their 60s, I'm amazed at how fast the time flew by. At this point in my life, I'm content to sit more often on the sidelines and watch. The thought of retirement has never crossed my mind, but I'd be foolish not to shift my priorities and adjust my sails.

I arose this morning pleased to find that my back didn't ache so much, managed to make a great cup of coffee, and boiled my eggs perfectly. I watched a business channel from the kitchen counter, and along came these advertisements: First, it was Flowmax – for old guys with "a going problem." Next, ex-basketball great Shaquille O'Neil appeared, promoting some kind of pain-relief patch and flashing his endearing and contagious smile. And then there was an ad for some miracle product to cover gray hair called "Just for Men."

As a marketeer, I watched and grinned, thinking: *Old guys rule!* ■

Ages 44 to 65 in Four Pages

SECRETLY, on a good day, I think I'm pretty damn cool for an old guy. But that illusion was recently shattered when a 30-something friend referred to me affectionately as "an old boomer dinosaur who needs to find some shade and retire."

His remark had some sting and reminded me how difficult it is to view ourselves as other people see us. It's hard to perceive one's own reflection. Cool or not, I'm fortunate to have had a good long run. I was raised by loving parents and two smart older brothers. My childhood played out on suburban baseball fields, on beaches, and in the forests of Big Sur. As a fifth-generation Californian, my entire life – with the exception of several sabbaticals – has been spent on the Central Coast.

I became immersed in American pop culture by the age of 12, and fascinated by politics starting at 16. My business career started at 19 with a variety of business partners, most of them remaining lifelong friends.

My good fortune leaves me with no valid excuse for some questionable choices and avoidable mistakes that I managed to stumble through during the first two decades of my adulthood. Writing about my past personal life makes me nervous, and some episodes are better left in the diary. Over the years, I've tried to make it my practice to apologize and make amends whenever it seemed necessary and possible.

Yet at some point the past simply has to become the past. Many times, the best I have been able to do is pick up what pieces I could, shake myself off, and move on.

An Attempt at Bachelorhood

After my second divorce, I seriously questioned my skills and capacity for maintaining a marriage, and vowed to live a single man's life. I shared a house for a year with Kevin Smith, the son of my business partner Jim Smith. I'd watched Kevin grow up, and by the mid 1990s he had a successful law practice and seemed to be (at that point) a confirmed bachelor.

I figured Kevin would be a good influence. During the time we lived together, we both tried our best to embrace a bachelor's philosophy, but it didn't last for either of us.

For a while, it seemed fun to be involved with much younger women, but I always felt a bit awkward, and I certainly received my share of death stares from the wives of my buddies.

In October of 1997, I was having a sandwich with Kevin at the Firestone Grill in downtown San Luis when I was introduced to Lynette Jordan. Lynette and I began talking, and we've never stopped.

Later that year, Kevin met Carolyn Johnson – they've also been together ever since.

Lynette is a fourth-generation Texas girl who grew up on Galveston Island among a family of traditional conservatives. She excelled in school and sports and graduated from the University of Texas. When I met her, Lynette was a single mom in the midst of a successful career – she was the senior vice president of a regional bank's mortgage division. I was sharing a house in San Luis with Kevin, but was also in the process of building a bachelor pad in Avila Valley. It was a time when I didn't have a *real job* – as an entrepreneur, I went from project to project.

After Lynette and I had been dating for several months, she commented about the fact that I was not "gainfully employed." She said with a grin: "At the bank I work for, they would view you as one of those guys with no visible means of support."

Regular job or not, our relationship soon became more than a romance, and within a year we committed to live together. Somehow I found myself disassembling my new office in my bachelor quarters, to create a bedroom for Tyler, Lynette's 6-year-old boy. I fell hard for both of them.

Lynette, Tyler and Cliff, 1998

Life Settles Down

Lynette and I were married in 2000, and in 2001 the three of us moved into a house we had constructed in Bassi Ranch, a residential development I'd completed in the '90s. We live there today.

During the past 17 years, Lynette and I have learned to appreciate our similarities and accept our philosophical differences. We grew up in very different environments and don't always share the same world view, and so we often have lively discussions. Lynette tells our friends that my thinking has *matured* under her influence. I might claim the reverse, that it's irrelevant, since the melting pot works.

For me, a wonderful part of getting older is gaining a sense of new freedom – I don't have to prove anything anymore, or fret over what others might think. I've grown comfortable with gray hair and my uniform of stretch-band khaki Dockers, a wrinkle-free shirt and New Balance tennis shoes. I drive to my office every day to work with people I truly like. I'm self-employed and don't suffer from the anxiety that some soulless corporation will eliminate my job or fire my ass. I've been lucky, especially given the depth of the most recent economic crisis.

How Did I Come To Write This?

In the beginning pages of this book, I described my concerns about my own health, and the fact that recent events have given me pause. I have close friends and family who are suffering from medical issues that have altered the course of their lives. Watching these situations unfold has reminded me that life is truly a gift – each and every day. As the people in my life struggle, I can only hope that they will get better as I stand by, wishing them my best.

As for my work life, the commercial property business remained depressed for several years, and my day-to-day management responsibilities became tedious. I decided to do something creative. Lynette had been encouraging me to "write something about our generation" to share with friends and family. She also reminded me that my stepson, Tyler, knew very few details of my life before he and I met in 1997 – although I'm sure he remembers my lectures against recreational drug use during his high school and college years. Of course, Tyler found out I hadn't been totally forthcoming about my own past when I handed him the first draft of this book. It's not that I lied to him, but I certainly never volunteered any detailed that at the time seemed better left unsaid.

Tyler with Abby, 1998

In the months that I've been working on this book, I've noticed that my overall mood has improved. Since I've spent almost all my spare time writing, I've had little time to watch the news or read the newspaper. I'm sure the world is still falling apart, but it is refreshing to take a break from learning all the grisly details. My wife has commented in the past that I read too much about politics and watch too many news programs, and she may be on to something. When I'm finished with this book, I plan to lighten up.

Somewhere along the road of our marriage, Lynette appointed herself my personal life coach, but I generally chafe against the constant generosity of her guidance. My wife considers me "a work in progress" – but from my point of view, it seems as if she's always nudging the bar higher. My good deeds have a short shelf life and my not-so-good deeds end up on my permanent record.

A couple of years ago, after listening to her *encouragement* to reconsider my selection of attire to wear at a dinner party, I ardently reminded Lynette that I had successfully made it through life for more than 40 years before we met. Without hesitation, she looked me in the eye, gave me a grin and proclaimed: "A miracle – only by the grace of God."

A Modern Family

My stepson came into my life during my late 40s, when he was 6 years old. He has been a blessing and a joy. When I first met Tyler, he often punched me in the stomach, but he eventually realized that I was there to stay and his punches turned into hugs.

Tyler with Lynette's father, Carl, late '90s

I remember one particular day, after we had all been living together for a while, when Lynette and I began "discussing life" during a short family road trip. Tyler was in the back seat of the car listening to our conversation. The poor kid had to endure a five-minute bickering match. It was nothing special – Lynette and I were debating the merits of something that I had recently said or done. My wife thought I'd been off base and I was making the case for the defense.

When Lynette and I finished squabbling and the car was quiet, I asked: "Tyler, what is your opinion on the matter?" Tyler answered, very clearly, in his young but wise voice: "Mom, honestly, I think you may be overreacting."

Cliff and Lynette with Tyler, Cal Poly graduation, 2012

In that instant, I knew that we had become a family. It was my good fortune to help raise the young lad, and he is now 23.

In contrast to my experience of growing up in the '60s, Tyler never went swimming unsupervised. There was no hitchhiking permitted, he was not allowed to own a gun and his mother said no to any street motorcycle. He always wore a helmet when riding his dirt bike, and played roller hockey padded up to the gills. ■

A Little Bit Texas

WHEN MY WIFE and I began dating, a few of our mutual friends (who knew us independently) wondered how a fifth-generation Californian and a fourth-generation Texan would find common ground. At times, throughout our years together, we've wondered the same thing.

Lynette and I were living together when her father, Carl, flew out from Texas to visit. I was 47 and Lynette was 37. Carl was a hunk of a man – about six-foot-two with broad shoulders.

The day after he arrived, Carl asked me to take him for a ride to see a construction project that I had mentioned. We hopped in my truck and after some causal chit-chat about college football, Carl turned toward me, looking me squarely in the eyes.

Galveston, 1962: Carl, Lynette and Marilyn Pehnke

He explained that he had come to California to find out what my intentions were regarding his daughter. He ended his comments with these exact words: "Son, in my part of the country, when a man and a woman live together, they get married."

I'd visited Texas before, but this conversation in the pickup was my first real introduction to the Lone Star State. I assured Lynette's father that my intentions were honorable, but I reminded him that his daughter was a grown woman, and informed him that we had not yet discussed marriage. Her father replied simply: "I suspect you will."

Carl was a wonderful man and we grew to be friends during his remaining years. I let several seasons pass before I told Lynette about her dad's inquisition. She cringed a bit at the story – but I told her that in my mind the exchange with Carl was a big plus: She had obviously grown up with a father who cared deeply about his daughter and his grandson.

Galveston

Galveston Island, Texas. Less than an hour's drive from downtown Houston, the island is home to 50,000 permanent residents and an influx of Houstonians and other tourists during spring and summer. Established in 1825, Galveston is the oldest port on the Gulf of Mexico west of New Orleans. It is equipped to handle a variety of cargo from around the world, and is home port to several cruise ship lines.

On one of my early trips to Galveston Island, I spent an afternoon with Lynette's grandmother, who lived a few doors down from the home where Lynette had grown up. We watched a Houston Rockets game together. Nanny (as she was called) was in her mid-80s at the time and a big Rockets fan.

She knew the skinny on every player on the team and candidly commented on the quality of their play – she was sharp as a tack. During a commercial, she looked me up and down, then asked, "How do you like Texas?"

She could see my hesitation as I tried to choose my words carefully, and then waved a hand in the air, indicating that I didn't have to answer. Nanny gave me a big smile and said, "Don't worry, honey, you'll grow to love this island – because of the people, and because the sand will get between your toes."

On a Texas visit about 10 years ago, Lynette and I attended her family reunion. I'm still not sure exactly how it happened, but before we left the island we ended up in escrow on a small home on the waters of Galveston Bay, next to the Galveston Country Club.

Lynette, left, with her sister Jill, their mother Marilyn, and grandmother Helen.

To be frank, for several years I was not a big fan of Texas, and I bitched and whined about the hassles of owning a second home. Once I made a snarky comment to Lynette: I said I thought Galveston was similar to a bad beach in California – with mosquitoes. My remark was a cheap shot, and I wished

Our home in Galveston

I could have taken it back the second I saw the expression on her face.

It was also not a fair assessment, because I found that Galveston has a long, rich history, and has much to offer. Lynette travels to Galveston frequently. I don't go as often, but I've spent my fair share of time in Texas over the past decade. We've remodeled the waterfront house twice – the second time in 2008, after the awful damage caused by Hurricane Ike. Galveston didn't receive much federal assistance after the disaster and I was amazed and impressed by how quickly the island was rebuilt.

The Galveston Museum is interesting. The city was the cultural and economic center of Texas, before the 1900 hurricane devastated the island. The Pier 21 Theater has an excellent documentary film on the storm, which still remains the deadliest natural disaster to ever strike the United States. Approximately 8,000 people perished. The island's nearly total destruction marked both the end of Galveston's preeminence as a financial center and the rise of Houston, 40 miles inland from the Gulf, as the state's economic hub. We've also visited other historic areas of the state, including the battleground and museum at San Jacinto.

The Sand Got Between My Toes

In spite of some of my initial misgivings, I found that Lynette's grandmother was right.

The Lone Star folks are very friendly, they'll go out of their way to help you, and they always seem to have a can-do attitude. Texans have tremendous pride in their state, and their economy has remained in much better shape than California's. The balmy summer nights are wonderful and you can swim in the Gulf almost year round.

And Texans know how to have a good time. They are wizards at barbecuing, love to drink and are not afraid to ask questions. Gas is cheap, and there is no state income tax. The boaters in Galveston have no fear of zooming around the very shallow bay, which keeps the local boat-repair business humming. If you get stuck, you can usually walk to the nearest shoreline.

I'll refrain from making any comment about Texas Governor Rick Perry, except to say that I am always surprised at how "moderate conservatives" describe their own governor. Apparently, Rick Perry may be a bit much, even for many Texas Republicans. When I'm in Texas, I find it's best to steer clear of politics. I just listen, and I avoid any discussion about the state of California.

Texas Comes to California

Lynette and I are good friends with our Galveston neighbors, and finally coaxed some of them to come visit in California.

Bill and Linda Frey were not familiar with the Central Coast, and during their stay we showed them much of San Luis Obispo and Monterey counties. At Big Sur, while gazing out from one of the majestic vistas, Linda remarked, "The California coast is even more breathtaking than it looks in the movies."

Our guests kept raving about the natural beauty of the area and its mild climate. As we drove past ranches, farms and vineyards, through mountains and beach towns, I began to see my own backyard with new, more appreciative eyes.

As a fifth-generation Californian, I again fell in love with my state, in spite of its overzealous public policies and pricey real estate. Our state government may have its issues – but California still has the magic. ■

Not a Smooth Operator

The Last Time I Flirted With a Young Woman

"SUPERCUTS" is the place I go for haircuts: They're fast, consistent and reasonably priced. One afternoon, about 10 years ago, I dropped in for my regular trim. The woman cutting my locks looked to be mid-30ish. I was captive in her barber's chair and captivated by her charm. She was very cute, chatted me up, and kept running her fingers through my gray hair. She seemed very open and very friendly, and for a moment I had a fleeting thought:

This woman is flirting with me.

The very idea caused me to sit up straighter in the chair. I pulled in my gut and made what I thought was a witty comment. We kept talking and I was doing my best to dial up the charm when she ran her fingers through my hair again and said sweetly:

"You really have the nicest gray hair … it reminds me so much of my father's."

I slumped back and released my stomach muscles as my lungs and ego deflated. Obviously, the attractive younger woman – snipping quickly as she talked – felt safe and comfortable in the presence of some harmless paternal figure.

I told Lynette the story and she laughed, gave me a long hug, and patted me on the back.

The Day I Turned Into My Father

A few years ago, I agreed to meet a much younger friend who asked me to join him for a drink, early on a Friday afternoon. We were to get together at Mother's Tavern (MoTav), where he worked – it's a downtown SLO hot spot frequented mostly by the youngsters from Cal Poly.

As I walked through the main doors, I noticed that the place was fairly empty. I glanced over at the bar and saw a group of *kids* sitting on a row of bar stools. All but one of them were downing straight shots of tequila. They looked about 17.

My visceral reaction was a mixture of shock and concern. *Who's letting these teenagers do shots?* I stood there watching with silent indignation.

MoTav

I glanced behind the oak bar at an older man with a frown of disapproval on his face. Suddenly, I recognized him – I was staring at my own reflection in the wide mirror behind the bar. I knew that look – it was *exactly* the same expression I'd seen many times on my father's face, when he'd just observed something that didn't meet with his approval.

My young friend approached and I quickly changed my demeanor, but he must have caught me glaring at the kids. He pointed toward the bar and explained, to ease my upset:

"It's a birthday party. The youngest turned 21 today. The guy on the left, with the soda – he's the designated driver."

All in a Day's Work

Throughout my life, I've been kind of klutzy. I try to blame it on my hyperactivity, but to tell the truth I just get so preoccupied with one thing or another that I turn into Mr. Magoo. I'm always on the verge of banging into things or tipping over something breakable.

My tendency for goofball stupid stuff has long been a known fact to my friends, and they make fun of me – with good reason.

In my younger years, I'd often go snow skiing or river rafting with a group of buddies. On a trip to Aspen, we'd finished skiing for the day and headed out to dinner. The party included Jim Smith, John King, Ben McAdams, Richard Blake and some doctors from San Luis whom I didn't know.

We ended up in a fancy restaurant, with an hour's wait for a table. We were sitting in the bar, all drinking, and I was really *hungry*.

The bartender was quite the showman and was entertaining the entire bar crowd with sleight-of-hand tricks. I was sitting at the end of the bar,

Colorado ski trip with the Kings, Smiths, Brett Whitaker

Left to right: Kerry, JG, John, Brett, Kevin, Cliff, Jim

parked right next to a full tray of prepared cocktail garnishes – olives, sliced oranges, etc. A few minutes later I realized I'd nearly chowed down the entire tray, as if it were my personal batch of *hors d'oeuvres.*

I was filling my mouth with the final four olives from the recently overflowing tray when the bartender – who must have been eyeballing me – lifted both hands high in the air until he had everyone's attention. Then he swiveled his body, tilting his head sarcastically in my direction, and asked loudly, "HEY, BIG GUY – GOT ENOUGH TO EAT DOWN THERE?"

Instantly, the whole bar was laughing at me, and with the olives stuffed in my mouth all I could do was turn a brighter shade of red. It was not one of my finest moments. After that little scene at the restaurant, for the rest of our ski trip I tried to become more conscious of my actions

But attempts at heightened awareness have never been of much use. I really don't try to embarrass myself – it just happens.

A Hand Dryer to the Rescue

A few years ago, Patti Giovannelli came to work in my office to help with property management. Patti was a good friend of Lynette's and had a background as a real estate escrow officer.

Patti hadn't been working for me very long when one afternoon I asked her to go with me on a quick trip down to Santa Maria, to a sit-down meeting with the management team from a prospective corporate tenant.

The company wanted a 20,000-square-foot building we owned that had been vacant since 2008, after the previous tenant had filed for bankruptcy.

I was anxious to make a good impression and secure a lease. It was a hot day, and Patti and I were running tight on time. When we got to Santa Maria, I said I was thirsty, so we made a quick stop at McDonald's for iced tea. We were only a couple of blocks from our meeting place – what could possibly go wrong?

The next several minutes passed like this:

I take the large iced tea from the lady at the drive-thru window, place it between my legs and drive off. For some reason, I have to hit the brakes and the plastic cover on the cup pops off. Several ounces of the icy tea spill into my lap before we are even out of the McDonald's parking lot.

To any objective observer, it now appears that *I've wet my pants*. Patti sees my soaked slacks and shakes her head, reminding me that our potential tenants are waiting for us.

I jump out of the car and hurry into the McDonald's restroom. With disbelief, I see there are no paper towels. I have no choice but to use a half roll of toilet paper to absorb the tea staining my crotch. But my pants still look awful and my options are running out.

I see an electric hand dryer projecting from the wall and think, *What the hell?* I move over in front of the dryer, unzipping my pants, and hit the button. The air dryer howls to life.

What else can I do? I'm late and I'm not going to meet potential tenants for the first time with huge stains on the front of my pants.

So I'm standing there, my hips arched toward the hand dryer, shaking my pants, with warm air blowing down at my crotch.

Everything is drying up just fine when the restroom door swings open and an older guy steps in. He stops in his tracks.

He stares for a second, taking in the scene, his eyes getting big before he exclaims, *"Oh my God!"* He pivots and shoots out the door.

I was sure he was rushing to call the police, or at least to alert the manager that a deviant was committing an unlawful act in his restroom. I zipped up and skedaddled.

Fortunately, my shameless action saved the day. I held my binder in front of my pants as I shook hands with the management team before we sat down. By the time the meeting was over, my pants were nearly dry, my pride had recovered and we had landed new tenants. ■

"Killer Cat" Lucy and her trusty companions, Lynette and Abby

A Quiet Evening at Home

On the same general "klutzy" subject, the following is an email that I sent my wife in 2010, while she was visiting her mother in Texas. I was at home, left unattended.

Hi Honey - I hope all is well. I know you can visualize this little scene - so here is a chuckle for the day:

Last night, I was looking forward to a quiet night at home. I dined on Lean Cuisine, read the newspaper, and then I decided to get ambitious. Since I had just replaced the bent drain-cover in our shower, I figured I'd also replace a loose tile near the drain and re-grout the entire shower floor. I was totally bare-assed except for my silver kneepads -- quite a sight. (Why screw up a pair of shorts with white grout?)

I was nearly finished grouting, minding my own business, when suddenly I hear screeching and barking sounds in the other room. The next scene rolled quickly:

I got up in all my glory and headed to the living room to see what all the commotion was. Killer-Cat Lucy had brought in a large, half-dead wood rat through the open patio door, and when she saw me, she dropped the big rat in the middle of the living room. Turns out, the rat was not quite dead and now I am watching Lucy chase it around the living room while Abby joins the fray with purposeful barks.

Lucy has now cornered the rat, and it's dazed, so I raced to the laundry room and snatched a big bath towel to throw over the poor rodent. I took the dead rat outside (still dressed in only my knee pads), and was heading back from behind the house, when I hear a car arrive in the driveway, so I quickly hid behind the fountain in the bushes to avoid being seen. I wasn't exactly dressed for visitors. It was cold in the bushes, but the mystery visitors soon left when they realized that no one was home.

I was really thirsty, so I went directly into the kitchen to make a smoothie. I knew I still had some blackberries and a banana, and just enough milk in the carton to do the trick. I neglected to turn on all the lights in the kitchen. Who needs much light to make a smoothie?

I filled the blender, placed the rubber lid on the top, and turned it on. There was an awful sound. Turns out, the clear plastic plug from the center of the rubber lid had somehow found its way to the bottom of the blender container. In the instant before I had time to turn off the blender, a gush of milk and blackberries splashed through the hole in the container lid, and dripped down on my chest and face.

I stood there in the kitchen, totally defeated, but then I noticed the real shocker -- the *reflection* in the kitchen window: There stood a chubby Albino-Zulu-War-Chief wearing nothing but silver knee pads, white grout steaks of war paint, and some black goop on his face. I dabbed off the mess with a paper towel and washed off with a garden hose on the patio. All I could do was go to bed - somewhere I might be safe. Come home.

Your loving husband -

A Boomer Looks Back

The informal essays that follow represent my observations on a number of social and political issues.

I am the first to admit that I'm not a qualified expert – a political scientist or a sociologist. My only credentials are those of an alert eyewitness who has paid close attention to the evolution of our American culture and our government institutions for the past 50 years.

My family and friends have their own opinions on the subjects I cover – which often differ from mine – so the following is no more or less than my own personal reflections.

See the U.S.A. today!

The Lone Ranger

Father Knows Best

Superman

Perry Mason

AMERICAN MADE

IT WAS very good to be a suburban kid in America during the 1950s. My childhood revolved around my immediate family, which was fine with me. Life got even better when my father brought home a new Magnavox TV and suddenly *The Lone Ranger* rode into our living room. A cowboy with a mask, silver bullets, a loyal Indian companion and a mysterious past was my first hero. Lured by the triumphant call of "Hi-ho, Silver!" and fortified by a big glass of milk and a stack of Oreos, I became glued to the TV.

The Lone Ranger was the No. 1-rated show on ABC in the early '50s.

The boomers were the first young American generation to learn the ways of the world via television. The bright moving images were exciting and came directly into the privacy of your home. The nation's newest source of fun and information didn't require the quiet discipline of reading a book or newspaper – you could *just sit there* and be entertained. There was a constant parade of new shows for kids, with advertisements that gave the inside scoop on the latest new Schwinn bicycles, Duncan yo-yos and board games like *Clue* and *Monopoly*.

I was hooked. All the kids I knew were hooked.

Popular programs like *Father Knows Best* and *The Donna Reed Show* always had pretty moms and kind fathers, happy endings and solid life lessons. The shows made it clear that parents, teachers and policemen were to be respected. Television taught kids that if they ignored the good advice of adults and behaved badly there would be a price to be paid.

Christmas was the big day that youngsters could count on to receive their biggest rewards for good behavior. School let out for a week and at home we enjoyed an endless supply of Christmas cookies and candy canes and often new kitchen appliances that thrilled my mother.

I remember being puzzled about why Santa Claus always seemed to give the very best toys to rich kids. That's when my oldest brother Tony explained how Christmas really worked, spilling the beans about Santa.

By the fourth grade I became infatuated with Superman, because the Man of Steel from the lost planet Krypton possessed *super powers,* and his adventures expanded my concept of the universe.

During fifth grade, real life became more interesting and I soon dumped *Superman* for *Perry Mason.* The unflappable big city lawyer held my keen interest for a couple of years. Mr. Mason defended innocent people who were charged with murder. Armed only with his wits, a loyal secretary and a private detective, Perry consistently outsmarted the real murderers, maneuvering them into dramatic courtroom confessions – just in the nick of time.

Each fall, a generous offering of new sitcoms and dramas reassured young boomers that life was based on fair, dependable rules and that bad people would inevitably suffer, in a manner appropriate to their misdeeds. In the golden era of television, each show's story had a "moral" and criminals were *always* caught. Life returned happily to normal by the end of each episode.

Like most boomers, I did some couch time watching *Leave It to Beaver.* When the show first aired in the late '50s, I was the age of the young main character, Beaver, and my brother, Greg, was the same age as Wally, Beaver's older brother. With all due respect to the legendary show, I confess that as a kid I thought that most of the episodes were lame. Beaver was too gullible or dumb to be believed, and the kids in *Mayfield* (wherever that was) didn't seem as smart as Larry Leslie and my other friends around Carmel Valley in California.

In 1959, Greg and I started watching a more sophisticated show with my Dad, called *The Twilight Zone.* Each episode was introduced by the writer Rod Serling, the program's creator, who smoked cigarettes, had heavy black eyebrows and spoke in a deep voice that was not so reassuring. He had tricks up his sleeve that he knew about and that his innocent viewers were about to discover. Each week different actors were caught in uncanny and often frightening predicaments, and many of the endings were darkly ironic if not downright chilling.

Another one of our favorites was *Have Gun – Will Travel*, starring Richard Boone as Paladin. Paladin was a gentlemen gunfighter with a strong code of conduct – "A knight without armor in a savage land" ran part of the theme song that opened each show. He was a *good guy* who wore black, had an engraved business card and was comfortably headquartered in a fancy hotel in San Francisco. He was fast on the draw and one cool dude.

Around 1960, I became so infatuated with the teenage, hot-rod driving Ed "Kookie" Byrnes – one of the stars of *77 Sunset Strip* – that I asked my parents if I could take "Kookie" as my middle name and become "Clifford Kookie Branch." For some strange reason, at my birth my parents had decided that they would let their youngest son pick his own middle name at some future date. My mom said "Okay" to my "Kookie" request, but a few weeks later I began to have second thoughts. When I checked back with my mother, I was relieved to find that she'd misplaced the official name-change paperwork.

"Kookie"

"Kookie, Kookie – Lend Me Your Comb" was a hit song, playing constantly on the radio. The catchy tune paid homage to Kookie's ducktail hairdo, which he combed on the show about every five minutes. I tried to grow my hair long like Kookie's but one day my baseball coach made fun of my attempt, so I immediately went back to my regular buzz haircut. And, to this day, I have no middle name.

If *The Twilight Zone* was one of the first TV shows to suggest that things don't always run like clockwork and turn out as we expect and hope, *The Fugitive*, starring David Janssen, was just a few years away and sent a similar if more personal message. It would first air the fateful fall of 1963, with the ominous words of an unseen narrator:

> Name: Richard Kimble. Profession: Doctor of medicine. Destination: Death Row, state prison. Richard Kimble has been tried and convicted for the murder of his wife. But laws are made by men, carried out by men. And men are imperfect. Richard Kimble is innocent. Proved guilty, what Richard Kimble could not prove was that moments before discovering his wife's body, he encountered a man running from the vicinity of his home. A man with one arm. A man who has not yet been found. Richard Kimble ponders his fate as he looks at the world for the last time. And sees only darkness. But in that darkness, fate moves its huge hand.

Kimble, wrongly accused, convicted, and sentenced to death for a crime he never committed, is saved by a train wreck on his way to his execution.

He will begin a long run from Lieutenant Philip Gerard, a policeman as determined as Javert, Jean Valjean's pursuer in *Les Miserables*. The story of the just man who must unjustly suffer to prove his innocence and save his own life would strike a new, strange and resonant note in American culture, and now seems a kind of omen as America began to face contradictions that it could no longer escape.

The '50s and early '60s were truly a TV era, but most of the more complicated and serious lessons about life were often learned in a dark theater. A soda, a bag of popcorn and some Milk Duds were the perfect nourishment to sustain me through the two- or three-hour sagas. John Wayne, Cary Grant and Gregory Peck were my favorite stars and each gave his unique take on how a real man should operate in the world.

My dad regularly took us to foreign films and Alfred Hitchcock mystery-thrillers. After a complicated movie by the *Master of Suspense*, my dad always asked Greg and me if we'd noticed "any holes in the plot," which made for fun discussions. My mother didn't like Hitchcock movies. She preferred to accompany us to "real theatre" – usually the corny stuff, like *My Fair Lady* or *The Sound of Music*.

President Eisenhower

America had been on a roll. By 1960, revered President Eisenhower was finishing his second term, and most middle-class American families had full refrigerators, vacuum cleaners and multi-cycle washing machines. It had been nearly 20 years since the attack on Pearl Harbor and for many millions of Americans our country was awash with abundance.

In 1961, John Kennedy, the rich and handsome PT-boat captain and war hero, was confidently in command of the White House. The television networks presented America's first family as royalty, although it wasn't until after JFK's death that *Camelot* became tied to his time in office. Jackie Kennedy told the historian Theodore White that Jack had always loved the

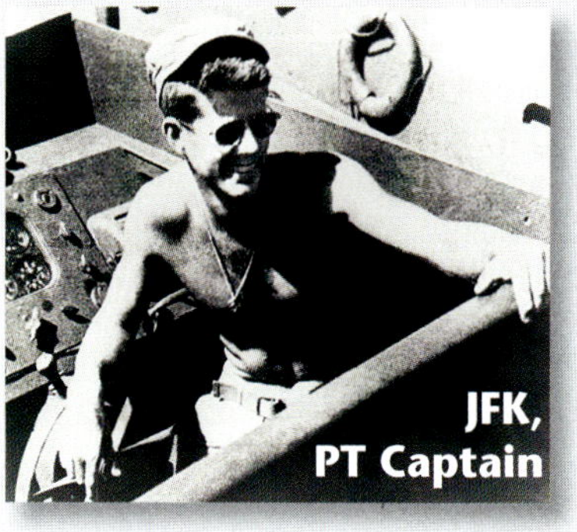

Jacqueline and President Kennedy

story of King Arthur and the Round Table and that he often listened to the album of the Broadway musical.

Of course there were a few bumps along the road leading up to our short-lived Camelot. Our nation was trying to shake off an imaginary mass invasion of crafty and amoral *communists* who were purportedly lurking in the shadows from sea to shining sea. Beginning in 1950, Joe McCarthy, a U. S. senator from Wisconsin, managed to whip up a Red-scare frenzy that obsessed many of our leaders. For a time, paranoia swept through the halls of the Capitol and across U.S. cities and towns. FBI boss J. Edgar Hoover ran a clandestine operation with hundreds of his G-men to ferret out American citizens who in his mind had secretly transformed themselves into avid communist sympathizers.

Joe McCarthy

Conservatives of every stripe were convinced that a large band of *commies* had taken up residence in Hollywood. In 1947 the House Committee on Un-American Activities struck fear into the lives of writers, actors and movie producers. Over 300 were placed on an industry "blacklist" and most of them were never able to rebuild their careers.

J. Edgar Hoover

Throughout much of the '50s, ministers and priests from across the land encouraged their flocks to keep a watchful eye for any signs of *communist activities* in their communities. Many churches led the rallying cry to ban rock 'n' roll music. Newspapers ran articles with helpful tips on "How to spot a communist." It was a time when politicians, claiming to be patriots, joined in a crusade to "save the soul" of America.

In all those years, I don't think I ever met a communist. The biggest danger in my life came from telephone poles. The first one found me when I was running for a pass on the playground at Carmelo Elementary

School. The second pole caught me at the bottom of a hill, when I ran off the road on my bicycle and was knocked unconscious. The ensuing visit to the ER was one of five before I was 12.

Some of my older boomer friends reminisce with pride about the era of soda fountains and bobby sox, but for me any nostalgia about the 1950s starts to grow thin when viewed through a wider lens. Our public schools in the South were segregated by race, as were restaurants and hotels across the country. Women were treated as second-class citizens.

Young segregationists

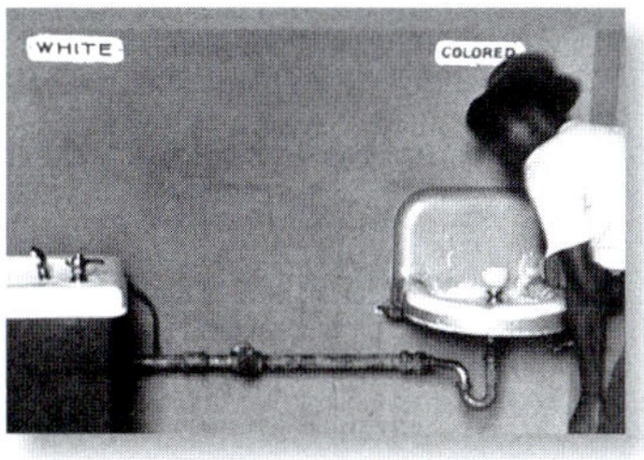

Signs of the time

I doubt that many African-Americans share fond boomer memories of '50s America. It was still a time when "Negroes" could face a prison sentence for using white bathrooms or drinking fountains. Other than a few sports heroes and gifted singers and musicians, I don't remember seeing many black people on television.

In 1950 we sent young men off to war in Korea, where some 400,000 American troops became bogged down in a military action that did not go as planned. America's Air Force ravaged North Korea, but the war soon turned into a quagmire and ended in a stalemate. Over 128,000 U.S. troops were killed or wounded.

The Soviet Union had developed an A-bomb in 1949, and the U.S. and Russia were locked in a "cold war" that terrified Americans. A couple of times in the early '60s, we practiced "duck and cover" exercises at school in anticipation of nuclear bombs exploding on U.S. soil, the drills a clear signal that at any given moment the world might come to an end. I remember being under my desk on my hands and knees, staring at Marsha Sherman's pale green underpants as she crouched under the desk in front of me. The experience left me wondering if our desks were really strong enough to protect us if the roof caved in – I worried that I'd never get to see a naked girl before I died.

1962

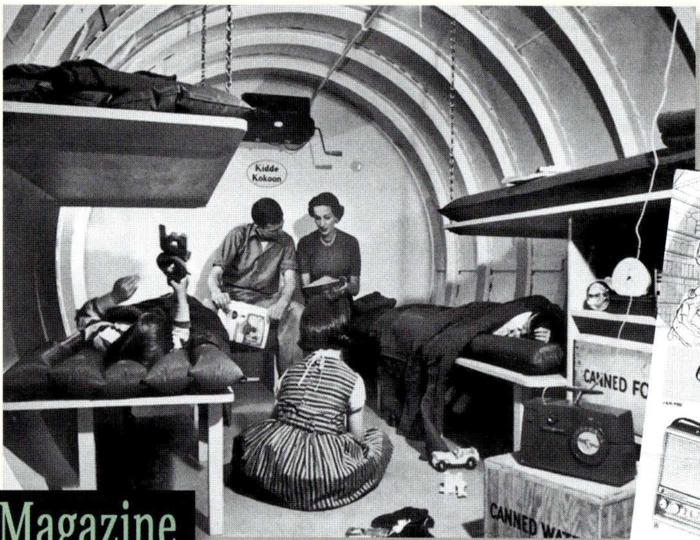

You Can Survive Atomic Fallout

- BLAST
- HEAT
- IMMEDIATE RADIATION
- FLYING DEBRIS
- FIRE
- FALLOUT RADIATION

45,800,000 AMERICANS— OR ONE-FOURTH OF THE POPULATION—MIGHT DIE!

IN A FAMILY FALLOUT SHELTER

97% CAN SURVIVE

General Merchandise Company
MILWAUKEE 1, WISCONSIN

WARNING! Tune to CONELRAD 640 or 1240 kc.

INFORMATION! Your contact with "the outside world"

EVACUATION! Receive full instructions

ALL-CLEAR SIGNAL! Lets you know when it's safe

Pay Only $46^{50}

SPECIALLY DESIGNED RADIOS ARE YOUR LINK WITH CIVIL DEFENSE HEADQUARTERS!

Pay Only $57^{62}

FOOD SUPPLEMENT

Pay Only $2^{98}

POWER FAILURE

Pay Only $7^{75}

You Can Build a Low-Cost Shelter Quickly

$30 . . . $97 . . . $280 — This can be the cost of materials for a family fallout shelter

NUCLEAR SCIENTISTS who have built shelters to protect their families against possible fallout radiation have, in many cases, put up simple, inexpensive structures that can be erected quickly. Following this example, *Popular Mechanics* presents on these pages the construction details of three previously unpublished plans prepared by the office of Civil Defense and one by a nuclear engineer. They include some of the low-cost and most rapidly-built shelters available.

UNDER THE PATIO

Nuclear testing, 1958

Since 1997, a character named "Vault Boy" has been central to a video game called *Fallout,* set in the mid-22nd century, in a world devastated by a 1960s nuclear war that began over dwindling petroleum supplies. *Fallout* features a violent post-apocalyptic storyline set in a mutated future. Vault Boy – bomb shelters are called "vaults" – is a recurring symbol in the game, a cartoon remnant of a pre-war ad campaign for a company that manufactured shelters, before the nukes finally fell. Seriously.

Fallout shelters were a hot topic in those days and some families spent their hard-earned savings on building concrete underground bunkers in their backyards. Most bomb-shelter dealers recommended the following basic provisions: dehydrated survival food, water, flashlights, first aid kit, a Bible, board games, cigarettes, playing cards, a box of ammo and a shotgun. Gas masks were optional.

Shelters seemed to make sense because our scientific community was busy inventing new weapons of mass destruction. Our military tested progressively larger nuclear warheads – blowing up parts of the Marshall Islands in the South Pacific and detonating nuclear blasts in Nevada, New Mexico, Colorado and other areas of the United States. In all, the military tested more than 900 nuclear warheads – about 250 of them above ground, in the open air.

In good faith and with God on our side, we spread tons of radioactive dust into our own atmosphere, all in the name of preparing for an inevitable war with the commies, or aliens, or with some other yet unidentified evildoer. During the '50s, American foreign aid was often a euphemism for supplying other countries with weapons of war. We kept our factories humming. Somehow, our government managed to sustain an economy based on war – in peacetime.

Leaders in our government and our pulpits were also vigilant when it came to enforcing morality in our bedrooms. Any sex between unmarried couples was strictly taboo and any *deviant* behavior (such as oral sex) was illegal. Some states even passed laws that forbade any discussion about masturbation with anyone under the age of 21. Adult magazines like *Playboy* were considered the work of the Devil. Any person who happened to be born homosexual in America lived with the fear of being exposed, humiliated or placed on trial and sent to the slammer.

During the '50s, our legislators may have been uptight about commies and sex, but not about smoking. Tobacco giant R. J. Reynolds ran national advertisements bragging that "More Doctors Smoke Camels than any other cigarette!" Full-page ads for Camels also appeared in *The Journal of the American Medical Association.*

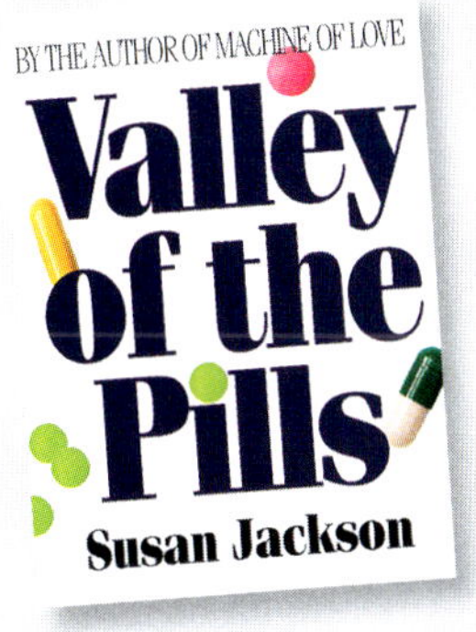

The American medical community promoted a new generation of tranquilizers and prescribed them to millions of housewives who consumed the *happy pills* like a new flavor of Chiclets, in an effort to cope with "modern-day anxiety."

Notwithstanding these issues, rock 'n' roll and Elvis prevailed.

The imperfections of Camelot did not generally interrupt the childhood of the majority of the 78 million growing boomers, except on rare occasions. Sometime during 1961, Larry Leslie shocked our class during Show and Tell when he announced, "I heard a man on the radio say that we were all going to die from the H-bomb." Larry's pronouncement seemed to catch our teacher, Mr. Glodd, by surprise. The entire class grew quiet as Mr. Glodd calmly reassured everyone that the man on the radio was misinformed. He explained that America was protected by two very large oceans, by the strongest military in the world, and by President Kennedy – who would keep us all safe.

That same night, at the dinner table, my parents confirmed Mr. Glodd's promise of security and peace. Such assurances, from parents and teachers across America, strengthened the core belief among boomers that our lives were solidly grounded in Superman's "truth, justice and the American way."

That's the most important stuff I remember about the '50s and the beginnings of the '60s. It was decades later that we learned that during the Cuban Missile Crisis our president was encouraged by our military leaders to drop nuclear bombs on Cuba, as a preemptive measure to teach Nikita Khrushchev and the Russians that we were still the biggest kid on the block.

President Kennedy chose not to push the red button, life went on and to most of us it was all water under the bridge. But the stand-off with the Soviet Union had scared us, them and the rest of the world. After those frightening days in October 1962, when JFK and his advisors were uncertain that we could avoid an atomic war, the White House and the Kremlin became connected by a hotline. The first faint glimmerings of an eventual end to the Cold War had begun to flicker in the darkness.

Most of the adults who ran the country between 1950 and 1962 are long gone and there's not much point in dwelling on what now seems like ancient history, except to understand that it lay the foundation for all the events that took place as the turbulent '60s unfolded.

"Boomers" are the subject of this section of the book. In 1963 I turned 14, which means I came of age as a member of the Pepsi Generation. It would be a tragic year for the country, although in October it seemed to

be ending on a very good note when the blazing fastball of southpaw Sandy Koufax brought prominence to the West Coast. The L.A. Dodgers toppled the New York Yankees in *four straight games* during the World Series and everything in my young teenage universe was blissfully aligned. It turned out to be a very brief moment in time.

A Voice Came Over the Intercom

It was a Friday afternoon and a short announcement came over the classroom intercom and our teacher quickly left the room. She returned in a few minutes and stood squarely in front of the class. With a quivering voice and tears steaming down her face, she gave us the news that the president of the United States had been shot and was dead.

Life stood still for the next couple of days. On November 25, 1963, I sat numbly with my family, watching the television coverage of President Kennedy's funeral procession.

I'd never witnessed so many adults openly weeping and it was the first time I remember seeing tears in my father's eyes.

It was the end of innocence for many in my generation, and it was certainly a turning point in my own life.

Fifty years have now gone by. It seemed like a good time for some personal reflection about what I experienced since that time. I had an urge to write some thoughts down, before I forget.

What follows is simply one boomer's perspective. ■

A Trip Back to the '60s

AS A BOOMER, I grew up during the 1960s. For nearly 50 years, I've worked as an entrepreneur in the business community. In those five decades I've also been an active participant in our democratic process. It's been my practice to pay close attention to candidates and issues – and then cast my vote. I have also encouraged others to vote. In this section, I look back at some of the public events that shaped our country as my generation matured and took over the leadership of our government. There are no academic credentials attached to my name. My thoughts on our cultural and political environment are based on my experience, reading and following "the news."

I speak from my own perspective, feeling comfortable in voicing opinions about events and personalities that have registered strongly on my personal radar. Writing this book was a creative expression – a sort of scrapbook of my own life. I have no agenda, and it's not my goal to convince anyone to do anything. My motive is to present ideas that may stimulate discussion about where our country has been and where it may be headed, and perhaps encourage others to increase their involvement in our democracy.

I've written these short essays from the specific viewpoint of a marketeer, a perspective that I know well. People who market "products" must pay very close attention to what their fellow citizens build and consume, because how Americans spend their money reflects our values and the nature of our society and what that society might want next. You could say that we are what we buy – or want to buy – whether we're speaking of consumer goods or lifestyles. We also express our values by voting for political leaders and the agendas they say they support.

Today, corporate and political platforms are like commodities – they are carefully crafted, "packaged" and presented to the public by marketing professionals.

Growing Up in the '60s

The term "boomer" appears often in this section, because I'm writing primarily about my own generation, and it's the most common label to describe those of us who grew up in the 1960s. My generation's name evolved from the *Baby Boom* – the population explosion created by parents who had survived both the Great Depression and World War II.

In the 25 years following the war – the period that spans the childhood, adolescence and early adulthood of the Boomer Generation – America was the preeminent force in the world. Our nation dominated as the most militarily powerful, culturally influential and richest country on Earth. The U.S. economy was firing on all cylinders, domestically and internationally.

The majority of boomers grew up with the presumption of economic security, and so my generation tends to be inherently optimistic about the future.

For most white middle-class children growing up in the States between 1946 and 1964, there seemed to be a never-ending stream of new goodies that were created for our pleasure. Wonderful, inexpensive items made from vinyl, plastic and nylon; shiny appliances and color television; endless new choices of cosmetics, prescription drugs and effortless TV dinners for all to enjoy. Every year brought an exciting crop of new automobiles – bigger, sexier and faster.

And yet, there were always contradictions and uncertainties. An undercurrent of social change and the threat of nuclear war with Russia was running through the apparent calm prosperity of the post-WWII, pre-Vietnam years.

The 1960s generation was the most privileged in the history of the world, but also the first generation of young people to witness multiple assassinations of our nation's leaders, the exploration of space, rapidly changing technology and constant social upheaval. As Charles Dickens began his 1859 novel, *A Tale of Two Cities*, "It was the best of times, it was the worst of times ...."

It's difficult to describe the boomers' experience without revisiting some of the significant cultural and political events that shaped our lives. The 1960s gave rise to an amazing mix of dramatic changes as Americans struggled to adapt to a rapidly evolving *new normal*.

In the next several pages – as context for some of the essays that follow – I've stitched together a fast-forward summary of the 1960s, highlighting key players and milestones that made a major impact on how we grew up and who we became. ■

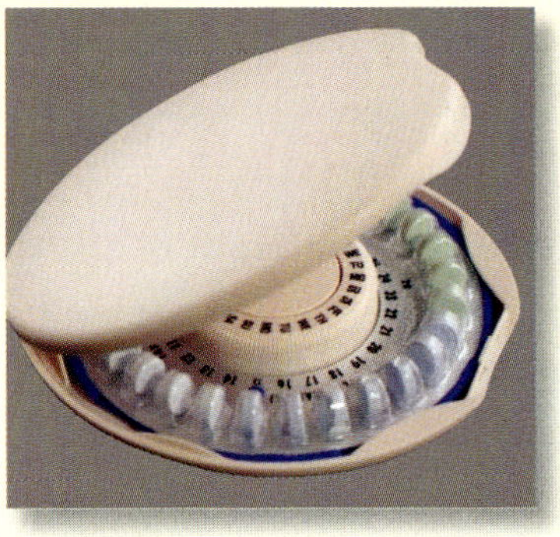

*The **Swinging '60s** began with the introduction of **The Pill**, making birth control widely available and triggering the start of the sexual revolution. The Puritan/Protestant roots of our culture were rocked to the core by the idea that sex could be recreational.*

*By 1960, **The Ed Sullivan Show** had become the most watched weekly event on television. Each Sunday night, American families sat down together to watch the variety show that introduced our nation to the world's best entertainers, ranging from opera singers to comedians. An array of the biggest stars came into our living rooms, from Jerry Lewis to Itzhak Perlman, and it was center stage for music – bringing the boomers their first look at Elvis Presley, The Beatles, The Rolling Stones, The Beach Boys and others. It was also the first show to introduce dozens of black artists on a national stage, including **The Supremes**, Louis Armstrong, Duke Ellington, Sammy Davis Jr. and Aretha Franklin.*

*America changed rapidly: When **Elvis** first rocked and shocked the older generation, a columnist in The New York Times commented: "Mr. Presley injected movements of the tongue and indulged in wordless singing that were distasteful. Overstimulating the physical impulses of teenagers was a gross national disservice." For better or worse, American mores were in rapid transition. By the late 1960s, Jim Morrison sang about psychedelic drugs in Light My Fire with the lyric: "Girl, we couldn't get much higher." It was a new era, and The Ed Sullivan Show would soon be off the air.*

Our nation was stunned in 1961 when a **Russian** *was the first man to travel into space, fostering the break-neck acceleration of our own space program. NASA later mesmerized the world when they landed an* **American astronaut** *on the moon.*

The United States unsuccessfully conducted the **Bay of Pigs** *invasion of Cuba in 1961. America remained on pins and needles during the 1962* **Cuban Missile Crisis***, and the threat of nuclear war lingered at our doorstep.*

Robert F. Kennedy and John F. Kennedy

In 1962 Rachel Carson published her book, ***Silent Spring****, about the overuse of pesticide, which fueled an underlying mistrust of big corporations and launched the environmental movement. The following year Betty Friedan published* ***Feminine Mystique****, kicking off the modern women's movement, as American women began to examine their roles in society and push back against the social status quo.*

In 1963, as many as 250,000 citizens marched on Washington, D.C., to hear **Dr. Martin Luther King Jr.** *deliver his famous I Have a Dream speech. The event was aired live on TV and watched by millions of Americans.*

The national television networks (ABC, NBC and CBS) became obsessed with three assassinations, playing loop after graphic loop of the video footage. In 1963, grief-stricken Americans watched the Zapruder film showing **President John F. Kennedy** *being shot while riding in his Dallas motorcade.*

April 1968 brought news of the **Martin Luther King Jr.** *assassination. Here he's shown with aides on a motel balcony in Memphis, Tennessee, just prior to being shot.*

In June 1968, the nation viewed footage of **Senator Robert Kennedy** *lying dead on the floor of a hotel in Los Angeles. He was shot at close range following a victory speech after winning a crucial Democratic primary.*

During the mid-'60s, the entire nation was stunned as we watched police in **Southern states** brutalize innocent black citizens simply for marching; Ku Klux Klan groups bombing black churches in Alabama; and riots on the streets of Los Angeles and other major cities. In South Africa, **Nelson Mandela** was sentenced to life in prison for speaking out against apartheid, and served 27 years.

The casualties from the **Vietnam War** *mounted throughout the decade, deeply dividing our nation. Americans saw the body bags of our soldiers being unloaded each day on television, and war protests sprang up on most major college campuses from coast to coast.*

Nearly 100,000 counterculture participants made the pilgrimage to San Francisco during the 1967 **Summer of Love** *social phenomenon. Hippies became a part of everyday life, while LSD and other psychedelic drugs became firmly entrenched in pop culture.*

That same year, World Heavyweight Champion **Muhammad Ali**, *winner of the Gold Medal for the United States in the Olympics, refused to be conscripted into the military. Ali cited his religious beliefs and opposition to the war in Vietnam. He was arrested, found guilty of draft evasion and stripped of his title. He was not allowed to box for nearly four years (during his prime), until the Supreme Court overturned his conviction in 1971.*

There was major conflict in the Middle East. Israel was triumphant in the **Six Day War** *with Egypt, Jordan and Syria in June 1967.*

In 1968, anchorman **Walter Cronkite**, *considered to be "the most trusted man in America," gave a closing statement on a CBS special news report that rocked the nation and accelerated the change in America's perception of the Vietnam War. Cronkite stated: "It seems more certain now than ever that the bloody experience of Vietnam is to end in a stalemate. … To say that we are closer to victory today is to believe, in the face of the evidence, the optimists who have been wrong in the past. … The only rational way out … will be to negotiate, not as victors, but as an honorable people who lived up to their pledge to defend democracy, and did the best they could."*

The Meaning of the '60s

(Talkin' 'bout my generation)

SOME BOOMERS feel considerable fondness for the '60s as a time of great freedom, exuberance and experimentation. Other boomers remember the period as one bad trip.

The past, like the present, is in the eye of the beholder.

The popular mid-'90s book by Judge Robert Bork of Nixon/Watergate fame made the case that the '60s were mostly bad juju perpetuated by left-leaning devils. The title of his best-seller, *Slouching Toward Gomorrah,* is a play on a line from the classic William Butler Yeats poem, *The Second Coming,* in which "The best lack all conviction, while the worst / Are full of passionate intensity."

Strong stuff from Judge Bork, though Newt Gingrich has probably been the most consistent and tireless critic of the Boomer Generation, arguing that cultural radicals in the '60s were responsible for the demise of traditional values in America. In subsequent years, Mr. Gingrich lightened up just a bit after leaving each of his previous two wives – both for younger women.

I suppose *love* can change a man.

It should be pointed out that many boomers never smoked pot or protested the Vietnam War – but they did join their peers, and society at large, in embracing some sort of cosmic optimism about the future. No one wanted to be thought of as *a square* – it was cool to be hip. Even businessmen shunned traditional dress codes in favor of fashionable new suits and colorful ties that displayed their individuality.

The Beatles and rock music became mainstream marketing tools. Popular movies, such as *The Graduate,* poignantly laid bare the hypocrisy in our society to a soundtrack by Simon and Garfunkel. The coming-of-age story, starring Dustin Hoffman, was an indictment of *the American establishment.* The movie, which won an Academy Award for director Mike Nichols, also explored sexuality in a manner not seen before in a mainstream popular film. The script, specifically targeted toward young people, hit a nerve with a much wider audience. Suburban Americans had fully embraced the Cultural Revolution.

Hugh Hefner's magazine *Playboy* opened up new horizons by combining well-written articles on a variety of subjects – including politics, art and sports – in a slick magazine that also featured a bevy of half-naked women. Hefner made no apology for his exploration (and exploitation) of sexuality. The pages of *Esquire* and *Cosmo* encouraged readers to shed their WASP guilt about the body and sensual pleasure. Advertisements from master ad man David Ogilvy linked products to the expression of a freer, less hung-up approach to life, persuading customers that self-expression was natural – a positive means of showing one's identity.

The '60s crescendo culminated in the motto: "If it feels good, do it!" This sentiment (generally presented in a more subtle manner) became the message that flowed from electronic media, profoundly affecting the nation's vision of what constituted *the good life.*

Marshall McLuhan had it right. Years before any of us ever heard the term internet, McLuhan was insisting that "our electronic media would become an extension of our central nervous system." His ground-breaking book – *The Medium Is the Message* – made the case that new technology would lead to "the electrical re-tribalization of the West."

McLuhan was a Canadian English professor – an erudite futurist who simultaneously stared in the rearview mirror at the past *and* through the windshield as the digital age precipitously approached. Watch his interviews on YouTube today and you'll find his foresight astonishingly insightful. In several interviews, McLuhan presented the idea that our society often searched for (and expressed) its identity through confrontation – whether through aggressive foreign military action, or at home (more peacefully) on the football field.

As with any historical period, the core meaning of the '60s is debatable, but regardless of your perspective it's hard to deny that it was a turbulent decade and a harbinger of the years to come. Every aspect of society was changing rapidly, sometimes with a vengeance, and often with a little help from master marketeers.

Madison Avenue Holds Up a Mirror

A current hit show on AMC goes to great lengths to accurately portray Madison Avenue and the increasing role of advertising in American culture after World War II. Jon Hamm (Don Draper) stars in the series as a partner in a large advertising firm. The show is appropriately called *Mad Men* and recounts and examines the time when the first boomers were beginning to come of age.

The series features well-developed characters and an interesting story line, and has garnered numerous Emmys and Golden Globes. It's definitely worth a watch. The first few seasons focused entirely on the late 1950s and early 1960s. *Mad Men* dramatizes human relationships in a quickly changing society and juxtaposes professional and private lives with many of the major political and cultural events that affected every American.

During the '60s, television advertising began to reflect both the psyche and hidden heart of the American consumer. Marketeers needed a direct hit on the hopes and dreams of their target market, so focus groups and hard data turned advertising into a science. Thomas Frank wrote about the "rise of hip consumerism" in his famous 1997 book, *The Conquest of Cool.*

Frank's central thesis was that corporations embraced the mythic – and mystic – aura of the American *counterculture* as a marketing strategy. To push their clients' products, Madison Avenue projected attractive images of an honest, rebellious and adventuresome new generation. Advertising agencies found that romanticizing the counterculture was the easiest way to capture the consumer loyalty of boomers and their wallets.

No company's success demonstrates the transforming power of Madison Avenue better than McDonald's. Starting in 1961, under the guidance of marketeer and owner Ray Crock, burger sales rose astronomically. By 1963, sales had tripled, and McDonald's was feeding the nation at a rate of one million burgers per day. Like mass-produced rainbows, the *Golden Arches* spread across America, and Ronald McDonald would soon become one of America's favorite icons for the young. The introduction of the Big Mac was just around the corner.

Madison Avenue Hits Its Stride

The appeal was direct: Boomers could show their individuality, reject conformism and express their true *inner self* by changing what they drove, wore and consumed.

Part of the attraction and glamour of the '60s "get real" movement was a rejection of the phony and the celebration of the genuine. Every suburban '50s kid idolized Fess Parker as Davy Crockett. American men wanted to identify with the macho guy on the horse who rode alone across our television screens, so they lit up Marlboros. American women were beginning to show their independence, so they smoked Virginia Slims, encouraged by that catchy phrase:

You've come a long way – baby.

The older members of Tom Brokaw's Greatest Generation, who grew up during the Depression era and fought in World War II, were beginning to retire. Marketeers began referring to the latter stages of American life as *The Golden Years*, selling prospective customers on the notion that a product or service might magically lead straight to the gates of Heaven.

Flash forward ...

The Boomers – 50 Years *After* the '60s

The Pepsi Generation took control of America.

Our political system and our corporations *are run* by boomers. The average age of a U.S. senator is 61, congressmen, 57. The average age of board members of S&P 500 companies is 62.

Men still control the country's agenda

American women and ethnic minorities have made tremendous advances in both business and government, but they had to fight for every inch, and still have a long run to catch the men who continue to run the show. Most boomer congressmen and businessmen seem to like it that way. We still live in a testosterone-driven society, at least in terms of who wields both financial and political power.

In the U.S. Senate, 95% of senators are white, and 83% are men. Even after a record number of women were elected to Congress in 2012, more than 80% of the U.S. House of Representatives are male, and 85% are white. And it's a wealthy group: More than 70% of senators are millionaires, as are 50% of congressmen.

The American dream is more elusive

Today, a widening range of economists and business commentators seems to come to the same conclusion: Economically, the chasm between the middle class and the wealthiest Americans has grown significantly. The United States can no longer claim to be number one among the countries of the world in upward social mobility or a financially secure middle class. The general media has given much attention to this shift of the nation's wealth to the mega-rich. The trend has been clear for some time and recent statistics tell the story: 10% of the population own approximately 85% of the nation's wealth, and, more to the point, only 1% owns approximately 40% of America's assets.

Pulitzer Prize-winning author Hedrick Smith details the financial crushing of the American middle class in his book, *Who Stole the American Dream?* Smith makes the case that this trend was no accident, no quirk of nature or coincidence. He carefully documents how corporate chieftains favor their own self-interests, and those of their major shareholders and lobbyists, over the economic health of their own employees. Smith makes a compelling argument that the American worker has been sold out with the blessing of U.S. presidents and the Congress – and by those U.S. Supreme Court justices who validate, by slim majorities, the decisions of mostly conservative lower court judges. It's a sobering read. In the past six years, profits for S&P 500 corporations have nearly doubled, yet wages remain stagnant.

Many of my conservative friends scoff at such observations, and are quick to point out, "Americans have every opportunity to pull themselves up by their bootstraps," "Entitlements only encourage slackers and promote laziness" and "People tend to get what they deserve." These sentiments are often voiced with irritation or even anger. Many take offense at any public resentment toward what they feel is simply their "well-earned success." Their feelings are all understandable, but I'm not sure that their conclusions are based entirely on fact. Our government has rarely offered a level playing field to all of its citizens. Moreover, American free enterprise has never been based on an economy of scarcity. As a nation, how we choose to allocate our abundant resources and capacities reflects our values. To some people, the fact that in America so few of our citizens control so much of our country's wealth may seem to be "the new reality of modern-day capitalism." For me, this trend is alarming and does not bode well for our country.

For the past decade, much of our government's attention was focused on the wars in Iraq and Afghanistan, distracting our nation from crucial domestic issues. The cost of these two wars is at least 20 times what was confidently projected by the Bush administration. And for the first time in more than 100 years, America went to war without imposing a war tax. The Wall Street crash and the ensuing recession greatly compromised our ability to repair our nation's crumbling infrastructure. Even the streets of Washington, D.C., are deeply rutted with potholes. Our health care system no longer even rates in the Top 10 among developed nations, and, to date, the implementation of "Affordable Health Care" has been miserable.

It's much harder these days to make a fact-based case for American exceptionalism, and a lot tougher for America to compete in what is now known as the global marketplace.

Boomer control not exactly transformative

During the '60s there was sincere idealism in the air about the transformation of the American character and redefining our national priorities, but very little change materialized.

John F. Kennedy's call to "Ask not what your country can do for you – ask what you can do for your country" faded into the mist, along with John Lennon's plea to "Give peace a chance."

In their eager and hopeful youth, the Pepsi Generation was especially outspoken about the hypocrisy they saw in the society around them. But as years passed and the Vietnam War ended, fearless younger Americans, so outspoken and opposed to President Nixon, disappeared into what Nixon referred to as the Silent Majority.

Most boomers quickly found themselves on detours. Marriage, children and careers replaced idealism. As John Lennon said: "Life is what happens when you're busy making other plans." The great majority of my generation never took "the road less traveled" but continued down many of the same paths of their parents. Under the stewardship of the boomers, there have been very few meaningful changes in our nation's practice, or brand, of capitalism.

The following examples are offered in a symbolic manner, indicative of the lack of social evolution to a wide range of corporations and/or industries.

Children still love a strawberry shake

By the time the children of boomers were toddlers, Ronald McDonald was their single most recognizable media personality. America's beloved hamburger clown is a true success story, a benchmark of American free capitalism and the advertising that supports and spreads it. Ronald McDonald was the front man and spokesperson for a company that grew from one burger stand to an ocean of shiny and identical fast-food shops feeding America. In fact, McDonald's represents a significant source of nutrition for boomer offspring.

I know I'm treading on sacred ground, but Ronald McDonald has been a questionable friend to America's children. The clown's company is still peddling the same *secret sauce* meal of Big Mac, fries and a Coke. Who but a clown would joyfully urge a child to enjoy a meal containing 1,050 calories, nearly half of those from fat?

And that's *before* kids are encouraged to say, "Super Size me!"

Not much has changed in the years since Morgan Spurlock's good-humored documentary *Super Size Me* hit the theaters and skewered the quick-food corporation. McDonald's didn't have much to say about the movie, but they did begin to give lip service to a "commitment to evolve their menu." Ten years later, they announced that they would promote juice and milk with their Happy Meals, in lieu of soda.

McDonald's has been successful with essentially the same menu for 50 years, so don't expect any game-changers: A McDonald's medium strawberry shake is currently listed on their website at 700 calories – including 21 grams of fat, a pinch of various chemicals and a whopping 100 grams of sugar.

McDonald's PR department does a great job publicizing McDonald's generosity in donating money to help families cope with childhood diseases. Ironically, it's a safe bet that someday we'll be reading about their plans to set up a worldwide chain of Ronald McDonald clinics to address the growing epidemic of childhood obesity and diabetes.

I apologize for singling out McDonald's. Burger King, Taco Bell and other fast-food chains are similar. Admittedly (as these corporations point out) the choice of what a child consumes falls squarely on the shoulders of the parents, so parents should "order wisely." My real point is simply that boomers continue to run corporate cultures mired in hypocritical double-speak. Coca-Cola has remained America's top gun in pushing soda for the past 40 years. A can of regular Coke, Pepsi or 7up still has about 40 grams of sugar.

Even hip-hop artist 50 Cent cashed in. When he began pushing Vitaminwater as some sort of "heath drink," sales skyrocketed. The superstar rapper was the national spokesperson for the Vitaminwater brand and received a cool $200 million when the company sold to Coca-Cola for billions. It's the "new healthy Coke." Of course the fine print on the back label concedes that a bottle of Vitaminwater contains about 32 grams of sugar, as well as "synthetic vitamins," but it was a great new name for sugar water.

Soft drink companies have no shame about having no shame.

Kellogg's is still pushing Frosted Flakes and Fruit Loops to children, and General Mills is still hawking Cocoa Puffs. Many of the breakfast cereals aimed directly at our young ones have sugar contents of 35% to 40% – or more.

When I was a boy, Tony the Tiger was a great promoter of Sugar Frosted Flakes. "It tastes *grrrreat*!" was his friendly growl to America's children watching the tube. In the mid-'80s, the word "sugar" was removed from the box title, although the Kellogg Corporation somehow forgot to remove the actual sugar.

Today the hot ticket from Wrigley's is the Hubba Bubba Squeeze Pop for kids, featuring 96 grams of sugar per 4-ounce serving!

According to an all-star team of marketing wizards, our fast-food industry has managed to magically transform processed ingredients into what they would have us believe are *health food.* Taco Bell now touts their Fresco Menu, and Subway offers up foot-long sandwiches that actually *empower* their customers to lose weight. Even health food stores offer 12 versions of *natural* energy bars – ludicrous to anyone who actually reads the wrappers' tiny table of contents confessing to 15 grams of sugar.

Boomer marketeers now peddle *perfect* food products that are highly addictive and highly profitable. Who can resist the call of *Nature Valley*?

Big Tobacco, Big Pharma and all-purpose snake oil march on

Cigarette smoking in the United States may have declined in recent years, but Altria – the new name of Phillip Morris Tobacco – never stops developing its markets. Altria is the parent company of Skoal, which offers a dozen flavors of chewing tobacco, packaged to attract teenagers. All tobacco kills, but the federal tax on other forms of tobacco is only about 10% the tax on cigarettes, keeping nicotine addiction affordable for its victims.

Altria is a sweet-sounding name for a company that markets cancer-causing products to young people worldwide. Of course, Altria isn't alone in targeting teenagers across the globe. Other American tobacco companies still market to the young in other countries. In spite of a U.S. court ban on the use of cartoon character Joe Camel in America, he still roams the world, luring children into addiction.

As I write this, Philip Morris International is pressing the U.S. government for legal language that will make it difficult for foreign countries that join a proposed Pacific Rim trade pact to require warning labels on cigarette packages. U.S. Senator Mitch McConnell is leading the charge to discourage any labeling that might dampen overseas cigarette sales – he argues that such restrictions might encourage black market cigarette makers. After all, our government is still subsidizing the U.S. tobacco industry with more than $1 billion tax dollars annually, so evidently Senator McConnell wants to protect the sales and profitability of cigarettes. Approximately 20% of American adults still smoke cigarettes. The health care cost is staggering and a sizable burden on non-smoking taxpayers.

In 2012, Phillip Morris spent approximately $10 million in lobbying Congress.

Tobacco companies never give up. Reynolds American is now peddling the *Natural American Spirit* brand of cigarettes that they advertise as "100% organic and additive free" and "grown in America," as if their cigarettes are somehow *healthier and more patriotic* than conventional cigarettes. R. J. Reynolds' advertisements claim that their Camel cigarettes are *inspired, passionate* and *original.* Cigarettes are still killing 1 in 5 Americans.

I've always wondered what the men who run the tobacco companies tell their own children when asked the inevitable question: "Daddy, what does your company do?" I doubt whether the father replies, "Well, kids, we produce cancer-causing tobacco products and market them to young people, but only in other countries. It's hard work, but someone has to do it."

Short-sighted business models from Wall Street

We live in a business climate where boomer CEOs go after their bonuses like sharks after blood. Shareholders demand dividends right along with their Frappuccinos. Our corporate culture is still based on short-term vision for short-term profits, all too often at the expense of our environment, our health and even our jobs. Corporations are quick to shut down manufacturing plants in America – instead of figuring out better long-term solutions to protect American workers. It seems that Wall Street is still our nation's most powerful guiding force.

Violence as a profit center

Under boomer leadership, America's appetite for viewing graphic violence has grown to seemingly insatiable levels. In the course of one generation, our entertainment industry has dramatically increased the exploitation of human depravity.

Cable television shows such as *Dexter, Breaking Bad* and *Sons of Anarchy* have set new standards in depicting gut-wrenching carnage. And by offering *CSI* programs and a wide variety of other "terrorist" dramas, even mainstream networks dwell on every minute detail of violent crime.

On the night before the Thanksgiving holiday, I watched a new prime-time show on ABC, *The Blacklist.* The episode culminated in a horrendous scene in which an innocent woman had her brains blown out at close range with a hand gun, with a gratuitous close-up of blood splatter filling the television screen. Lovely.

The former *peace and love generation* has loaded up America's prime time with crime shows whose central plots revolve around the lurid details of rape, murder and other perverse activity. Throw in a mix of dark humor and sexual tension between the star characters and it's a winning combination for better ratings and bigger profits. Of course Americans can also choose from nine different reality shows, most of which are light on violence but long on idiocy. Should a citizen prefer to watch endless remakes of action-hero movies, or play the most popular video games, gratuitous violence is available in a wide range of flavors.

It seems odd to me that boomers still make such a fuss if a bare breast or "crude" dancing is aired, while scenes of gruesome murder are accepted as part of everyday fare. A psychologist might conclude that we live in a sick society, but at least we still have the consolation of knowing that our nation is still *shocked and incredulous* every time a senseless act of bloodshed (as glamorized on TV) becomes reality and is featured on the nightly news.

Paradise lost to disco, drugs and infomercials

Until the mid-'70s, some boomers still had the illusion that a "paradigm shift" was moving us toward a more holistic, humane and balanced society. Without much fanfare, the Age of Aquarius somehow disappeared into the ether – lost under the spell of *Saturday Night Fever* and the magic of the disco ball.

The War on Drugs, originally launched by the Nixon administration and continued by boomer presidents Clinton, Bush and Obama, has failed. Under my generation's guidance, powerful drugs (both legal and illegal) have proliferated in every major city and small town. America's medicine cabinets overflow with prescription drugs, while illicit substances are secretly stashed in the closet. Americans crave their drugs and are constantly seeking new ones.

However, when it came to dispensing contraceptive drugs to young Americans, our Congress extended the Reagan administration's *Just Say No* position on recreational drugs to birth control: For teenagers, abstinence from sex, like abstinence from marijuana, was pushed as the best policy. This attempt to use social engineering to control youthful hormones was (pardon the pun) not well conceived. In the past several years, the states that spent millions of federal tax dollars promoting sexual abstinence programs (while discouraging easy access to birth control) registered the *highest* teen pregnancy rates in the country.

The ultimate consumer society reaches new heights

If there is one area in which America continues to excel, it's in finding new and more effective ways to market consumer goods and services.

Most people became familiar with Amazon.com as a bookseller. But in less than two decades, Amazon has become the store where America truly loves to shop – for *everything.* Jeff Bezos has perfected the one-stop internet marketplace, offering customers everything from Kindle reading devices to sexual wellness merchandise and high-end art and fashion. Amazon now employs nearly 100,000 people and brings in about $75 billion a year. Amazon is now America's biggest seller and their mission is simple: "Anything you want on Earth will eventually be available from Amazon."

Smaller companies like QVC – Quality-Value-Convenience – dedicate themselves to niche markets through television merchandising. Joseph Segel's network offers viewers 24/7 stay-at-home shopping. In 2013, QVC pushed $8.6 billion in specialized non-essential gadgets out their door. HSN – Home Shopping Network – offers a similar service. Boomers have developed and marketed an endless supply of commodities no one really needs. Sophisticated sellers *create* demand. Our closets, our garages and our mini-storage units are full of *stuff.*

A myriad of lotions, potions and miracle creams fill our bathroom cabinets – all with some guarantee of a better life. Even All-American superstar quarterback Joe Theismann has started carrying the ball for instant fixes, as he now stars in an infomercial hawking Super Beta Prostate pills.

The infomercial has wormed its way into nearly every aspect of our lives. Entire networks are devoted exclusively to these advertisements masquerading as helpful, honest documentaries. Most of the information we receive today about goods and services is either pablum or propaganda. Talk-show format infomercials feature a gaggle of questionable *experts* who babble incessantly about their breakthrough products. Even *Happy Days* star Henry Winkler ("Fonzie") now informs us about the benefits of reverse mortgages.

Television isn't the only source of authoritative-sounding but self-serving information. Magazines regularly insert sections called "advertorials" where *super lawyers* and other ambitious business professionals receive special newsy attention and spurious awards. To fool the reader, these phony write-ups use the same typeface and layout design as standard editorial copy, floating the illusion that their content was factually written by some objective third party.

Newspapers allow these questionable full-page ads that look and read like a concerned columnist's opinion piece, letting advertisers bury the word *advertisement*. These same papers run articles about the perils of consumer fraud, or editorials pleading for ecology, while stuffing their Sunday edition with two pounds of junk mail and throwaway flyers.

Our internet is now polluted with an infuriating stream of pop-up junk ads.

In short, American culture has run off the rails into the Twilight Zone. If one of America's Founding Fathers surfed our cable channels he might quickly conclude that his countrymen had all gone insane:

Click – a violent murder scene from CSI. *Click* – a scene from reality show *Duck Dynasty. Click* – an ad for *Hooters. Click* – an evangelist preacher pleading for money in the name of Jesus. *Click* – QVC selling fancy dog beds. *Click* – a clip from *The Texas Chainsaw Massacre* to push a DVD collection of horror films. *Click* – an infomercial for erectile dysfunction pills. *Click* – a rapper doing a promo for MTV. *Click* – a replay of Roseanne Barr singing the national anthem.

I rest my case.

Contemplating the Cialis Moment

Most of what we see today is simply a continuation of old-school marketing, but you can count on the drug companies to pioneer new ground. It's interesting to note that the United States is the only country in the world (besides New Zealand) that allows pharmaceutical companies to advertise prescription drugs on television directly aimed at consumers.

One of the newest trends in advertising features senior citizens happily riding bicycles, hiking in forests or practicing yoga. We're promised entry to a mythical land, where boomer couples sit blissfully in bathtubs by the ocean, contemplating their Cialis moment. The Marlboro Man has also matured – he cleverly pulls his horse trailer out of the mud with his own horse before going home to pop a Viagra.

Drug companies give boomers the hope that they can remain forever young, pain free and vital, as long as they swallow the right pill. If Big Pharma sponsors a study to identify a new syndrome, it's a good bet that an expensive capsule has already been developed to fix the problem. Selling psychoactive medicine to old people is the new frontier in marketing. Pushing feel-better drugs requires clever advertisements that pluck at the heartstrings – because many of these expensive *medicines* provide only questionable benefits and come with a mountain of nasty side effects. At the end of each ad the familiar warnings arrive, the litany of potential dangers, which always seem to include headaches and/or diarrhea and/or dry mouth, followed by that catch-all phrase: "Check with your doctor before engaging in sexual activity." Charming.

The price tag for a specific drug often bears little relation to its production cost. It's common for drug companies to charge *whatever the traffic will bear*, as long as they can figure out *an angle* to demand a higher reimbursement from Medicare. For instance, Genentech (a division of Roche) sells two virtually identical drugs, both commonly used for the treatment of macular degeneration: Avistan costs $50 per shot and Lucentis $2,000, but Medicare still commonly pays for Lucentis. According to an article published by the AARP, providing Lucentis to patients results in "the single largest medication expense for Medicare, based on 2010 data."

To make matters worse, the mega-brand name manufacturers often seek to extend a drug's exclusivity, by paying smaller generic drug makers sizable sums to drop legal challenges. This common tactic delays the introduction of less expensive generic drugs. It's a sick practice.

A detailed study by PLoS Medicine, published in a journal of the Public Library of Health, asserts that the drug industry spends at least twice as much on marketing as it does on research and development. The industry claims otherwise, but independent sources say that the PLoS findings are conservative in estimating the lopsided ratio between R&D and marketing. A study conducted from the late-'90s through 2006 – and published by the non-partisan Center for Public Integrity – found that drug companies had spent almost $1 billion on lobbying activities – more than any other industry.

Pharmaceutical companies also focus their marketing efforts on the medical community: In 1990, there were approximately 585,000 children in America on psychoactive medication for ADHD, and today the number is 3.5 million.

Are there really *six times* more children who now need to be medicated?

Over the past two decades, the big drug companies have transformed themselves into shameless drug pushers who especially target the aging-boomer market to create a demand. Unfortunately, when it comes to boomers, we all know that all of the drugs that offer to postpone or even reverse the aging process belie a chilling reality that is just around the corner.

Is the boomers' party over?

The boomers may have started out as the Pepsi Generation, but somehow the flower children are finding themselves knee deep in the quicksand of heart disease, diabetes and cancer, and often struggle with depression.

But wait, there's more: In addition to facing the humbling experience of physical decline and an onset of the blues, many boomers will soon end up in a fog, a condition once simply referred to as "senility." A click on the Alzheimer's Association website reveals a startling prediction – in the near future the number of people diagnosed with the disease will increase by 40%. Seven million Americans will soon suffer from some sort of dementia.

The boomers will be at least a decade too late to be saved by any stem-cell bullet. What they can expect for treatment are long waits, complicated insurance forms, and little compassion from companies prone to deny coverage at the drop of a hat. It's no accident that the largest buildings in most major cities bear the name of insurance corporations.

And, insurance companies always employ three proven accomplices: Mr. Fear, Mr. Lobbyist, and Mr. Politician. It's an unbeatable combination.

The tape-measure perspective

As I write this, most boomers are still reeling from the gut punches of the Great Recession, with more implications yet to unfold. Many of my generation will still be able to afford spending their *sunset years* in newly minted versions of what were once called assisted living facilities, which have recently evolved into *active senior living communities.*

For those without sufficient financial assets, things will be more difficult. Boomers relished the idea of living for the moment. Sadly, the moments have passed, and large numbers of the '60s generation are too old to work and have too little savings to live comfortably in their Golden Years. Millions of old people will fall through the cracks as inflation inevitably rears its ugly head. Worse, a significant portion of boomers will endure their closing years on Earth hovering near the poverty line, homeless and forgotten.

The topic of aging seems to come up more often these days when I socialize with friends. A few of us *older guys* were having coffee the other day, commiserating, when I mentioned that

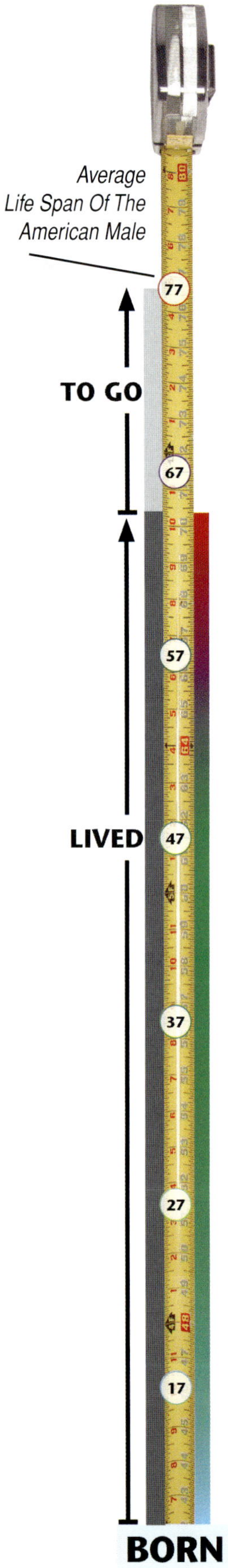

the average life span of the American male is about 77. My friend Jim Agee (who always has an interesting perspective) grabbed a metal tape measure from one of the other guys at the table and said: "Gentlemen, you may be pushing up daisies sooner than you think."

Jim pulled out 77 inches of the tape and laid it across our table. He then dramatically ran his finger from 0 inches all the way up to the 65-inch mark, and stopped.

"Ok, *Mr. Branch*," Jim said, "look at how far my finger ran up the blade. Now check out the very short piece of tape that's left. You should start making your bucket list."

The visual was stunning – it's hard to argue with the marks on a tape measure.

About 65 years ago, bandleader Guy Lombardo wrote a catchy tune with the memorable lyric: "Go ahead, enjoy yourself, it's later than you think." It was a big hit.

Now the Good News

The majority of boomers still believe that our generation remains at the center of the universe.

As a group, we still make up the largest, wealthiest and most powerful segment of the population. More than any previous generation, boomers are in a position to use their wisdom and wealth to help their fellow inhabitants of the Earth.

My generation seems to have an innate pursuit-of-happiness impulse, although we certainly did not invent or discover the idea that human life should be rewarding, enjoyable and fun. After all, our forefathers codified the concept by writing it into our Declaration of Independence as an unalienable right. The search for happiness became a mandate, the main trail to the American Dream.

Much of this essay is not a pretty reflection of the past or the future, but I should point out that all of my downbeat prognostications are merely personal conjecture.

It was my goal to encourage some thought and discussion.

Most people still in their 50s or early 60s are much too busy working their asses off to worry about this morbid stuff. Many of my friends, when they read this, will respond: "Hey, I feel great. And why would anyone dwell on these negative thoughts?"

It's really a good point. Long before boomers kick the bucket, we will see exciting and profound changes in technology and bio-science that will continue to improve the world.

A lot of boomers remain in terrific physical condition, and engage in activities that once belonged only to the young. Jamie Moyer still plays professional baseball at 50, Fred Couples is still winning big in his mid-50s, and the band members of Earth, Wind & Fire are currently touring in their 60s. In December 2013, we spent a night listening to Jerry Jeff Walker and his band at The Grand 1894 Opera House in Galveston. At 71, the country singer who wrote Mr. Bojangles sounded as good as ever and received a standing ovation.

There is no reason that boomers need be isolated as they grow older. It's never been easier to stay connected. PCs and iPads are a source of endless enjoyment, and allow us a stream of emails and photos from friends and family. They supply an endless selection of new information about the world around us. An inexpensive wristwatch will be able to monitor your health, remind you to take your pills, locate any lost item, and serve as your phone and internet connection. If you get lost, it will give you voice commands to find your way home.

Our 21st-century technology provides an inexhaustible supply of entertainment. Sporting events look terrific on new HD televisions with surround sound, and the price of a large flat-screen is reasonable. DVRs let you view your favorite shows whenever you want. Any book is available at the click of a mouse.

Many of the children of boomers are finally independent and out in the world, allowing lucky parents to once again walk around the house naked. Medicare benefits are just around the corner along with a Social Security check. Walmart now sells prescriptions for $4.

Advancing age brings clarity about what is important, reminds you who your real friends are, and gives you the confidence to speak your mind freely. Many boomers have to take periodic health tests to monitor one thing or another, but each time the results come back clean, it's time to celebrate.

Carpe diem!

Several books have been written about how the boomers will change the experience of aging, and how they are determined not to give up on life's possibilities. It is this emphatic engagement with life that drives many of us.

As the siren song of the Golden Years grows louder, each of us will be faced with the question of how to spend our remaining time, and what kind of legacy we want to leave to the younger generations.

Those remaining chapters have yet to be written. ■

FACEBOOK TWITTER YOU TUBE PINTEREST GOOGLE+

The Millennial Generation

My stepson, Tyler, is a member of the Millennial Generation – those born after 1980, and the first generation of Americans to grow up during the social media/technological revolution. Like many young people his age, he is part of a new wave of "digital natives," whose prized possessions are cell phones, computers and video games. Tyler will undoubtedly shake his head with amusement when he reads my take on the millennials, but it will not be a shock to his system. He recently graduated from Cal Poly and wants to pursue a career in computer programming.

Tyler and his contemporaries view the World Wide Web as their personal yellow brick road – instant access to information, entertainment and adventure. The web is also the gateway into the wacky, the weird and the forbidden. Google, Facebook and YouTube are ubiquitous. Every book or video, and much of recorded human history, is just a mouse click away.

Many boomers have reservations about young people who know only a world where kids can read, see or hear anything they desire instantly and privately. A good deal of scientific research shows that more of the brain is activated while *interacting* with a website than when reading a book. Interactive websites and games engage young minds in ways never imagined. Millennial brains function like search engines. The young simply sit down at a keyboard or flip out a smartphone and enter a universe that has no bounds.

YouTube may not kill off television, but it's rapidly changing global viewing habits, especially among the millennials. YouTube was acquired by Google in 2006 for $1.6 billion. Many scoffed at the internet giant paying so much for a company that had barely celebrated its one-year anniversary. Google was undaunted and the acquisition has proven to be momentous. In 36 months, videos viewed on YouTube grew from approximately 60 billion to 130 billion – *per month.* According to Nielsen research, 18- to 24-year-olds now view 2.5 hours of online video – *per week.*

YouTube's purchase marked an important advance in Google's mission to gather, organize and disseminate all of the world's information, but YouTube is only one of more than 120 companies that Google has absorbed in the past decade. It's a new Google world, and we've just seen the beginning.

Jeffery Katzenberg from DreamWorks purchased a new company, called "Awesomeness TV," which is a new kind of network: It offers an open platform and may grow to rival traditional cable networks like Cox Communications or Comcast. Viewers will be able to post content and YouTube will share in the ad revenue. Similar youth-oriented "YouTube" networks will surely follow.

The globalization process Thomas Freidman described in his 2005 book, *The World Is Flat,* has arrived. Millions of miles of fiber optic cable make geographical and national boundaries increasingly irrelevant. The internet has created greater, more equal access to business opportunities, allowing small companies to compete with corporations in the global marketplace.

World-class instruction is now available 24/7 through Khan Academy, or edX, and Wikipedia provides a treasure trove of information on anything and everything. An ever-exploding universe of "apps" is instantly ready to assist and entertain users.

Want to view the world? Anyone can fly around via Google Earth.

Every time I type in an address and see "Google Earth" start rushing toward me on the screen, I have to giggle, because it's just so much fun. The other day I was sitting in my underwear, sipping coffee, taking a 3D tour down 5th Avenue in New York, for free.

For better or worse, the internet's impact on the world is ever-present, profound and expanding. Apple, Microsoft, Google and Amazon are leading us into the future and have become top American brands, surpassing traditional heavyweights like Coca-Cola. Moore's Law (named after Intel co-founder Gordon F. Moore) suggests that the growth of computer power is exponential, and we can sense this increase in speed and efficiency in our daily lives. Our tasks are becoming more automated and almost instant, whether we're punching in instructions on our new "smart refrigerator" or requesting an airline boarding pass. Moore's Law, and the projections of former Intel executive David House, predicted that computer-chip performance would double every 18 months.

Boomers grew up with three TV channels – ABC, NBC and CBS – a newspaper, and access to usually outdated volumes of *Encyclopedia Britannica.* Any research or other additional reading material was found on the shelves of the public library or in a bookstore. A visit to the library required a drive to town, and once there (as I remember all too well) you had to sit still and be quiet.

Oh, These Kids Today

Many of my generation bemoan the fact that the young have no real knowledge of the pre-internet world, and some view this as a problem. Boomers constantly worry that kids today have too much of a sense of entitlement and that they dwell in their narcissistic Facebook fantasy lives.

This criticism strikes me as ironic and somewhat hypocritical, coming from my fellow members of the "Me" Generation.

Human resource directors of corporations, both large and small, grouse about how job applicants from Generations X and Y have unrealistic expectations. Young employees seem to blatantly place their own personal priorities ahead of company goals. It's all true, but it's not necessarily all bad. Why aspire to be a workaholic? Why should we care so much about corporations? Kids have grown up watching how corporations treat their employees. Corporate history is hardly a story about compassion and/or loyalty. The realities of outsourcing, mergers, bankruptcies, plant shutdowns and pension failures are well-known to millennials.

Trophies Abound

The Millennial Generation has been continually maligned for playing too many video games and being too absorbed in social media. My contemporaries lament that the new generation suffers from not leading more physically active childhoods, unlike the hardy children in our Leave-It-to-Beaver memories. It may be true that young people suffer from increasingly sedentary habits, but no one should blame the internet for lack of parental guidance in promoting healthy lifestyles. Few would claim that the internet can build character, or that it can provide wisdom or love. Any deficit in good parenting should fall squarely on the shoulders of parents.

At the same time, this new generation is indeed different, primarily as a result of how they experienced childhood, adolescence and early adulthood. Their entitled attitude came naturally, because they (for the most part) were raised by boomers in an abundant world of opportunity and entertainment. Their environment was child-friendly, and most kids were told they were special. American culture proclaimed that every girl and boy was a winner. "Building self-esteem" was often a primary goal of many boomer parents. Every kid received a trophy for *something.*

How would these kids not feel entitled?

In other areas, today's new adults are remarkably similar to boomers – they're irreverent toward their elders and highly skeptical of government and big business.

Millennials may not respect authority, but they tend to obey the rules – maybe more than we ever did. For better or worse, the laws of the road of computer software and video games have trained kids to stay within a strict set of guidelines.

The younger generation participates in a wider variety of sports and other social activities. They have a more diverse selection of stars from which to choose their role models and heroes. Watch some old episodes of *Gossip Girl,* or better yet, a few episodes of the hit TV series *Glee* – it's immediately obvious that the new teenage idols come from a far different planet than the one inhabited by my generation. The characters and subject matter of the typical youth-oriented TV show are a far cry from what appeared on *Happy Days.*

Young Women Redefining Their World

There is a new reality for the millennial women who grew up taking Title IX, which guarantees equal access in athletics, education and employment, for granted. Today's young women can recite the liberating lyrics of the mega-stars who inspire them – Beyoncé, Taylor Swift, Katy Perry, Lady Gaga, or Pink, to name a few. Together these five female singers have sold over 350 million records worldwide. Each of them runs her own mega-corporation, and none has much patience for men controlling her career or the nature of her health care.

They are the masters of their own universe.

Serena Williams plays tennis on an entirely different level from our generation's star, Chris Everett. Danica Patrick qualified for the pole position at the Daytona 500, clocking in at 196 miles per hour. Mo'ne Davis, 13, was the first female World Series Little Leaguer to throw a shutout and grace the cover of *Sports Illustrated*.

Country star Taylor Swift, at age 22, was already the CEO of a multi-hundred-million-dollar enterprise. Why not? Ms. Swift grew up observing how women like Carrie Underwood rocketed from obscurity to win *American Idol,* then went on to garner six Grammys and 10 Academy of Country Music Awards. Underwood takes a back seat to no man – she graduated *magna cum laude* from Northeastern State University, with a degree in mass communication. Like her successful contemporaries, she controls her own corporation.

Ms. Underwood and Ms. Swift each project a different persona than super star Angelina Jolie, but before their successful careers began they must have noted that Ms. Jolie had already shattered several feminine stereotypes. Jolie first emerged as a cultural role model, starring as a "kick-ass" heroine in adventure movies. Now she also serves as an official spokesperson for the United Nations, flies her own plane, is a mother of a large, multi-cultural family, and goes home to Brad Pitt – as an equal. Between her stardom and her philanthropic work, Jolie has become one of the world's most popular celebrity ambassadors.

I remember watching a teenage Angelina Jolie in the late '90s movie *Girl Interrupted*, and thinking that a new day was dawning for young American women.

Michelle Obama grew up in a modest home with little money but graduated from Princeton, then Harvard Law. She went on to become a successful attorney, then a mother, a successful administrator and first lady. If that's not enough, Mrs. Obama can also do 20 push-ups.

All of these women are widely admired and powerful role models. The remaining layers of the glass ceiling are finally beginning to shatter.

In contrast, when I was in high school, I took my girlfriend to watch Annette Funicello in *Beach Blanket Bingo* and Sally Field in *The Flying Nun*. Marlo Thomas, as *That Girl* at the end of the '60s, and single and independent TV reporter Mary Tyler Moore through the '70s, helped to push the envelope, but it was only the beginning.

The '60s and '70s were also a time when "in real life" a host of women came forward to lead, including Gloria Steinem, Betty Friedan and Bella Abzug – all co-founders of the National Women's Political Caucus. It was Friedan who joined Congresswoman Shirley Chisholm and Muriel Fox to found the National Organization for Women (NOW). Barbara Jordan, a member of Congress from Texas, and boomers Hillary Clinton and tennis player Billie Jean King were just a few of the other strong women who were steadfast in their beliefs, undaunted by men who called them "women's libbers" and the constant harassment from the likes of Rush Limbaugh, who proclaimed to the world that all such modern feminists were "femi-Nazis."

America's changing perception of women can be seen in the movies that were made between 1960 and 1980, when the screen's sex symbols and "docile wives" began to give way to female characters who had lives of their own and whose identities weren't dictated by men. In 1979, nominees for Best Actress at the Academy Awards all played self-motivated, independent heroines: Meryl Streep in *Kramer v. Kramer,* Bette Midler in *The Rose,* Marsha Mason in *Chapter Two,* Jane Fonda in *The China Syndrome,* Jill Clayburgh in *Starting Over,* and Oscar-winner Sally Field in *Norma Rae.* Field had come a long way since playing the Flying Nun and sidekick to macho Burt Reynolds in *Smokey and the Bandit.* Helen Reddy's 1972 hit song, "I Am Woman," became an anthem for the women's liberation movement.

Watching My Mother

From a young age, I saw firsthand how my mom struggled with the reality of second-class citizenship for women. Her work outside the home constantly brought her into contact with men who felt women had a defined, limited role in society, but she would not be intimidated. She was involved with the woman's equality movement long before it became fashionable. Without knowing it, I was being educated by my mother's example and by my father's innate respect for her. It certainly took me some time, but as I matured as a man, I began to see more clearly just how poorly women have been treated all over the world.

The world's future will be brighter when all women have a truly equal say in everything. Even older politicians and conservative religious leaders now give more lip service to women's equality – although their hypocrisy becomes apparent anytime the rubber meets the road during the legislative process.

In 2012, Republican Congressman Darrell Issa convened his House Committee on Oversight and Government Reform to discuss women's health issues in front of the entire nation, on network television. There was not a single woman on his panel.

All the members of Issa's committee were aging boomers who looked like me. As I watched the hearing on the nightly news, I burst out laughing and thought to myself, *Why are these old men still making all the decisions about women's health issues? I guess it's going to take a number of funerals before these men give up power.* No woman I know wants some man telling her what she can do with her body. If I'd been a panel member, I would have looked around the table and asked, "Hey, where are the women? What are you guys thinking?"

Apparently these men live in a bubble, and were not even savvy enough to anticipate how badly a male-only panel would play out in the media. I can understand why women ignore or reject any politician or religious authority that does not truly honor women's equality.

Not the Boomers' Biggest Fans

It's no surprise that the younger generations are not all that impressed with the boomer legacy. Today's young adults *do not dance to our beat,* and they are keenly aware of the hypocrisy that runs rampant throughout our culture. Why would the generations coming after us want to follow our lead? Our children are quick to point out that boomers have failed on so many levels – especially when it comes to the economy, health care and the war on drugs. There is even a book titled *Why Boomers Suck.* No doubt it will be one of many.

Generation X (1965-1980) and Generation Y (millennials, 1981-1996) naturally resent being burdened with boomer mistakes and boomer debt. It's become clear that their elders are leaving them a colossal mess. They watch us fumble with new technology, or become confused by new software, and they conclude: *Old people are not that smart.*

That's not to say that the young don't have boomer-aged heroes. Satirists Jon Stewart and Stephen Colbert are well received, but of course they spend most of their time poking fun at boomer politicians. *The Daily Show* with Stewart seems to tackle subjects no network will touch. What makes the program unique is the ability of his cast to be humorous but not mean-spirited.

Stewart is one of those rare satirists whose sharp intellect is always expressed with a sense of decency on a wide variety of subjects, lampooning fellow boomers of the media and politicians in all camps and in every country. Although Stewart is a "boomer," his honest and funny political and social insights hit a nerve with younger generations. In 2010 Stewart's show produced a book titled *Earth – A Visitor's Guide to the Human Race,* which was a bit hit, especially among millennials. It's hilarious – I haven't seen anyone pick up the book and not start laughing within 60 seconds.

Boomers Still Write the Checks

The fact remains that however Generations X and Y view "old people," the boomers are still in the demographic majority, and people over 50 vote in greater numbers than their younger fellow citizens. No one should expect boomers to relinquish their hold on power or fade away quietly. We still write the checks. The Pepsi Generation has total control of the U.S. Congress and of nearly all the Fortune 500 companies. Boomers own the nation's wealth.

When I was in my 20s, we had a popular motto: "Don't trust anyone over 30." Now, at 65, I find myself in an ironic position, suggesting that people under 30 should learn as much as possible from boomers, despite all the blunders and mistakes we've made.

It's important to remember the long list of accomplishments associated with the Boomer Generation, especially in civil rights and concern for the environment. It's no longer acceptable to openly disparage ethnic groups or gay people, or to patronize women. Nowadays there is much more awareness of legal penalties for spousal and child abuse, and for workplace sexual harassment.

Boomers Bill Gates and Steve Jobs brought the world revolutionary technology. Stephen Spielberg, George Lucas and Ron Howard gave life to some of the world's best movies. Our music continues to rock. Boomer "writers" still supply the nation's best novels – they grew up before email, texting and video games made the complete sentence nearly obsolete.

Most importantly, members of the '60s generation will soon be the last living bearers of their ancestors' accumulated store of knowledge and wisdom, and of our nation's collective memory of traditions and events predating the advent of the Computer Age. Boomers will be the last women and men alive who registered firsthand the revolutionary changes that swept America between the end of World War II and the closing of the 20th century.

Taking Care of 78 Million Old People

However they view their parents, the younger generations will have to provide a massive stream of economic support to take care of 78 million boomers drifting off into the sunset. If our children fail in that mission, perhaps our grandchildren will invent a hi-tech version of Soylent Green, the nutritious product that gave its name to the 1973 sci-fi movie in which old people were lured to "gentle euthanasia centers" and their bodies turned into recycled protein – to feed the starving masses. In any event, countless retirement centers will soon be packed with feeble boomers requiring constant attention. It won't be long before the last traces of any sense of entitlement for millennials slip away, as their helpless elders hold up the mirror of mortality.

In short order, this new generation will have to look up from their smartphones and laptops long enough to address complex problems, and make the hard choices that we and our politicians ignored – or failed to make.

Rebuilding America's infrastructure, updating our educational system and revising health care should be at the top of their to-do list. And the biggest challenge in tackling these monumental issues will be dealing with the darker sides of America's corporate structure.

May the force be with the Millennials. ■

Democracy is a device
that ensures we shall be governed
no better than we deserve.

– George Bernard Shaw

LIVING UNDER BOOMER RULE

IN 1983 *The Big Chill* was a smash hit that captured the hearts of my generation. The movie starred Glenn Close, William Hurt, Tom Berenger and Kevin Kline. Thirty years later, the soundtrack still sells like crazy. The comedy-drama was centered squarely on boomer growing pains and was nominated for three Oscars, including Best Picture.

In the early '80s marketers began referring to the Pepsi Generation as "thirtysomethings." The name stuck for several years, with the TV show *Thirtysomething* becoming an immensely popular series after it first aired in 1987. How popular? The show was nominated for 41 Emmys and ranks high on the list of *TV Guide*'s greatest series of all time.

The subject matter of the movie and the television series confirmed that – by and large – those born after World War II had enjoyed the longest adolescence in American history. While most boomers had settled into "responsible lifestyles," some were still knee-deep in rock 'n' roll, extracurricular sex, recreational drugs and big drama.

After the deaths of Robert Kennedy and Martin Luther King – and worn out by the war in Vietnam – thirtysomethings began a quiet retreat to the political sidelines.

During the 1990s my generation started to enter its fifth decade, and a youthful and handsome Arkansas governor named Bill Clinton ended the long run of Republican presidents Ronald Reagan and George H. Bush.

Who could resist a New Age boomer in cool dark shades, blowing a bluesy solo on his saxophone during a surprise visit to the *Arsenio Hall Show*?

An updated model of the American character began to emerge.

Boomers found themselves in uncharted territory. Life got serious as *fiftysomethings* rapidly took control of Fortune 500 corporations, the U. S. Congress and the White House. The Soviet Union had collapsed and with it the Cold War. In the early '90s, the American-led Operation Desert Storm had freed Kuwait from Saddam Hussein with a quick and decisive victory, which boosted U.S. morale. Nelson Mandela was president of a post-apartheid South Africa, and Hillary Clinton was our first lady. In 1997, a young Tiger Woods won the Masters by an eye-popping 12 strokes and graced the cover of *Sports Illustrated.*

The same era was a difficult time for President Clinton, because the Biggest Story involved a blue dress. The scandal surrounding Bill Clinton eventually passed, although righteous indignation still lingered over his affair with Monica Lewinski. Many of my conservative friends wanted to see Clinton tossed out on his ear for lying to the nation about his sexual indiscretions. On the other hand, the U.S. government actually had a budget surplus for the first time in years, and Clinton was a steadfast friend to big business. Scandals involving our presidents are not exactly uncommon in our history. The conservatives loudly proclaimed their disgust with Clinton's "immorality," but they were unsuccessful in their attempt to throw him out of office. Ironically, Newt Gingrich was among the most vocal critics – until his own "indiscretions" came under scrutiny.

In 2000, the country voted to return to a more conservative direction, and George W. Bush became our 43rd president and our second boomer president.

I didn't find myself in tune with many of the social policies advocated by the new administration, but I admired the fact that George Bush had dramatically turned his personal life around to become the governor of Texas, and then successfully used the governorship as a stepping stone into the White House. Since I was never a fan of Al Gore, I was more than willing to keep an open mind about our new president.

All in all, I was optimistic about the future.

But the next eight years turned out to be painful and disastrous for our country. On September 11, 2001, terrorism reached American soil on a massive scale and forever altered our national psyche. Our government's first action involved "seeking justice" in Afghanistan, but within a short time we had launched a major invasion of Iraq. In March 2003, during a four-day period, the U.S. fired 2,000 guided missiles into the Iraqi cities of Baghdad, Kirkuk and Mosul. More than 100,000 U.S. troops were assembled on the ground and began their invasion to take over control of the country. The Iraq war did not go as planned. *[See page 295]*

By 2008, the United States was mired in two failing military conflicts in the Middle East, the American banking system was on the verge of collapse, and financial markets were near a free fall. Between its high mark in 2007 and its low point in 2009, the Dow had lost almost 50% of its value, and the NASDAQ index had fallen by more than 50%. Millions of boomer investors faced margin calls on their stock holdings. Others sold their stocks in desperation, simply because they could not afford any further losses.

It was the worst financial crisis in three generations.

Millions of Americans had lost their jobs, homes and savings – the economic meltdown rocked our national mindset like nothing since the Great Depression of the 1930s.

President Bush left office with the lowest approval rating in American history.

Our nation – evermore divided

Since 2008, our culture has become highly polarized, more divided than at any time since the Vietnam Era. Today about 50% of Americans dislike our current president and about half that group seem to be downright hostile. Many conservatives appear eager for the president of the United States to fail (or even be impeached) simply "to prove" their particular point of view. I can understand their frustration with the current president, but given the history of the most recent Republican administration, neither party has any claim to a stellar track record. Fox News, Rush Limbaugh, Bill O'Reilly, and a gang of other ultraconservative pundits spew their hatred toward Obama – relentlessly.

It's no wonder that any semblance of political civility has evaporated.

America has had a tough go in the first 14 years of the 21st century. Under the Obama administration, the Great Recession continued, year after year. For most of the decade before Obama entered the White House, and in the six years since, America's middle class has endured gut punch after gut punch. President Obama has been unable or unwilling to keep many of his promises, and our national health care system has become ever more complicated and confusing. *[See page 227]*

• • •

It seems to me that there are larger underlying concerns, like submerged, connected icebergs, that have plagued our country for decades. These ongoing issues have remained unaddressed by either political party and now appear to be hard-wired elements of the American system.

I'm going to try to step back a few paces and throw in my two cents about what I've seen during the past 50 years, and how the same chronic problems have affected our past and present and most likely will influence our future.

Our national priorities are easier to identify when viewed from a distance and I'll quickly list them, then describe how I think they're all interwoven and aid and abet one another in damaging our country and its citizens.

Taxation: Historically, a cornerstone of American democracy is fair taxation. The government is empowered to collect taxes in an equitable fashion from its citizens for the common good. Over time, the way a democracy spends its tax revenues creates a telling portrait of its values.

Wars: We've been fighting "preemptive wars" for 50 years and this practice appears to have become (more or less) institutionalized. Our federal budget represents what our countrymen think is important – or more accurately, what our elected leaders think is important. In my lifetime, preemptive war has become a major aspect of American foreign policy.

Education: The state of our educational system is also a reflection of national priorities. By almost every educational measurement standard, our schools are failing when compared to the education offered in most other industrialized nations.

Prisons: The decline of American schools (especially in low-income areas) has contributed to the ever-expanding prison population and the rise of a rapidly growing, increasingly privatized prison industry.

How do these four subjects tie together?

If you can tolerate a bit of rambling, I'll attempt to address some of the connections between taxes, wars, education and prisons, subjects that are inexorably linked.

It begins with the world's most complicated tax system

Individuals have their own spin on who is responsible for America's incomprehensible tax code and our current economic predicament. Most wealthy people believe that they pay too much in taxes, and were relieved when George W. Bush became president in 2000 and implemented the Bush tax cuts. Conversely, middle-class citizens intuitively feel that the wealthy and large corporations receive the biggest tax breaks and don't pay their fair share.

Economists and pundits on both sides conjure up different figures to support their claims.

Whatever your personal viewpoint, one thing is clear: For the past 15 years, our national government has been spending more money than it takes in. The current deficit started and expanded under the Bush administration, and grew tremendously during the early years of the Obama presidency. A significant portion of the deficit increase was a result of bailout commitments made during the financial crisis that began under President Bush in the winter of 2007. Subsequent emergency funds were doled out at the discretion of the Obama administration. These expenditures were meant to prevent a financial meltdown and ease the effects of the national recession. The measures introduced by Obama may (or may not) have positive long-term effects on our economy, depending on the politician, pundit or fellow citizen you happen to listen to.

As I write this, it appears that the economy has finally dug itself out of a deep, dark hole.

The interest accumulating on our national debt may impair any graceful solution to our economic problems, but in the past few years the U.S. budget deficit, as a percentage of gross domestic product (GDP), has been steadily declining and the overall economy seems to be stabilizing. We've had other long stretches of deficits – the last one from 1970 through 1997 – so the sky is not falling.

The myth of equitable taxation

The incomprehensible volumes of tax regulations have been cobbled together by Congress over the past 50 years. An *entire industry* has been created simply to help Americans navigate the muddy waters of our tax codes.

My business partner and I have used the same accounting firm for the past 37 years. Each December, we give our accountants all of our numbers and a few weeks later they tell us how much we owe in taxes. There is no way that we can prepare our own tax returns, because the state and federal tax forms require almost 200 pages of complicated accounting documentation.

In the course of the year, we meet regularly with our accountants, who give us "tax planning guidance" and assure us that they are taking advantage of all allowable tax breaks. I'll be the first to admit that my partner and I have never seen a tax break we didn't like, and we don't include any gratuity when sending our payments to Uncle Sam.

During the 2012 presidential campaign, we heard a lot of media chatter as Americans learned that the Romney family had consistently paid an "actual tax rate" of around 14% on their yearly earnings. Some citizens were taken aback at how the wealthy seem to hold on to a much larger percentage of their income, yet no one ever claimed that the Romneys had broken any U.S. tax laws.

The fact that an American family worth several hundred million dollars could be taxed at a rate 50% lower than a schoolteacher or a construction worker caused only minor outrage. When it came to light that Romney and other mega-rich Americans regularly park portions of their savings in certain foreign countries for additional tax breaks, many more Americans were disturbed, although moving funds off shore is legal. The effective tax rate on deposits held in other countries can range between 10% and 20%, or in some cases, less. *Money flows naturally* – to the most inviting climate.

When it comes to working the tax system, the private equity fund managers on Wall Street and the law firms that specialize in corporate tax law are in a league of their own.

The rich continue to roll, but it's been ugly for the middle class

Alan Krueger, a Princeton University economist and former undersecretary of the treasury department, has been named among the world's 50 most important economists and currently chairs President Obama's White House Council of Economic Advisors. Professor Krueger recently pointed out that from 1979 to 2011 approximately 80% of our nation's increase in income went to the wealthiest 1% of the population. Similar statistics have emerged in recent years from a variety of sources, so this upward redistribution of wealth is old news. The 2012 Citigroup brochure for the super-rich, titled *The Wealth Report,* noted that the economic period spanning the last three decades has generated the largest concentration of wealth in the fewest hands since the Gilded Age of the late 1800s.

While the average CEO has gotten a raise of nearly 40% since 2009, average American workers earn no more now than they did in 1978 (adjusted for inflation), according to the U.S. Census Bureau (2010 Census). That's 30 years of stagnant water for the middle class. Women are typically paid between 10% to 15% less than men for the same job. Even when a husband and wife both work, as most couples do, making ends meet can be a far from easy and often a harrowing experience.

Americans have also learned that many of our nation's most prestigious companies, such as Apple, keep a significant portion of their profits outside the United States and pay very little income tax. The media took note of Apple's ongoing tax strategy, and Tim Cook, Apple CEO, was indignant when called on the carpet to answer questions from a congressional committee. He reminded legislators that "Apple pays all the taxes legally owed."

Cook was right – big corporations are simply taking advantage of legal loopholes put in place by the same politicians who publically appeared to be outraged. Of course it was those same politicians who previously had no issue with large campaign donations.

Apple has recently aired artful advertisements emphasizing that their products are "designed" in California, which is a clever turn of phrase – almost all of their products are manufactured in Chinese mega-sweatshops. It's all part of the game. The Citigroup *Wealth Report* concludes, "There has never been more opportunity for the rich."

It's not rocket science: Our political leaders (on both sides) do not seem motivated to disappoint the sponsors who help keep them in office.

Tax rules written by lobbyists, for people with accountants

We live in a society where average citizens, who dutifully work for a company and perform a traditional middle-class job, never have a chance to touch the 35% to 40% of their incomes that is deducted *before* they even receive their paychecks. And yet huge tax breaks are given to a long list of industries, including oil, pharmaceutical, tobacco, Hollywood, Wall Street, etc.

The tax system continues to cast shame on our lawmakers, who give lip service to initiating reform but do nothing. More than 50% of our congressmen and 70% of our senators are millionaires. Major portions of their campaign funds are derived from other millionaires, who happen to run the successful industries that receive generous tax benefits.

Far more troubling is the fact that these same representatives of the people routinely become lobbyists after their retirement and gain a big pay raise when they go to work for special-interest groups. These private entities and the clients they represent make their contacts with our elected officials before congressional members leave office, so it's naïve to think that influence isn't peddled from day one. In the first seven decades of the 20th century, fewer than 10% of our elected leaders became lobbyists. Starting in the 1980s this figure began to shift dramatically – now approximately 33% of Democratic and 50% of Republican politicians eventually become lobbyists for special interests, including Wall Street. When ultraconservative Congressman Eric Cantor lost his election in Virginia, he was earning a government salary of approximately $220,000. A year later he inked a personal contract for *$3.4 million* to "help guide" Moelis and Co. – a Wall Street investment bank.

Lobbyists have been largely responsible for drafting much of the U.S. tax code, as well as other governmental regulations. It's a complicated, illogical mess.

Matt Taibbi, the renowned journalist who has closely covered Wall Street for the past decade, came to this conclusion:

"By creating an urgent crisis that only can be solved by those fluent in a language too complex for ordinary people to understand, the Wall Street crowd has turned the vast majority of Americans into nonparticipants in their own political future."

Sad but true: American democracy now operates on a system of the rich returning favors to the rich. The citizen/politician who goes to Washington can find an easy path to a lucrative payday by staying close to the Beltway in the wake of retirement or electoral defeat. Leaving Congress can be a good thing when politicians want to increase their personal wealth.

Mix in the prospect of a prestigious job with the frailties of human nature, and the result is a tax system that remains a hodgepodge code written by the wealthy for the wealthy.

Although the pundits on Fox News constantly complain that America has one of the highest corporate tax rates in the world (up to 40%), almost everyone in the business community knows that the actual percentage paid on corporate profits is much lower, due to copious tax loopholes – holes you can drive a truck through.

American corporations receive tax incentives and employ a long list of gimmicks expertly obtained by their lobbyists. The *real tax rate* large corporations pay on profits is somewhere between 10% and 25%, depending on your source of information. There is a long list of well-known companies that have learned to carefully structure their operations to avoid most U.S. taxes, with "off-shoring" one of the leading techniques to skip out on tax liability. Burger King recently transferred its corporate headquarters from the U.S. to Canada and suddenly became famous for more than their hamburgers.

Taxes for Social Security and health care

It's constructive to keep in mind that the Social Security system is entirely self-funded by payroll deductions, monies that have come out of workers' paychecks. Most seniors depend upon receiving their regular monthly check, especially as private company pensions fade into history. Social Security has become even more critical for elderly Americans trying to stay afloat in tough economic times.

Social Security is financially solvent at this point, and the anticipated shortfalls can be fixed with equitable adjustments. Common sense seems to point to a humane, practical overhaul of our Social Security and health care systems, rather than a total dismantling of these programs.

What seems ironic is that the politicians who are most aggressive about the need to spend huge sums on our military are generally the same ones preaching the economics of austerity in all other areas of government. In their eyes, we simply have to cut big government and citizen benefit programs. Many in the Tea Party still contend that the nation's financial growth is dependent on trickle-down economics: Cut taxes, deregulate and free up the private sector, and our unfettered, *laissez-faire* capitalist system will take care of the rest.

America put that theory to a test beginning in 2000, and by 2008 the economy had nearly melted down. Anyone who thinks we can allow corporations and banks to self-regulate has not paid much attention to recent history.

There is constant grumbling among conservatives that our real budget problems stem from the health care system and entitlements. These critics have a point – although few have proposed practical solutions. It's self-evident that our health care system is bloated and inefficient, and we know that the United States spends a far greater percentage of its GDP on health care than any other industrialized nation – for mediocre results. Most conservatives decry governmental involvement in national health insurance, and many suggest that access to medical care is not a civil right.

This viewpoint brings up valid questions: Why should those citizens who produce and pay taxes be expected to pay for "slackers?" Why should anyone suffer a penalty for not purchasing health care insurance? Why should young people suddenly pay for the baggage of aging boomers? Are we truly just creating a nanny state where citizens will no longer assume any personal responsibility for their own lives?

Many conservatives claim that if we allow health care services to respond to free-market forces, the health care system will fix itself – that somehow our existing insurance companies and hospital chains, if left unregulated by government, will bring us salvation. Their prescription for America is a mega-dose of Ayn Rand's brand of capitalism.

According to that chain of logic, all we need to do is trust in the good will and integrity of both our existing insurance companies and Wall Street. Some suggest government should never be empowered to regulate health care insurance, which again begs the question about our national priorities: Is health care a *commodity*, or is it "a necessity in the modern world" – like having clean water and breathable air.

Can we compromise somewhere between a nanny state and Ayn Rand?

From a pragmatic point of view, there is no question that budget cuts in our health benefits programs are necessary. Cuts are both essential and doable, in ways that will still provide basic health coverage for all Americans. For instance, it's far more practical to treat acute illnesses in clinics during the first onset of disease or infection, than through visits to the emergency room. ER care is a costly service, eventually paid for by taxpayers. Some suggest we should simply bar the uninsured from the door leading to our hospital emergency rooms.

Whatever your view, there has been little progress in decreasing the cost or expanding the delivery of quality American health care. Insurance companies continue to rake in staggering profits, and our lawmakers keep fighting along party lines while health costs still rise and many Americans fail to receive the medical attention they need. *[See page 227]*

In recent years, conservatives have openly ridiculed "Obamacare," i.e., The Affordable Care Act, which has acquired the flavor of sour grapes. The new health care laws were passed by the U.S. Congress and upheld by the Supreme Court, and – good, bad or indifferent – have become U.S. law. If conservatives want to repeal Obamacare, they should convince Americans to vote Republicans back into control of the Senate and/or elect a Republican president, and repeal the laws by rules set out in our U.S. Constitution. Our nation may well benefit by cutting back certain entitlements, but if we repeal the Affordable Care Act, then what?

In the past, both parties have had to live with laws passed and political appointments confirmed by the opposing party in power. In November 2012, The Affordable Care Act was one of the major issues in the presidential election. House Speaker Boehner acknowledged as much to the press: "It's pretty clear the president was elected, and The Affordable Care Act is the law of the land."

The 2014 mid-term elections

Over the last several years, Speaker John Boehner has lost control of his own Republican House members to conservative extremists who will do whatever they can to see President Obama fail. The RNC continues to allow itself to be heavily influenced by a small group of reactionaries. The 2014 mid-terms only exacerbated the situation.

The feistiest of the new Republican congressional representatives hail from gerrymandered districts, so they have no fear of losing their seats. One of the brightest stars for the Tea Party is Texas Senator Ted Cruz, who reigns as the titular leader and seems to be the Pied Piper of Republican infighting. This ideologue craves the camera, often to the annoyance of moderate Republicans. It's a good bet he intends to run for president in 2016. He's a protégé of Jim DeMint, the former South Carolina Republican senator and president of the Heritage Foundation, the famous conservative think tank tied to Heritage Action, a well-funded 501 PAC that has expressed its fondness and support for Senator Cruz.

Millennials and minorities rarely show up for mid-term elections and a good portion of older Democrats are lethargic when it comes to Obama, so it comes as no surprise that Republicans ran the table in the mid-terms. Conservatives now have a one-vote majority in the Senate and even better control of the House. Gridlock will continue and Republicans will have to decide whether to defer to "reactionary demands" in order to keep all conservative votes in line. However, if moderate conservatives defer to Tea Party demands, the RNC may learn the "2012 lesson" all over again in 2016. Should Republicans nominate Cruz, or any Cruz-type candidate, the Democrats will be delighted, because it will draw women, millennials and minorities back to the ballot box in droves.

Perhaps Republicans can find a more moderate conservative (a leader more along the lines of Eisenhower, Reagan or George Bush Sr.) who can unite their party. DeMint and Cruz and their allies may be able to sway some citizens to their brand of conservatism, but they have yet to understand the demographic trends of the American electorate. The other day my mainstream moderate Republican wife lamented: *"I'm a woman without a party."*

Military Spending

America continues to be the world's biggest spender on defense. More than 50% of our nation's discretionary expenditures are currently committed, in some form or fashion, to our military, yet it's difficult to know exactly where all this money goes. The Department of Defense is an organization whose bookkeeping methods defy auditing.

The portion of our federal budget allotted to military spending suggests a preference uniquely American. We spend more on our military than the combined total spent by China, Russia, the UK, France, Japan, India, Saudi Arabia, Italy, South Korea, Australia and Canada. Approximately 5% of the world's population lives in the United States, but nearly 50% of the world's military expenditures come out of the pockets of American taxpayers.

We have fought in five major conflicts since WW II: Korea, Vietnam, Iraq (twice) and Afghanistan. We've also engaged in numerous other military operations – all on foreign soil – and have recently embarked on an armed effort to stop ISIS, the extreme Islamist terrorist group attempting to set up a "caliphate" in Syria and Iraq. Our nation has already managed to pour more than $1 trillion into Iraq, while simultaneously burdening college graduates with educational loan debt that exceeds $1 trillion.

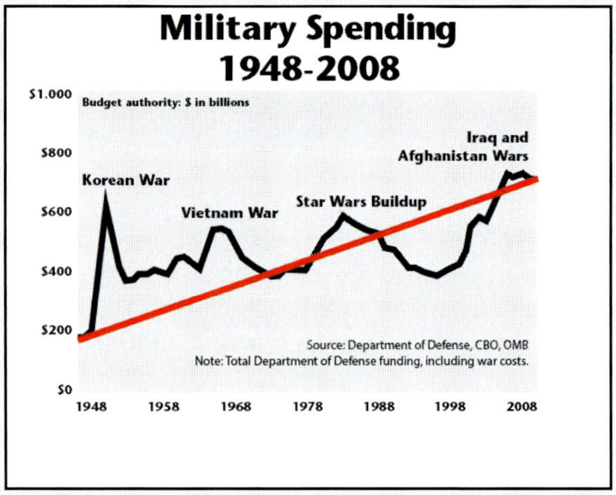

Most Americans would probably agree that the war that followed our 2003 invasion of Iraq did not go as Cheney, Rumsfeld and Rove had arrogantly predicted. In his book, *Before the First Shots Were Fired*, retired Marine Corps General Anthony Zinni, former commander of the United States Central Command (CENTCOM), carefully argues that the invasion of Iraq was a monumental mistake. General Zinni suggests that American war planners had no sense of the long-term repercussions of an Iraq invasion, and only "further destabilized" the Middle East. "In the lead-up to the Iraq war and its later conduct, I saw, at a minimum, true dereliction, negligence and irresponsibility – at worst, lying, incompetence and corruption."

The quickest overview of America's ever-increasing emphasis on military spending was brought to my attention by Jim Agee, who emailed me a short video produced by Axel Gerdau of *The New York Times*. The video is only two minutes long – it's very well done and worth a watch. Go to YouTube: Axel Gerdau Thinking Back: The Military Budget

A few highlights from the U.S. military budget

- A significant portion of the Defense Department's accounting is done by the Defense Finance and Accounting Service, which relies on a computer system from the 1970s – although outmoded hardware and software are not the only problems preventing a clear and accurate reporting of where our defense dollars are going. Some of the obvious disarray in the DOD's $650 billion budget is no doubt intentional, simply to camouflage politically sensitive military spending and operations.

- The special operations of some of the most powerful agencies of the U.S. government – for example, the CIA (Central Intelligence Agency), DEA (Drug Enforcement Agency), NSA (National Security Agency), CSS (Central Security Service) and the U.S. Cyber Command (USCYBERCOM) – are conceived somewhere in the Twilight Zone, in an obscure dimension which is off limits to any American without the highest security clearances. How these elite arms of our government use our tax dollars is most often a mystery, all classified "to protect U.S. interests." As citizens, we know little about what these agencies really do, how much money they receive, and where they spend it. The people who do know rarely tell.

In 2005, General Keith Alexander was appointed by President Bush to simultaneously direct three highly secret and powerful intelligence services. For almost a decade, General Alexander served in an unprecedented role as the head of the NSA (the world's largest intelligence service), the CSS *and* the U.S. CYBERCOM. No one officer in military intelligence has ever had so many people under his command, or shrouded agencies' activities in such secrecy – a secrecy that was recently shattered.

In 2013, during Alexander's ongoing tenure under the current administration, ex-CIA employee Edward Snowden unleashed a torrent of top-secret (and disturbing) NSA documents to the media. Many of our government's vast domestic and foreign eavesdropping activities came to light – the nature of the previously clandestine information, and its unauthorized release, embarrassed our government and its intelligence wings and opened America's secret spying activities to increased national and international scrutiny.

Our government has since been back-pedaling under congressional and media pressure, NSA polices are being "reviewed," and Admiral Michael S. Rogers has been named as commander of the NSA and U.S. CYBERCOM.

- Before our invasions of Iraq and Afghanistan, every major conflict that the United States had fought since the Civil War had been financed by a war tax imposed by Washington. Warfare is always extraordinarily expensive and Americans understood that if they wanted war they had to pay for it.

  The Bush administration broke with 140 years of history – and the long line of former presidents of both parties – by initiating two wars in the Middle East without imposing any war tax. And there were no contingency plans in place to raise needed, additional revenues if the wars grew longer and more costly. To make matters worse, the Bush administration offered tax cuts, primarily to the wealthy, during the period our troops were fighting overseas.

- America uses 6% of its discretionary spending budget to care for military veterans. It's doubtful that 6% will be sufficient to meet our responsibilities to the men and women who risk their lives for our country. We all agree that our service personnel need and deserve the best health benefits available, but the sad fact is that they are not receiving adequate or timely medical attention. The recent exposure of the poor services provided at Veterans' Hospitals – and the hospitals' unethical reporting practices – is a national disgrace. Veterans' outpatient services are also in disarray, with medical staff unable to properly treat tens of thousands of veterans suffering from post-traumatic stress syndrome and/or other war-related ailments.

The cost of war does not end when the fighting is over or when our troops come home.

As I write this it appears that we may headed for a prolonged war against ISIS, which will mandate additional military expenditures. Our military invasion of the Middle East in 2003 still fosters a catalog of unintended consequences.

It's too easy to place the blame for a failed system on teachers. As a society, if we want the best educational system, we need to attract our best and brightest minds – or those gifted individuals will continue to choose other professions. As long as "good salespeople" in most industries can earn more in commissions than the yearly salary of a high school teacher, our education system will suffer and keep falling further behind those of other countries, where educators receive salaries more commensurate with their crucial contribution to society.

Finally, an unfortunate trend during the last 20 years has been a de-emphasis on traditional civics education. A recent study by Tufts University found that schools in most states still require some sort of American government course, but students in fewer than half our states are given a state-designed civics exam. Only nine states require a student to pass a civics test in order to graduate from high school. If democracy is based on an informed electorate, these are worrisome figures.

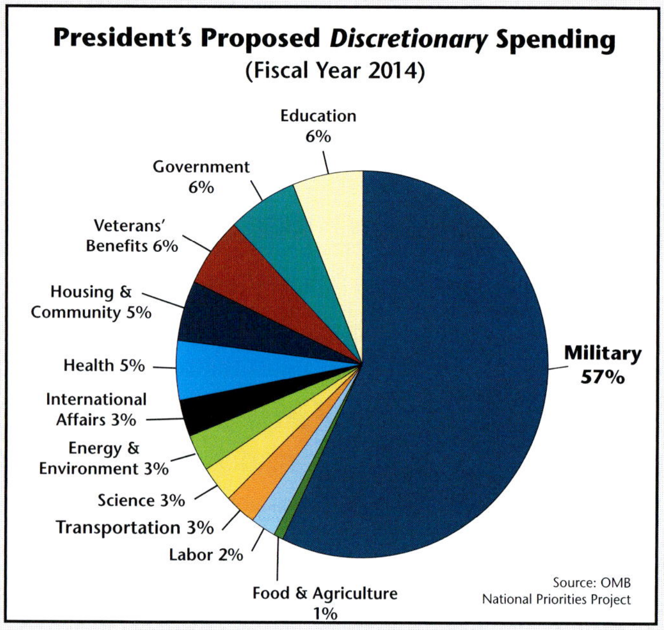

American students need to learn about our constitutional system and democratic processes at a young age. They should be encouraged to follow legislation and elections, and prepare themselves to make well-informed decisions by their 18th birthday, when they obtain the privilege to vote. Whatever one's personal political persuasion, we should be able to agree that our country's future depends on a nation of informed citizens, not just eager consumers.

Prison, Inc.

America has the highest incarceration rate of any nation in the world. Our country has about 5% of the world's population, but approximately 25% of the world's prison population. The U.S. Department of Justice reports that approximately 7 million of our citizens are currently in prison, on parole or on probation. We lock up our fellow Americans at a much higher rate than China, and at more than six times the rate of other industrial nations such as Canada, England, Germany and Japan.

In response to what we perceive as a society growing more violent – and because we choose to imprison even non-violent drug offenders – we're building more jails and penitentiaries. The prison industry has grown so rapidly that it is now referred to as the "prison/industrial complex." Increasing imprisonment is providing fertile ground for *defense contractors* who use lobbyists to persuade Congress to privatize our entire prison system.

It's a lucrative business, because as a nation, we currently spend in the neighborhood of $30,000 per year to house each and every inmate. The emphasis might be placed on "house" – we do little to rehabilitate inmates to help them successfully rejoin society upon their release.

Studies reveal that a high percentage of adults who end up in prison were, in some form or fashion, neglected and/or abused as children and many of them have never learned to read with any proficiency. It's obvious that the best way to address America's epidemic of incarceration is to provide both security and education during Americans' early years of life. Our federal spending on child nutrition and education reflects a government that does not make these issues a top priority, even though there is simply no better return on investment if our desire is to nurture healthy, well-informed, law-abiding citizens.

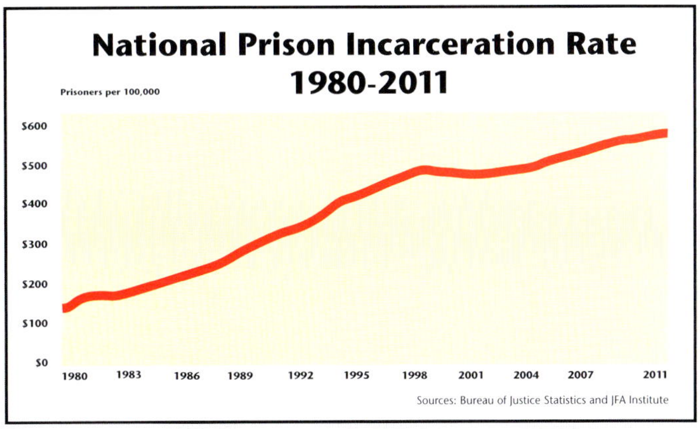

If we don't lay down a good foundation, the results are all too predictable.

Over the decades we have not given adequate attention and support to our own children. The grim reality is that one in five American children lives below the poverty line. According to the U.S. Department of Agriculture, more than 17 million American households are "food insecure," a bureaucratic term meaning a whole lot of kids still go to bed hungry in the world's richest country. This widespread lack of sufficient nourishment is particularly strange when you learn that American citizens throw away approximately 25% of the food they buy, according to the USDA and several independent studies. A report by a United Nation's Children's Fund on the well-being of children in 35 developed nations ranks the United States at 34th, just above Romania.

As early as 1953, President Eisenhower, a conservative, made a compelling point:

"Every gun that is made, every warship launched, every rocket fired signifies, in the final sense, a theft from those who hunger and are not fed, those who are cold and are not clothed."

Caring for America's children is essential because neglected problems of early childhood compound, especially for boys, when adolescence comes knocking. To an immature young man who has not benefited from a decent childhood and education, the world can seem very hostile, and his often negative frame of mind should not be surprising or hard to describe:

> *If I'm a white, black, or brown 17-year-old male in America who dropped out of school and I don't talk like the educated boys talk – I'm instinctively pissed off. I find myself in a one-down position where everything seems stacked against me and I'm angry.*
>
> *I have my pride, so my male mojo kicks in and I begin to look for ways to strike back to even the score. I'll be packing a gun, so I mean business. I may not be educated, and I may not*

speak very well, but I'm not afraid to kick some ass. I figured out a new set of rules – my rules. In my mind, I've got nothing to lose.

It's a pretty simple proposition. America can invest early in all of our children, to encourage the development of productive citizens, or keep kicking the can down the road with the same tragic results.

For decades our country has been in denial about the failings of our prison system, torn between wanting to punish and hoping to rehabilitate. Addressing either issue by building more prisons has never worked and never will. Prisoner rehabilitation has proven to be elusive. The recidivism rate is startling: 50% of released inmates go on to commit additional crimes. Are we simply going to throw more money at an ill-conceived system?

Setting National Priorities

Until we curb our country's propensity to fight preemptive foreign wars and start shifting more of our attention and support to public education, we will never genuinely evolve as a humane and rational society. The military/industrial freight train we created over 70 years ago – as World War II ended and the Cold War with the Communist bloc began – is perhaps our single biggest dilemma. Once again, President Eisenhower, one of our revered military leaders and a true Republican, famously alerted America to what was coming in his 1961 farewell address to the nation:

"Until the latest of our world conflicts, the United States had no armaments industry … We have been compelled to create a permanent armaments industry of vast proportions … We annually spend on military security more than the net income of all United States corporations. The total influence – economic, political and spiritual – is felt in every city, every state house and every office of the federal government. Our toil, resources and livelihood are all involved; so is the very structure of our society. In the councils of government, we must guard against the acquisition of unwarranted influence, where sought or unsought by the military industrial complex. The potential for the disastrous rise of this misplaced power exists and will persist … Only an alert and knowledgeable citizenry can compel the proper meshing of the huge industrial and military machinery of defense with our peaceful methods and goals, so that security and liberty may prosper together."

Eisenhower's warning about the perils of institutionalizing an economy centered on military pursuits is only part of his speech, one of the most compelling and prophetic by a modern president. The full video of President Eisenhower's address is instantly available on YouTube.

Full circle to education

Human capital is the single most important driver of a nation's economy. Developing a society of well-educated people who feel that they are true stakeholders in their country's destiny is a necessity and a long-term challenge. Education remains the single best answer for nurturing a better-informed citizenry, growing a robust economy and reducing our enormous and unsustainable prison population.

Creating an improved educational system is just common sense, and it's unfortunate that a Wall Street mentality sets the tone for how our country tries to move forward. All of our major corporations, banks and brokerage houses have a preoccupation with short-term profits. The financial world operates quarter by quarter and year by year. This short-sighted concept of "progress" limits our future and our potential as a free nation. Wall Street does not care where human capital comes from, as long as it's available right now to use for immediate profit.

Quality of life is not a line item on the Wall Street balance sheet.

Once again: America's most significant underlying problem is the growing educational gap among our socioeconomic groups. This disparity starts early and widens in the later years of schooling. Investing in the education of our lower-income citizens is not only an ethical imperative but also a solid financial investment because most of the economic advances in the future global economy will be generated by a knowledge-based workforce.

A good education sets the stage for an alert electorate, the indispensable factor for a thriving, self-sustaining democracy. Our public schools forge a common culture and introduce our children to their fellow citizens from a variety of backgrounds. Learning about America's history and our nation's ideals – expressed but still unmet – binds apparently disparate citizens together in a common cause.

What Lies Ahead?

The Congress of the United States now has its lowest approval rating in our country's history, and there's a growing contempt for all things governmental. Ronald Reagan may have meant well when he coined the phrase, "Government is the problem," but it casts a shadow on our joint efforts to face the unfolding 21st century. Disdain for government is thick in the air – the media and our citizens speak continually about the incompetence of our duly elected leaders, and many candidates run against "those people in Washington." There is now visceral distrust of government. This does not bode well for attracting a new talented generation to American politics and institutions. Who wants to join a team that is held in such low esteem?

Even worse, "the news" thrives almost entirely on controversy and diverts the nation's attention from one daily crisis to another, because media corporations gain the highest TV ratings and are most profitable when they bombard the national psyche with constant sensationalism of one kind or another. From covering the sexual antics of ex-Democratic Congressman Anthony Weiner to the public reading of Dr. Seuss by Ted Cruz (during his flamboyant 21-hour filibuster), the drama goes on 24/7/365. It's so easy to get caught up in the heat of the moment and lose perspective on issues that are immediately and, in the long run, vitally important.

These days, pious politicians line up *demanding action* to fight the threats of ISIS and Ebola, insisting, "America has a sacred duty to do *whatever it takes* to save American lives!" Some of our leaders even sent National Guardsmen to secure our southern border, and demanded that we erect additional walls to stop *illegal aliens* entering from Mexico. The same passionate voices urging battle against external dangers go strangely silent when confronting *the most deadly annual killers* of Americans: cigarettes (400,000), gun violence (30,000) and drunk-driving (6,000 young people). When it comes to tobacco, booze or packing a handgun – these issues ironically fall under the folds of "the flag of freedom."

What's even more concerning is that our traditional political process is losing control of our elections to political mercenaries and billionaire moneymen who are adept in manipulating the media. Given the recent rulings of our more conservative Supreme Court, the trend toward money-driven politics and policy is unlikely to end anytime soon. *Big money* now controls our country.

Elections were once the domain of grassroots movements and political parties. Candidates actually paid for their own ads and/or disclosed the names of campaign contributors. By 2016, campaigns will be dominated by unknown operatives and highly paid political hit squads. Elections will be significantly controlled by billionaires like the Koch brothers, the petrochemical giants whose political network raised $400 million during the 2012 election season. Very rich groups of individuals and powerful corporations will spend massive amounts to obtain the political outcomes they desire. In Washington, D.C., both sides of the aisle will bow to the influence of money – with the caveat that the "one percenters," who control the largest portion of wealth in America, are for the most part very conservative. It's logical that they will have an advantage, given the new campaign finance rules.

The best example of the increased leverage exerted by moneyed segments of our society is a group called America Rising. This new venture was devised by three powerful GOP operatives: Tim Miller and Joe Pounder, who have left the Republican National Committee, and Matt Rhoades, who managed Mitt Romney's unsuccessful 2012 presidential campaign. Their operation is unregulated by current federal election rules, doesn't have to disclose donors or donor affiliations, and is free to make profits from its services to those clients who can pay the price. The money is rolling in and America Rising can collect its loot from very murky waters, with little accountability. So far, the focus of America Rising has been to dig up dirt to discredit "liberal" candidates and help ensure conservative victories in the 2014 mid-term elections. It's just the beginning of a new era in politics, and it's ugly. Campaign spending has increased at an alarming rate. Both Democrats and Republicans should be ashamed.

No one to blame but ourselves

During the past 20 years, Americans have grown increasingly critical of their duly elected leaders. Clinton left the oval office tarnished by scandal and George W. Bush left the White House after eight years with the lowest approval rating of any prior American president. Our current president seems to have disappointed many people who voted for him and further alienated those who didn't. A number of our government bureaucracies have been mired in their own blunders, and Supreme Court rulings have allowed a significant increase in the powerful influence of moneyed interests. Not a pretty picture.

And yet, we continue to live in a democracy, however compromised it is.

It gives me no pleasure to point out that the *overwhelming majority* of senators, congressmen and board members of Fortune 500 companies are white, male boomers. Presidents Clinton, Bush, Obama – all boomers. My own generation might want to look in the mirror before we begin placing blame for America's many shortcomings.

As George Bernard Shaw said, "Democracy is a device that ensures we shall be governed no better than we deserve." His observation remains a fair criticism of our experiment in self-rule, and my age group has been steering the ship of state for almost a quarter of a century.

Politicians, pundits and citizens who promote the fuzzy concept that the "demise of America" is somehow tied to "welfare cheats" and "illegal aliens" speak with righteous conviction, but they simply spread fear and distrust. The truth is that the vast majority of Americans, of all stripes, remain hard at work and obey the law. It's unfair to cast blame on minority groups, who are the very people who have the least amount of political power and earn the lowest incomes. They have never had control of our government, not in the past and certainly not in the present.

Keeping the faith

America, for all its faults and failures to live up to its stated ideals, still has a process in place to elect leaders able to identify and address national priorities in a positive fashion – *if our citizens choose to become informed and involved and to vote.*

I'm proud to live in the country that remains the brightest light for so many people across the globe, many of whom sometimes risk their lives to live in freedom, determined to follow their vision of the American Dream. Our country, for all its flaws, remains the world's best hope. ■

He who opens a school door, closes a prison.

– Victor Hugo

A New Day for Education

WE CAN only imagine – given the rapid technological advances of the last 15 years – what's in store for the children of our children. The latest smartphones, iPads and laptops are dazzling, but they are just a preview of more amazing tools to appear. Our children intuitively gravitate to cutting-edge technology and take to new social media and apps like ducks to water.

Like it or not, every aspect of our lives will be affected by further advances in technology and the World Wide Web. Yet none of this remarkable hardware and software will bring meaningful rewards unless we discover how to wisely integrate them into our educational system.

To date, our leaders have not made this one of our national priorities.

Most of our senators and congressmen are in their 60s, so it may be hard for them to fully understand the technology, and what's at stake. If we fail to fully integrate the newest technology into our educational system, our nation's cultural and economic viability will remain a question mark in the 21st century.

At this point, our boomer leaders merely argue over the *basic philosophical standards of 20th-century education.*

The Common Core Standards recently adopted by most of our states represent an attempt to bring some consistency to the educational curricula across the nation. It's too early to know how well the new system may work, or the full extent of the political resistance that will try to waylay these potentially transformational reforms. Texas, our second most populous state, hasn't yet adopted the new standards. Florida – fourth largest in population – may "phase in" the standards over several years, but the Tea Party is pressuring the state to reconsider that tentative decision.

The new curriculum will have a much better chance of acceptance and success if we can more equitably fund America's entire public school system. Sufficient funding would allow educators to employ a variety of promising learning technologies, even in the poorest school districts. These advancements in ways of teaching and learning should be revolutionary when in place in every classroom.

One of the newest trends in education is the use of *adaptive learning technologies* that blend high tech with teaching and are being developed by a wave of forward-looking companies. Adaptive learning aims to integrate specific data from each student to personalize teaching and transcend the one-size-fits-all approach common to most U.S. schools. Many experts in the forefront of improving education believe these technologies are the key to saving America's school system. Tech breakthroughs will allow one-on-one teaching on a mass scale, with subject matter and the speed of its presentation tailored to the present abilities of each student. (Check out Knewton.com for an overview of the technology.)

Online education is another remarkable advance in instruction. You may be familiar with the Khan Academy, iTunes University, or edX.org, and already sense the great educational potential of learning centers on the World Wide Web – a recent development that can reach millions of students of all ages, everywhere on Earth.

The Khan Academy offers a free online collection of more than 4,000 lectures via video tutorials stored on YouTube. There are presentations on history, mathematics, biology, medicine, finance, physics, chemistry, astronomy, economics, cosmology, organic chemistry, American civics, art history and computer science. To date, the Khan Academy has delivered over 450 million lessons.

For a quick overview of how the internet will affect the future of education globally, visit KhanAcadamy.org. At the bottom of the screen, click the icon bar marked "What Khan Academy is all about" to watch a short video about the academy. The clip features Salman Khan (the academy's creator), along with Bill Gates, at the 2011 TED conference – it's an excellent summary of the advantages of online learning. The Bill and Melinda Gates Foundation and Google have added financial clout to this non-profit organization, which appears to be on solid financial ground. Best of all, learning at the Khan Academy is free.

Another educational site to look into is edX.org, which offers courses from the world's best universities, including MIT, Harvard, Berkeley, University of Texas, Boston University, Rice and Wellesley, to name a few. Like Khan Academy classes, its courses are free. Online instruction is the growing trend and is also available from Penn State, Pepperdine, Northeastern University and many other institutions.

The Georgia Institute of Technology College of Computing now offers a master of science in computer science that can be earned through its online program. The big news is not just state-of-the-art educational technology, but also the affordable price. The tuition for the two-year program is $6,600 – as opposed to the cost of traditional instruction, which runs about $45,000. The program is virtually identical to the standard Georgia Tech curriculum – and better in many ways. The benefits of learning from a top-tier university and faculty through a dynamic, interactive web program can be enjoyed by thousands, as opposed to the few hundred who could pursue instruction onsite. Online education helps defray rising tuition rates, easing the debt burden our students incur through current student loan programs.

Online learning is still in its trial stages and will face a few inevitable hurdles: the reluctance of a generation of educators who feel threatened by new technology; the politics of "old school" universities that view online learning as a disruption to the status quo and fear the financial implications; and the difficulty in understanding how to merge or integrate the hands-on classroom experience with new technology in a manner that truly moves us forward.

A Front-Row Seat for Everyone

Cameras of every shape and variety are being coupled with computers, and are now becoming important features of many learning environments. Google Glass and similar technologies allow the teacher's eyes and the student's eyes to see exactly the same thing at the same time. Already several medical schools incorporate Google Glass during surgical operations. Our future doctors have a real-time front-row seat, up close and personal, to observe every detail of what the surgeon does, and instructors can interact with students during the operation. These filmed step-by-step procedures are saved and can be viewed again on the student's personal laptop. This is only one example of how *wearable tech* will transform how the wearer and the watchers experience the world.

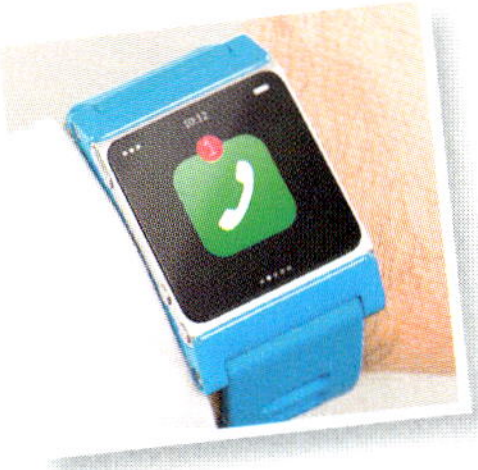

Just a decade ago, it was hard to imagine that smartphones would become such an intimate part of our lives, on a *moment-by-moment* basis. Just watch any crowd on a plane or sitting in a park and half the people are glued to their devices: talking to someone, reading their emails, watching videos, listening to music, playing a game or shopping online. The approaching wearable-tech revolution may spread even faster than the smartphone, allowing users to further cut the "time lapse" between *intention* and *action*. Remember when it took Google five seconds to complete a search? Now you enter a few key words, and Google has the answer, *before you're even finished typing*. Wearable technology will soon *anticipate* our needs and desires by learning our tech-use patterns and reading habits.

Smartphones are portable, but they can distract you from reality and separate you from your environment. You have to focus on digital information on a tiny screen. Wearable tech will augment reality, providing a less-intrusive data delivery, about any subject – without distracting the eyes from the surrounding world. The wearer remains grounded in immediate, concrete reality. Wearable tech is going to be both awesome and transformative. Who knows what unforeseen consequences will arise and where they will lead?

The potential applications of Google Glass and other technologies (such as Apple iWatch and Sony's Smart Band) for improving education, as well as business and government operations, appear nearly endless. Google Glass is expected to start offering its product in the $1,000 to $1,500 range, but surely the price will be $499 before you know it. Samsung's remarkable new Galaxy smart watch sells for $299, a great deal for Dick Tracy's sci-fi timepiece. If you find a wristwatch too cumbersome, why not try the new "NFC" ring? It looks like a hi-tech wedding band and features an embedded radio chip that will open your front door (or other security doors) and make your monthly payments.

While I was working on this book, Tom Spalding suggested that we attend the CES (Consumer Electronics Show) in Las Vegas. He flew his Cirrus plane into San Luis Obispo, picked me up, and we spent a couple of days walking through the convention, marveling at the vast array of futuristic electronic gear – wearable technologies, remote-controlled devices and equipment of every description, and the latest high tech advances in music/audio programming and ultra-high-definition TV. To put it mildly, the CES has changed dramatically since we first attended shows in Chicago, 40 years ago. I returned home with a heightened awareness that continued breakthroughs in electronic technology will transform how we live, work, learn and play, and especially how a modernized American educational system could radically improve student performance.

Collaborative learning

GitHub, a web-based hosting service for programmers, is transforming the opportunities for truly collaborative work and study in a number of fields, including education. GitHub was launched in 2008 as a platform for shared development of software, but has evolved to include aspects of popular social networking sites. The website shows the world what you're working on, stores your project progress information and invites anyone to comment. In its first year, the site attracted about 50,000 users.

Today, GitHub is used by nearly 4 million software developers (coders). The concept of online tracking of real-time creation is quickly expanding, and has gained the attention of governmental agencies interested in providing more open access to information. Soon textbooks, 3D designs, and even legislation can be created in a team-based manner. Advancements in medicine are developing at a much faster rate as a result of collaborative research made possible by the internet. 3D printing technology will profoundly impact bioscience as well as numerous other industries – from food production to car manufacturing.

ResearchGate is another venture that promotes collaborative learning. The enterprise was backed by Bill Gates and received $35 million in funding. ResearchGate applies the dynamics of social networking with the culture of academia – sort of a Facebook for scientists. The sharing of information about successful and unsuccessful experiments allows scientists to receive feedback from outside the traditional *behind-closed-doors* peer review. This site may help bring academia into the 21st century by encouraging communication among scientists from around the world, which can speed the research process.

Online learning and other related new technologies signal a new era for the education of our young people and increase the democratization of higher education. Electronic teaching will allow anyone who wants an education to receive it, regardless of economic status or living location – even if it's presently behind prison walls. Employers will certainly be more likely to give released prisoners a second chance if they've shown initiative – via online instruction – to complete their education.

Technical and Trade Schools

Many modern learning technologies can be used to improve job skills and technical expertise required in manual labor. Our society tends to marginalize jobs that require good old-fashioned hard work, which is a shame. To rebuild America's infrastructure, we will need legions of skilled workers, including welders, plumbers, carpenters, masons, electricians, and other trade professionals. Vocational programs, like Career and Technical Education (CTE), need more support from both business and government. U.S. Secretary of Education Arne Duncan has long been a supporter of CTE, but Congress continues to cut CTE funding.

Shining a Light on Educational Innovators

Chris Whittle is co-founder and CEO of Edison Schools, the organization that helped pioneer the charter school movement. He's also the CEO of ***Avenues,*** the new "world school" in Manhattan. Recently, for an educational think tank, he drafted an essay titled "Would Steve Jobs Be A Hero if He Had Built An Education Company Every Bit As Good As Apple?"

Sadly, probably not. One key point in Mr. Whittle's essay is that the media, the government and the politics of academia keep our educational system rooted in the past. All of them are slow to embrace any new player or innovation – and by ingrained habit and territorial instinct resist the pioneering and/or controversial. [*Go to* **avenues.org** / *See page 356*]

Maybe one day our children will be able to name the nation's greatest scientist as quickly as they can name their favorite athlete or pop star. Many of our citizens would be hard pressed to name their U.S. senators or congressmen, or even the U.S. secretary of education as quickly as they can identify one or more *American Idol* winners.

It's an odd fact that as a nation we don't value intellect or public service as much as athletic performance or singing ability.

Success requires talent, and attracting the best and brightest minds to education and science will require salaries and benefits like those awarded to the people who run our corporations. A teacher, scientist or engineer earns a decent salary in America, yet a competent stockbroker on Wall Street earns perhaps 5 or 20 times as much – mostly on the backs of other people's productivity. Is this what our forefathers envisioned?

America's future prospects will improve when our nation takes a long-term view by investing heavily in public education – for all of its citizens. ■

America's health care system
is neither healthy, caring, or a system.

– WALTER CRONKITE, CIRCA 1980

America's Health Care

Another Profit Center

HISTORIANS often point out that an important measurement of a civilized society is how well it cares for its very young, very old and those who simply cannot take care of themselves.

By that measure, America is losing ground.

Somehow we have created a society in which a host of corporations of every configuration have manipulated ways to intrude into the private relationship between doctor and patient.

Everyone wants a front-row seat in the health care profit center.

When an American needs a medical procedure that requires an extended hospital stay, the experience can be harrowing for both the patient and the patient's family, and a new and different crisis can arise after the patient returns home. Concerned family members fear for the health of their loved one, but even good outcomes are often followed by financial devastation: Hospitals routinely send invoices totaling $125,000 or more – the price of a new home in some parts of the country.

60% of bankruptcies due to medical bills

According to a report published in *The American Journal of Medicine,* bankruptcies increased by nearly 50% in the six-year period from 2001 to 2007, and most of those who filed for bankruptcy were middle class and well educated. The lead author of the study, Steffie Woolhandler, M.D., of Harvard Medical School, concluded: "Unless you're a Warren Buffett or Bill Gates, you're one illness away from financial ruin in this country. If an illness is long enough and expensive enough, private insurance offers very little protection against medical bankruptcy, and that's the major finding in our study."

We have a health care system that seems to extract its profits from customers when they are most vulnerable. Insurance companies have one overriding concern – their bottom line. Most people would rather go to the dentist for a root canal than face a legal fight with their insurance company – bankruptcy becomes the least painful way out.

None of this happened overnight. The American health care system was diagnosed with *incurable greed and bureaucracy* long before Pelosi, Reid and Obama stirred the pot. The pricing policies of hospitals and insurance companies have not had any basis in reality for decades. The selling price of even standard medical procedures can vary by 200% – within the same city.

The Affordable Health Care Act – a moon shot

By November 2014, approximately 10 million Americans had signed up for "Obamacare," but the program still remains anathema to a large segment of my countrymen. However you see it, the latest attempt at heath care reform may have been conceived with good intentions, but implementation has been, at best, a mixed bag. The odds for The Affordable Care Act actually working as planned were improbable.

Unfortunately, with the mishandling of the roll-out of The Affordable Care Act, Fox News tried to convince its audience that Obamacare's emergence signaled the apocalypse – but it didn't.

However, the program was oversold to the public.

There was virtually no chance that such an ambitious plan could cover so many people without causing some pain and misery to one group or another, because our population is so diverse. Every American family has specific health needs and an individual budget from which health care costs must come.

Our old health care system may have been broken, but at least it functioned at a mediocre level. People had grown used to the devil they knew. The Obama administration can complain that Republicans tried to obstruct the new plan, but the Democrats were quite capable of making a bad situation worse all by themselves. For the past several decades, Americans have concluded that government is incompetent, and The Affordable Care Act's debut confirmed that sentiment.

From the very beginning, the failure to beta test the system should have been a big red flag. The president was first elected in large part because of his savvy implementation of new technologies to reach a wide variety of demographic groups, yet when it came to Affordable Health Care, the performance of his team was thoroughly disappointing.

For starters, the insurance companies have teams of handsomely paid lawyers who can always outmaneuver government and devise ways to twist any new program to their advantage, even before it's launched. The insurance industry is not in the business of caring for the health of U.S. citizens – it cares about profits, and the tailoring of medical legislation to protect its own financial well-being.

To make matters worse, the Republicans began bashing President Obama as soon as he took office and were fully vested in the program failing. The Tea Party's growing influence over the GOP makes it almost certain that the "debate" over health care will continue to resemble an episode of The Jerry Springer Show.

The real irony is that none of our politicians (on either side) have ever been the primary authors of any of our health care legislation.

Over many decades, a hodgepodge of laws has been drafted and pushed through the U.S. Congress by insurance and other medical industry lobbyists. Those are the same people who help fund congressional campaigns, so they have the keen attention of lawmakers.

Conservatives would now like everyone to believe that heath care was just fine before Obamacare – but it's just not the case. The good old days of health care are a myth. In 1948, President Harry Truman encouraged Congress to enact national health care insurance, but when the legislation passed, paying for health care had somehow become the employer's responsibility, by contracting with private insurance companies.

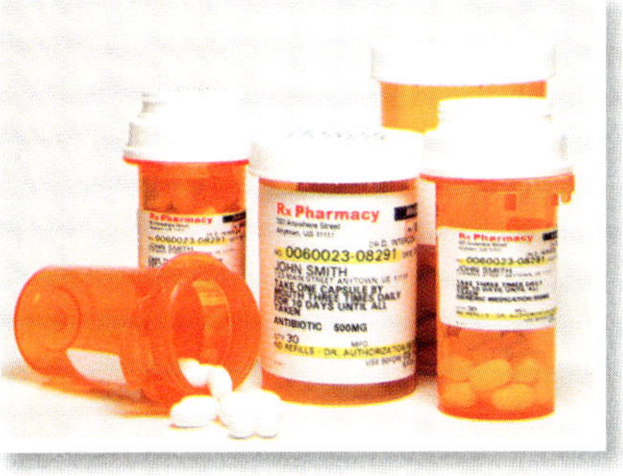

Senator Ted Kennedy was promising to reform the health care system long before young Hillary Clinton charged into the fray in 1993. Clinton had several good ideas, but she was quickly devoured by the lobbyists and by the old guys on both sides of the aisle, who portrayed her as an uppity young woman sticking her nose where it didn't belong. All subsequent attempts at substantial health care reform – including measures introduced by both Bush presidents – were derailed by political pressure exerted by entrenched corporate powers.

There is virtually no political will to confront the existing crisis that many boomers are now facing with their own parents, who have too little savings and can't fend for themselves. Congress has no plan to fix our health care system, at least not in the next decade. We can argue about how we've reached the present impasse, but the inevitable train wreck is coming as 78 million boomers enter their "sunset years," demanding new drugs and expensive medical procedures to treat the aliments of old age.

The sound and fury from both political parties about who should receive health care and who should pay for it is just background noise. Everybody points the finger, and no politician wants to face these ugly questions:

The heart of the matter

- How did Americans come to pay a much higher price for the same level of health care delivered in so many other industrialized countries? We live in a nation that spends a whopping 18% of its GDP on health care, a cost which affects our nation's ability to invest and compete globally.

- Why do insurance companies make such staggering profits, when they really have little to do with the actual hands-on delivery of health care to patients?

- How did we come to live in a society that allows our oldest and most vulnerable citizens to fall into the hands of corporate-managed hospitals during their final days, where they routinely suffer without dignity and without power to make decisions about their own care. Archaic rules and bureaucratic meddling and/or pressure from organized religion often artificially prolong the suffering of the terminally ill. An estimated 20% of all terminal patients spend their final days in ICU, hooked up to IVs and breathing machines – at a cost $50 billion a year. And yet, we remain short on funds for the prenatal care of young women or basic dental care for the nation's children.

- Why is the entire American health care system so deeply rooted in making money from outdated practices, rather than oriented toward the future? There are very few hospitals in our country that plan care delivery based primarily on the best possible services for patients rather than on profitability.

- How did we decide to drastically cut funding for research by the Centers of Disease Control, to the lowest level since 2003?

- Why don't we better protect and educate our children, until they are mature enough to make informed health decisions on their own? American corporations spend billions to capture the hearts and minds of our nation's young, urging them to crave food that will place them squarely on the road to diabetes and/or heart disease. Teaching our children about diet and exercise has not been a high priority. We've eliminated physical education from many of our schools, and rarely teach practical life skills. We have created a ticking time bomb that virtually guarantees that Americans' health care costs will continue to skyrocket.

The prognosis

Sad to say, it is unlikely that any president can successfully battle the corporate powers which own and operate the insurance industry, hospital chains and the pharmaceutical industry. Other special interest groups lurk on the sidelines, lawyers in tow, each searching for a slice of the health care profits. Short of a change in human nature, I am not optimistic about any short-term reform.

As Winston Churchill once said:

"America will always do the right thing, but only after exhausting all other options."

I never considered a difference of opinion in politics, in religion, in philosophy, as cause for withdrawing from a friend.

– Thomas Jefferson

It Makes Me Nervous When They Take God Indoors

Would Jesus be political If He came back to Earth?
And admit He's talked to all them preachers
Who say they've been talkin' to Him?
If He came back tomorrow
Well there's somethin' I'd like to know: Could ya tell me?
Would Jesus wear a Rolex on His television show?

Excerpted lyrics from "Would Jesus Wear a Rolex,"
a country song written by Chet Atkins and recorded by Ray Stevens

MY FRIEND Jim Agee brought this song to my attention some time ago, and I couldn't help but hear it echoing in my ear as I watched the pomp and circumstance of Pope Benedict's retirement ceremony.

In August 2013 every major television network covered the two-day event from start to finish. The pope exited the Vatican wearing his white formal robes, adorned with gold medallions, walking in his famous hand-made red Prada shoes. I certainly mean no disrespect to Pope Benedict XVI as a person, but I found it odd that he climbed into a shiny black Mercedes to ride a very short distance to the Vatican's pearly white multi-million-dollar custom Bell Jet 407 helicopter – all for a seven-minute ride to his new residence.

To some Americans who are not big fans of organized religion, the spectacle demonstrated that the Church remains in its own rarefied universe. The pope's carefully orchestrated farewell was performed on the world stage and seen globally by more than a billion television viewers. The elaborate event must have struck a fair number of people as a bit over the top and set them wondering if the Catholic Church might have made better use of its funds, especially with the severe economic recession in Europe.

On the day of the broadcast I was having lunch at the counter of a local restaurant, while a young man sitting near me was watching the event on television. He commented that the Jesus that he worshiped would have been dismayed by the ostentatious show of wealth. Actually, what the young man said about the Church was far less respectful and not worth repeating.

Of course not one television commentator dared to mention the irony of Jesus' commitment to the poor and dispossessed in contrast to the lavish public extravaganza honoring the pope's retirement. The strange disconnect – between the Church's professed concern for the down-trodden, and the vast resources it spent on the televised spectacle – surely crossed the minds of TV journalists, but no network wants to alienate conservative sponsors and their customers.

The new pope took the name of St. Francis of Assisi, the first Franciscan, who lived in poverty and preached a love of all creatures and creation. He brought a breath of fresh air – he has the kind, "common touch," and has dispensed with many of the trappings and ceremonies of rank that Pope Benedict enjoyed. The previous pope was a strong defender of traditional Church doctrine, and frequently described his vision of a "purer" church. Pope Francis speaks openly about a more inclusive church, "a home for all." Francis has been critical, insisting that the Church places dogma above love, and adherence to strict codes of personal behavior before Jesus' commitment to serve the poor.

Late in 2013, the Vatican released an 85-page document titled *Apostolic Exhortations*, a mission statement from Pope Francis. The new pope derided the widening gap between rich and poor, and condemned "the new idolatry of money." He emphasized that economic disparity is a result "of ideologies which defend the autonomy of the marketplace and financial speculation." Francis wrote: "I beg the Lord to grant us more politicians who are genuinely disturbed by the state of society." The new pope has even taken a "moral stand" against trickle-down economics.

There was no change when it came to a woman's right to abortion, or the possibility of female priests: "These are not questions open to discussion."

During his first two years in the Vatican, Pope Francis has certainly endeavored to change the public image of the papacy. It remains to be seen if there will be a demonstrable long-term shift in how the Church actually functions, or whether it truly intends to use its considerable wealth to increase Church programs that help the poor and dispossessed.

Empty Seats in the Church

So far one thing is still clear: Organized religion is losing ground. In the lifetime of the boomers, church attendance has fallen dramatically in the United States, especially among Catholics. In the last decade, the media's constant revelations that pedophile priests had (for a long period of time) molested parishioners' children in dioceses around the world shocked Catholics and everyone else. These disclosures resulted in many lawsuits and large settlements that the Church was required to pay to victims of sexual abuse. Few of the priests guilty of molestation faced criminal charges and in too many cases their crimes were hushed up by the Church, and offenders were shuttled to other churches to conceal their abuse of children.

The suffering inflicted on young church members reflected an ethical breakdown at the highest levels of Church leadership. This sad state of affairs became evident as the systematic and decades-long cover-ups were slowly pieced together. The truth came to light not from the Church, but from journalists, the courts and the pain-filled public accusations made by countless victims. The Church was not exactly cooperative with the investigation of its failure to protect its young flock and punish their victimizers – a dereliction that led many people to question the moral compass of Church leadership. This is not to be construed as a negative comment about priests in general – only a small percentage of priests engaged in criminal activities.

I have never attended church on a regular basis, but I do believe in the concept of a higher power, and particularly in religious freedom. Americans are fortunate to have a constitution that guarantees their right to follow the religion of their choosing.

When it comes to the *history* of organized religion, I'm not a fan. Too often a professed love of God has been translated into intolerance of others and senseless wars. Organized religion has often been wrong (but never in doubt) back to the days when the church persecuted those who dared suggest that the world was round. George Bernard Shaw had a solid point when he said, "All great truths begin as blasphemies." From my perspective, organized religion still has too much to do with power and control and too little to do with love.

I tend to scratch my head when people are interviewed on television after *something good* happens to them – such as surviving cancer, or walking away from a car accident, or scoring the winning touchdown in the final seconds of a football game. They often point their hands toward the sky and say with conviction: "All Glory to God." Yet when an innocent person is murdered, or a young child dies from cancer, no one ever seems to mention God, except perhaps to say: "Well, it's all part of God's plan" – as if they are absolutely certain there is a total rhythm and reason to the universe. I imagine it would be a comfort to have such faith.

My dad used to take our family to the beach on Sundays, or other natural settings where we could enjoy sun and open air. He was raised in a church-going family, but he always told us that it made him nervous "anytime anyone tries to take God indoors."

Involvement in Modern Politics

Today, organized religion has become an active participant in politics.

Many churches have spent millions of tax-free church dollars trying to block a woman's right to choose and to discourage easy access to birth control. According to UN studies, women in the least economically developed nations are 300 times more likely to die during childbirth than women in the UK and other similarly advantaged countries. The Catholic and other churches have traditionally hindered efforts to bring birth control to women living under deplorable conditions, in dire poverty and without modern medical attention. How does that ease the suffering of women and the poor?

The majority of Americans – and particularly those under 30 – support a woman's right to choose and contraception use, as well as and gay rights. It should come as no surprise then that over half of our citizens view organized religion as dogmatic and/or irrelevant.

According to the Pew Research Center, the generation born after 1979 is 50% less likely than boomers to claim church affiliation. America's younger generations are religious – but the majority of them are avoiding traditional organized religions.

In 2006, Sam Harris penned a controversial bestseller, *Letter to a Christian Nation*. His critique of American Christianity was, to say the least, *unflattering*. Maybe the author's harsh tone partly reflected his response to the hate mail he received from conservative Christians after his previous books appeared. Mr. Harris' *brutal honesty* does register some compelling points, about the dark side of organized religion's effect on the world.

It may seem a bit odd to our young people that organized religion can be so outspoken and politically active about social causes – except when it comes to war. There was no big fuss from organized religion in America when our political leaders made the decision to invade Iraq, starting with the indiscriminate bombing of Baghdad. Our religious leaders don't seem to be interested in talking publicly about the morality of using drones to bomb residential areas in other countries in hopes of killing one individual whom our government wants dead at the expense of innocent women and children.

Death With Dignity

Organized religion has also been actively engaged in thwarting any progress on *death-with-dignity* legislation. Many churches warned that assisted suicide will skyrocket if the terminally ill are allowed to receive aid in ending their pain and suffering. And yet, the state of Oregon passed death with dignity legislation many years ago and there has been no onslaught of elderly suicides or the intervention of death panels, as predicted by many ultra-conservatives.

Churches and other religious organizations have exerted considerable effort to impose their morality on the dying, and on the families of the dying, and have expressed very little real-world compassion for the plight of terminal patients. This lack of concern for the hopelessly ill and their caretakers was epitomized in the famous Terri Schiavo case that received worldwide attention at the beginning of George W. Bush's second term. The federal government intervened, with the encouragement and support of organized religion, to prolong the life of Mrs. Schiavo, who had been in a long-term vegetative state following a catastrophic stroke in 1990. The government not only overruled her own written end-of-life wishes, but also ignored the decision of her husband, who had watched her survive for 15 years on life support, until she was finally allowed to die in 2005.

"Please do not let my loved one suffer" is the most common request families make to doctors when a family member is diagnosed with a terminal condition. But many patients often endure terrible, unnecessary suffering, due to the unresponsiveness of hospital and governmental bureaucracies and the hurdles raised by legal concerns. Families are burdened with both emotional agony and mounting medical bills that drain their financial resources.

'Traditional' Marriage in America

I'm not exactly sure what preachers mean when I hear them speak so passionately about saving "traditional marriage." Historically, even in our own country, *marrying for love* has rarely been the primary motivation for matrimony. In America, our ideas about marriage can be traced to a Judeo/Christian religious/social model, a romantic model, or a rational model, which are all different concepts about why one person should marry another.

Arranged marriages were common during much of human history and were based on economic, political or other pragmatic concerns. For centuries, in civilized nations, traditional marriage was by arrangement of the bride's and groom's parents, but these marriages chosen by others were certainly never "traditional" by American standards.

In 1967, the U.S. Supreme Court ruled that all state laws forbidding intermarriage between the races were unconstitutional. The official, legal term for such unthinkable unions was *miscegenation*, a joining of different races or ethnicities, which was considered immoral by most Christian churches. In the long, slow wake of the Civil Rights movement, mixed-race marriage was finally sanctioned by organized religion and society.

The truth about "traditional" marriage in America is that it has traditionally evolved.

God's Children All Deserve the Same Rights

I cannot figure out why organized religion feels so threatened by gay people marrying one another. If many churches had their way, the gay couple portrayed in TV's *Modern Family* would be left in the closet, and certainly wouldn't be allowed to adopt a child. In most states in America, gay couples who have lived together for decades are still denied the same Social Security benefits and other legal rights enjoyed by heterosexual couples.

The United Methodist Church, the nation's third-largest Christian denomination, recently defrocked Pastor Frank Schaefer, who had led his congregation for more than 10 years. Pastor Schaefer defied church doctrine by presiding over the marriage of his own gay son, in 2007, in Massachusetts – after same-sex marriage had become legal. John Lomperis, the United Methodist director at the Institute of Religion and Democracy, has referred to gay marriages as "publicity stunts."

Ironically, it would be hard for anyone to claim that our current version of heterosexual matrimony is a shining testament to the sanctity of American marriage. Over 50% of marriages between women and men end in divorce, and a significant number of couples who stay married live together in quiet desperation, or by financial necessity. Essentially, the long-term "success rate" of "traditional" heterosexual marriage is, at best, about 35%.

How can we deny gay couples who commit to the institution of marriage the legal benefits and rights "regular" married people enjoy?

Perhaps one day both our churches and our government can find their way out of our bedrooms and away from our deathbeds, and steer clear of intruding on the privacy of American women who are fully capable of making their own decisions about reproductive health issues.

It's my hope that some day organized religion will focus a larger portion of its resources toward helping the less fortunate attain sufficient food, decent shelter and good medical care – along with spiritual comfort.

Amen. ■

MISSING IN ACTION

Growing Up on Violent Sights and Sounds

Video Games

Most boomers think they know about today's video games, but my guess is that very few have any real clue. People in my generation may have memories of *Pac Man* or *Donkey Kong*, but I imagine that my contemporaries would be shocked if they actually sat down and watched today's most popular video games, which can make *Clockwork Orange* look like a fairy tale.

Our nation's children and teenagers often spend more hours playing video games than interacting with parents, doing homework or socializing with friends. Since boomers generally control the companies that sell these games to our children, I thought I'd stick in my two cents about what we now promote as *children's amusement.*

If you are over 50, commit yourself to viewing 15 minutes of the latest version of *Grand Theft Auto* or *Call of Duty.* For accuracy's sake, take in this experience like a typical young boy would, by watching the games on a 20-inch or larger HD video screen with the accompanying sound track *blasting* through speakers and a subwoofer, or a pair of high quality headphones.

My bet is that in less than 10 minutes you might feel compelled to stand up and scream, "*STOP!*"

The two titles I've mentioned are among the bestselling video games in America. Their graphic portrayal of senseless killing is enough to repulse most adults over 45, regardless of one's political persuasion.

After watching a small dose of the carnage, try to imagine the impact that thousands of hours of make-believe participation in such extreme violence must have on our children and grandchildren.

Grand Theft Auto has long been a popular video game in which killing cops is a fun and integral part of the action, and stealing cars and creating havoc are cool. A player can hire a prostitute, and if he wants a refund on services rendered, he can shoot the "ho" or slice her throat – the violence against women (and others) never stops.

Like it or not, *GTA* has become a favorite pastime for our youth. When *Grand Theft Auto 5* was released, teenagers lined up at midnight to snag a copy. At about $60 a pop, the new installment of mayhem flew off the shelves – revenues exceeded $1 billion during the *first three days* of sales. That's twice the sales rate of the last *Harry Potter* book.

I can understand why you might make the assumption that "This is rap music," but hip-hop as an art form is not all that different from visual art. Hip-hop commands our respect in the same manner that your generation respects rock 'n' roll, and yet there is music from punk or heavy-metal rock groups that many people (in my generation and yours) find tasteless or offensive.

The cultural origin of rap also makes it difficult for some older people to relate. People like Bill O'Reilly constantly point to Ludacris and Cam'ron, and disparage all rap music as if the nation is in peril because of the music of two artists among hundreds of other and different rap artists.

Hip-hop did not even exist when your generation was born, and most Americans from affluent backgrounds cannot relate to life in the inner city. Rap in America is a genre that was started by African-Americans and Hispanics during the late '70s in the impoverished parts of the Bronx. Today there are rappers of every color who produce their art in a variety of languages around the globe.

Hip-hop has many sub-genres: political hip-hop, alternative hip-hop, g-funk, Christian hip-hop, and trip-hop, to name a few. Much of this music can be political, introspective and poetic, and it sheds light on problems in troubled communities. The CD I am giving you will demonstrate this.

One last item: For some in your generation, over-generalizing about rap can be an easy and more acceptable way of talking about the state of minority groups without sounding blatantly racist. This can be offensive and disrespectful to the thousands of rappers and their listeners who choose not to conform to the standards of MTV or Top 40 radio stations.

It is unfortunate and ironic that so many older people cast a shadow over all rap music. Much of your own writing keenly skewers the hypocrisy rampant in your own generation - the generation who bathes our society in movie and television violence. Keep your mind open as you listen to the CD.

Thomas

Postscript

I did listen to the rap CD that Thomas dropped off and found some of the music interesting – especially when I could figure out the lyrics. The letter from Thomas has valid points. After all, boomers are the world's biggest marketers of violence, so I should not be pointing fingers. Hypocrisy aside, I'm staying with more traditional rock, blues, pop and country – which generally focus on non-violent subjects.

In that regard, Lynette and I took a trip down to the Hollywood Bowl to catch the Zac Brown Band. The group has been around for a decade, but they only appeared on my old-guy radar after Lynette downloaded one of their albums a couple of years ago. I became a fan. The Bowl sold out all 18,000 seats. It was a little disconcerting to find that I was a *grandpa* among a sea of 20- to 35-year-olds, but I settled in, curious to see if the band could faithfully recreate their studio-produced sounds.

L.A. crowds are not easily impressed, so it was fun to watch the band bring all 18,000 in the audience to their feet. All seven members of the group are seasoned star performers who Zac Brown recruited over several years. Their sound is hard to pigeonhole, as they play a variety of genres, from pop-country to Jimmy Buffet-style reggae to rock. Zac Brown's voice is wonderfully pure, and two other band members also sing lead vocals. Their harmonies can be haunting, harkening back to Crosby, Stills, Nash & Young when those boomers were in their prime.

Most refreshing was the obvious affection that the band members have for each other and their fans. In a music world full of showboating, lip-syncing and gimmicks, these guys seem to be genuinely humble, with a level of musicianship off the charts. They had the crowd in the palm of their hand for almost three hours. This "new" pop-country band is the real deal. ■

I have a love interest
in every one of my films – a gun.

ARNOLD SCHWARZENEGGER, 1988

IT'S GOOD TO BE A GUN IN AMERICA

BOOMERS *love* firepower. Firearms continue to be lighter, faster and more powerful, and sales are soaring. The right to gun ownership lies deep within the American psyche, so passions run hot when anyone questions what the love affair with guns might mean or if it will change someday.

Currently, we live in a country with nearly 300 million firearms, several million of them assault rifles. Americans make up less than 5% of the world's population, but we purchase more than 50% of the world's guns meant for personal use. Nearly 600,000 *new* firearms find their way into the hands of our citizens *each month.* Guns are glamorized in our motion pictures, in our video games and in nine flavors of "police dramas" on television.

No other culture glorifies the gun on such a monumental scale.

The Supreme Court Weighs In

American scholars will continue to debate the intent and meaning of the Bill of Right's Second Amendment to the U.S. Constitution until the cows come home. In 1939, the Supreme Court ruled in *U.S. v. Miller* that the amendment protects arms that have a "reasonable relationship to the preservation of a well-regulated militia," a finding that seems logical, given the amendment's wording.

In more recent times, it was Ronald Reagan who threw his considerable political clout behind two of the major pieces of gun legislation passed by Congress in the last three decades. Reagan's ardent support of the Assault Weapons Ban secured the bill's narrow passage, by a two-vote majority. Congressmen Scott Klug and Dick Sweet credited Reagan's public endorsement of the ban – and his personal appeals to members of Congress – as key factors in their decision to vote for the new gun legislation.

By 2008, Supreme Court justices more conservative than their FDR-era predecessors viewed the Second Amendment in a different light. The court ruled in *District of Columbia v. Heller* that the amendment "protects an individual's right to possess a firearm unconnected with service in a militia." The court's new interpretation seems to be "pro-gun ownership." For all practical purposes, our present federal law assures Americans that they have the *right* to possess an unlimited number of firearms.

In America, anyone who appears to be an adult and has $200 cash can easily buy a firearm without undergoing a mandatory background check. Buying or selling guns without the required review is technically *illegal*, but citizens in most states can visit the parking lot of a local arms show and quickly purchase a weapon, no questions asked, or go online to locate a willing private seller. Money is the only restriction for individuals who want to assemble a personal arsenal.

The National Rifle Association (NRA) is a powerful marketing organization that excels in promoting its own interpretation of the Second Amendment, under the guise of "protecting our freedom." The NRA's apparent core agenda was expressed in a battle cry delivered by actor Charlton Heston (when he was NRA president) as he addressed its 2000 convention. Raising a rifle above his head, Heston passionately declared, "I'll give them my gun when they pry it from my cold, dead hands."

The NRA has three million dues-paying members, but evidently it doesn't speak for *at least one* gun enthusiast, whose differing view of firearm regulation caused him serious trouble with mainstream gun lovers. My friend Jim Agee sent me the disturbing article from *The New York Times,* with his appended comment: "Apparently, gun advocates seem to think that the Second Amendment trumps the First Amendment."

The *Times* article concerned Dick Metcalf, one of the preeminent gun journalists in America, an avid hunter and a gun enthusiast. Metcalf is a former Yale University history professor who has written about firearms for decades – his monthly column was a fixture on the back page of *Guns and Ammo* magazine.

In late 2013, Metcalf wrote a column titled "Let's Talk Limits," which appeared in Guns and Ammo. His subject was America's gun laws, and he dared to express his overview on the pros and cons of gun regulation: "The fact is, all constitutional rights are regulated and always have been."

Of course, his point implied that gun laws were not "written in stone" and could be amended, like any other legislation, which is true.

The response was fast and absolute: Readers threatened to cancel lifelong subscriptions, and gun manufactures warned they would pull their advertising. Metcalf received death threats, was fired as a columnist, and his television show was taken off the air. Jan Libourel, a former editor of *Guns and Ammo* and *Gun World,* explained Metcalf's immediate dismissal from the magazine: "The editors only want editorial content for their key advertisers."

In one week, the admired, longtime writer on firearms and hunting was vilified, stripped of his employment, and cast out from America's gun community.

Gun control proponents take a different view and suggest that the NRA's primary concern is the protection of profits of gun manufacturers. Sales of firearms and ammo sales have never been stronger, and the gun lobbyists fight hard to increase their clients' business. Firearms are currently a $12 billion industry, with Walmart leading as the nation's largest retailer of guns.

Not Much Likely to Change

No American president has ever suggested that citizens don't have the right to own guns. Any politician who speaks up for gun control becomes a target of the NRA, and the organization is a formidable foe.

It seems more convenient for most politicians to ignore the steady stream of sobering statistics flowing from our governmental agencies, including the FBI, the CDC (Centers for Disease Control) and the Department of Defense:

- Approximately 100,000 of our citizens are shot each year – that's an average of 300 people shot each day. (It should be noted that approximately 50% of the poor souls who die from gunshots take their own lives, a gun simply being the most convenient tool.)

  Even so, one person dies by a firearm in America about every 17 minutes. From 2000 to 2010, more than 330,000 of our citizens – a number greater than the population of Cincinnati – were killed by gunfire. *Every 3 days,* more young people under 19 die from firearms than died in the 2012 Newtown, Connecticut, massacre.

- Gun-related death rates in the United States are *6 to 8 times higher* than in countries that economically and politically resemble our own. Developed countries with strict gun laws have dramatically reduced gun violence.

- Under pressure from the NRA, funding has been drastically cut for research and the collection of data on gun violence. A recent study by *The New York Times* and other sources document that gun accidents involving children are grossly underreported in the United States.

- Americans have to pass a written exam and a driving test to obtain a license to drive a car. Given the firepower of modern weapons, why not consider requiring a license to own a gun?

The road ahead looks familiar, but where is it headed?

Given the history of the NRA and its sizable funding from the gun manufacturers, not much change is on the horizon. As I read the pro-gun-rights information from the NRA, I just kept wondering: *Where is all this gun proliferation headed and what kind of road are we on?*

Gun & Ammo Sales

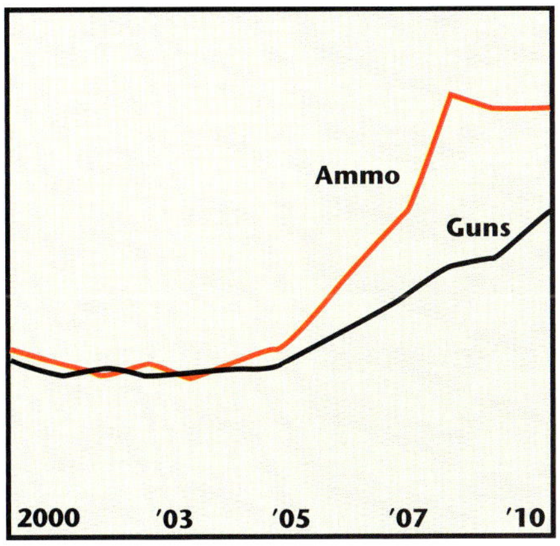

It's undeniable that these lethal products have a long shelf life. Each firearm that is sold will last for decades. More than *six million* firearms are produced each year. Millions of additional firearms will pass into more and more hands in an exponential increase in gun ownership. Based on public records, there is a "national theft rate" of 35,000 firearms per month. As these weapons continue to accumulate in our neighborhoods, businesses and public venues, common sense suggests that the probability that a firearm will be involved in some sort of crime or accident will only increase:

- Bumper stickers proclaim *Only a good guy with a gun can stop a bad guy with a gun.* Perhaps, but that wasn't recently the case in Florida when a "good guy" – with a newly obtained concealed handgun permit – decided to take action against a "bad guy" fleeing from a robbery, with a policeman in hot pursuit. The well-intended 86-year-old opened fire and everyone in the vicinity *including the police officer* hit the ground while the bad guy escaped.
- Then there's 71-year-old Curtis Williams – previously considered a "good guy" – who carried a new, concealed weapons permit and lost his temper in a movie theater, shooting and killing a young man who was "constantly texting" during the film and who refused to stop.
- Even more depressing is the recent story of a "fun family outing" at a California "shooting park," which ended in tragedy when a 9-year-old girl accidentally killed her gun instructor after she lost control of her *assault weapon.*

U.S. Ammunition Prices

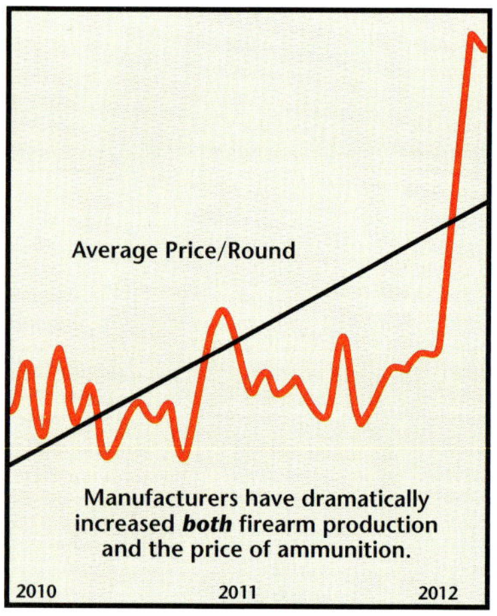

Admittedly, these are "isolated cases" and the NRA still maintains the opposite case: *More* citizens, *armed with more guns,* will produce less violence. Ok, even if we are to buy into that counter-intuitive line of reasoning, what is the end game? Will we be safer when there are *two* firearms for every man, woman and child in America? Should schools begin "firearm training" for our children so they can be safe in the midst of all these guns? Some Americans believe that we should arm our teachers to safeguard their classrooms. The Texas House actually proposed legislation to allow college students to carry weapons on campus.

Where does it end?

A Look at Other Countries

Other countries, including Canada, Japan and England, have long demonstrated that "freedom" and "packing heat" don't have to go hand in hand.

Australians finally became fed up with gun violence after a mass shooting killed 35 people, and in the late 1990s the government banned both automatic and semi-automatic weapons. The political fallout was fierce, but amazingly, Australians turned in over 700,000 firearms for destruction. Since that time, gun homicides have been down by more than 50%, and there has been a 60% drop in gun-related suicides. Australia suffered more than a dozen mass shootings in the two decades prior to the new gun laws, but since then, none have occurred.

For better or worse, Americans still possess a 19th century mentality about firearms. At some point we might try looking at a new approach. We are truly a nation in denial if we continue to allow the NRA and firearm manufacturers to dominate the discussion and the future of gun control.

Firearm technology was very different during the time when our forefathers wrote: "A well-regulated militia, being necessary to the security of a free state, the right of the people to keep and bear arms shall not be infringed."

When the Second Amendment was adopted in 1791, a citizen could string a new arrow to a bow more quickly than reload a gun. Guns were handmade by a gunsmith, were "single shot" and were loaded through the muzzle.

To some, it may be un-American to point out that the very men who actually wrote the Second Amendment would probably be stunned by modern firearm technology, and dumbfounded that any American today can possess the firepower to kill 25 or more fellow citizens *in less than 50 seconds.* One man bearing assault weapons now has the power to act as his own private "well-regulated militia."

Our nation's love affair with firearms will continue to foster unintended consequences. It seems that most Americans seem to be defiant about their "freedom" to possess semi-automatic hand guns, and assault weapons that hold *lots* of bullets.

In the coming years, boomers will turn over their control of gun laws.

My generation will pass on more than 400 million firearms to the younger generations.

Quite a legacy. ■

It appears to me that no one has learned a thing; that Wall Street is still operating as if 2008 never happened.

– Colin C. Peterson, U.S. Congressman

Shameless on Wall $treet

This is a cautionary tale about shameless politicians outwitted by scoundrels and other soulless con men, who prospered after ruining the lives of millions of Americans. Yet none of the bad guys went to jail.

THE TELEVISION series *House of Cards* delivers a raw slice of modern American politics. The Emmy Award-winning series was ground-breaking, partly because it was produced by Netflix – instead of one of the traditional networks – and because it is cast with feature film stars Kevin Spacey and Robin Wright. The political drama resembles *The Sopranos* meets *The West Wing,* but even the creepiest characters are based in reality, so the story cuts close to the bone. The drama is an entertaining portrayal of life inside Washington, D.C.'s beltway, and Spacey's character is spellbinding.

In 2008, an equally riveting political drama played out in real life.

The Big Bank Meltdown Cometh

The *real* criminal drama involved a motley crew who managed to swindle Americans out of billions. When the financial crash came, all the Wall Street players scurried back to their mansions, donned their corporate armor, lawyered up and avoided jail. The nation's economic crisis began in 2007 and became a big story before it faded from the headlines.

America has a short attention span for white-collar crime, so the country was quickly distracted by another tragic random shooting spree, a natural disaster, the never-ending exploits of the Kardashians, or the "Real Housewives" from … *somewhere.* The subsequent deluge of vacuous media was certainly less painful and far more entertaining.

When the smoke finally cleared, the money-grubbers had managed to slither back into the murky depths of the Wall Street lagoon, unpunished and unrepentant. Given their record, it's only a matter of time before they resurface to run their next con.

I'm a businessman and a bit of a political nerd, so my attention lingered on the financial crash. I watched the financial debacle as it continued to unfold. Before the meltdown, any screenwriter who approached a producer with such an improbable script would have been quickly dismissed as an author who was smoking too much weed. But truth can be stranger than fiction.

In real life, a cast of perhaps 25 major players triggered the worst economic meltdown since the Great Depression, but I'll focus on just two of the key players: Henry M. Paulson and Phil Gramm.

Henry Paulson and Phil Gramm Play Star Roles in the Saga

Mr. Paulson was the CEO of Goldman Sachs when President George W. Bush appointed him U.S. treasury secretary in 2006. Paulson had been the highest-paid CEO on Wall Street and was able to cash in his chips at Goldman Sachs for approximately *$500 million.* It was a nice payday for Paulson, but it didn't raise many eyebrows: Goldman Sachs executives always seem to end up extremely rich. It was also not unusual for a former Goldman Sachs executive to end up in the U.S. Treasury Department. Paulson was another Phi Beta Kappa and Harvard man selected to run the club.

A Wall Street CEO protects the taxpayers' piggy-bank

Ironically, in his first public appearance as treasury secretary, Paulson identified an alarming and growing gap between the richest and poorest Americans, and stated that this disparity was near the *top of his list* of major economic issues that needed addressing. In short, we had a Wall Street CEO who claimed one of his primary goals was "to help the middle class."

Deregulation had already gained momentum

By 2000, banks were allowed to further expand the scope of their business outside the bounds of traditional banking. The relaxing of certain long-standing banking regulations also permitted the banks to increase their deposit leverage ratios to *as much as 40 to 1.* This process of bank deregulation started under the Clinton administration with the repeal of the Glass-Steagall Act, through legislation introduced by Texas Senator Phil Gramm. Many aspects of Glass-Steagall had already been challenged and deemed to be elastic, as Citibank's affiliation with the stock brokerage firm Salomon Smith Barney was given the green light by the Federal Reserve Board's interpretation of the existing law.

President Clinton had declared, "The Glass-Steagall law is no longer appropriate." But after the Bush administration took office in 2000, banking deregulation went into overdrive. The theory was that less regulation would only *slightly* increase risk while offering more freedom for U.S. banks to compete and prosper in a global economy.

Free enterprise turned out not to be so free

A cornerstone of the Bush presidency's economic plan was an emphasis on increasing the rate of homeownership, in large part due to the relaxation of mortgage lending policies. The White House press secretary often boasted about how the rate of home homeownership had soared since the year 2000.

By 2005, U.S. banks could lend to nearly anyone with a pulse. As the White House's chief spokesman on economic issues, Henry Paulson emphasized to the world that America's economic growth was strong and sustained, and that a current dip in the housing market was about to turn around. In 2006 (and into 2007) Mr. Paulson was publicly upbeat in his assessment of the U.S. economy, repeatedly assuring the nation that the financial markets were healthy – even robust.

Paulson's 'structurally sound' economy

In 2007 and into 2008, the U.S. treasury secretary also informed the business community that the emerging U.S. sub-prime mortgage crisis remained largely contained, due to what he called "the strongest global economy in decades." In mid-2008, Paulson again assured the nation that the U.S. financial markets were emerging from the ongoing credit crunch, and that he believed the worst was now behind us.

In 2008, after IndyMac Bank failed, Paulson told the press, "It's a safe banking system, a sound banking system. Our regulators are on top of it. This is a very manageable situation." Even as late as August 2008, Paulson appeared on Meet the Press and stated that he had no plans to inject any capital into Fannie Mae or Freddie Mac. Nonetheless, both institutions went into conservatorship within a few weeks of Paulson's statement. Only weeks before the presidential election, Paulson, the White House and Senator John McCain continued to reassure the nation, ***"The economy is structurally sound."***

Anyone who challenged these statements was quickly ridiculed as being an "unpatriotic alarmist." In typical fashion, Fox News spoke disdainfully about any politician who openly questioned the continuing assurances given by John McCain or the Bush administration.

I wanted to believe that Paulson, Bush and McCain were right, because I care about the well-being of our country, and, from a personal standpoint, I was nearing retirement. I wanted to give the Bush administration and their financial experts every benefit of the doubt when they assured the world that our economy remained stable. I told myself that although the White House may have misconceived and mismanaged the Iraq War, at least the administration was business friendly and had cut income taxes. It seemed reasonable to believe that the Bush administration, over its eight years in office, had fortified the financial foundation for the nation's economy.

The power couple from Texas

Phil Gramm was an outspoken conservative, a former U.S. senator, and chief economic advisor and co-chair for Senator John McCain's presidential campaign. Gramm and his wife, Wendy, made quite the power couple: Mrs. Gramm was also an economist and sat on the board of directors of Enron and on Enron's audit committee.

Ex-Senator Gramm was also the former chairman of the U.S. Senate Committee on Banking, Housing and Urban Affairs and had spearheaded the push to pass banking deregulation laws, including the landmark Gramm-Leach-Bliley Act of 1999. His support was a key element in passing the Commodity Futures Act of 2000, which kept derivative transactions and credit default swaps free of government regulation.

Gramm's efforts – which were aided by other sympathetic politicians and backed by lobbyists – removed or modified many of the laws that for decades had effectively separated banking, insurance and brokerage operations. Now bankers had more flexibility to conduct transactions across a wider range of financial activity.

The music stops and Gramm disappears

Throughout the year 2008, it was hard to turn on the news without hearing John McCain, Phil Gramm and the White House repeat the good economy story – until one day they suddenly stopped.

Phil Gramm abruptly stepped down as McCain's campaign co-chairman and top economic advisor. It was only weeks later, in September 2008, that all of the television networks interrupted their programming with a special announcement: President Bush would be speaking to the nation on an important matter.

The 'structurally sound economy' crumbles

America watched as a somber-looking President Bush walked to the podium. The president informed the nation of the bad news:

(A) The U.S. banking system and financial markets were on the verge of collapse.

(B) As president, he was invoking his emergency powers to immediately inject hundreds of billions of dollars of taxpayer funds into the banking system. Bush emphasized that it was "an urgent situation" and that there was no time for the standard congressional oversight. The president informed the nation that Hank Paulson, treasury secretary, would have the authority needed to oversee the emergency program.

I stared at the television in disbelief: *Say what?* A financial crisis? The nation suddenly needed a "Troubled Asset Relief Program" for banks? How did our "fundamentally sound economy" disintegrate in less than 60 days? On that day, the term "TARP" instantly became the most ubiquitous term in the financial community. The rest of us called it "The Bailout."

BUSINESS

Friday, October 10, 2008

Nightmare on Wall St.

More big losses

Panic selling – Dow to its lowest level since 2003

We all know the rest of the bailout story, but what we didn't know at that time was a sobering fact that was later revealed: Between 2002 and 2007 – during the Bush administration's economic expansion – the income of the wealthiest 1% of our citizens grew 10 times faster than the income of the remaining 99%. That means that the income of roughly 3 million people grew 10 times faster than the total income of the remaining 310 million Americans – or, said differently, two-thirds of total income gains went to the richest 1% of our population. In 2007, the "one percenters" had a larger share of America's total income than at any time since the late 1920s – just prior to the Great Depression.

The same players stay in the game

President Obama inherited Bush's TARP program, and kept it in place, along with the same financial team who kept running the same financial plays. The new president even stepped up the bailouts in an effort to keep the sinking ship afloat, all with taxpayer money.

I felt some empathy for President Bush, because my guess was that he'd been misinformed by his senior economic advisors in the months leading up to the crisis. Certainly, both the president and the Republican National Committee (RNC) would have preferred that the financial crisis had surfaced after the 2008 election. President Bush must have understood that his "emergency press conference" would make his previous rosy statements about the "strong economy" appear ludicrous, or at best inept and ill-informed. It must have been a hard pill to swallow. I don't envy the White House advisor who delivered the stark message just weeks before the election:

"Mr. President, we are making a recommendation that you stand up in front of the nation next week to say that America's banking system is on the verge of collapse."

On a cynical note, it should be pointed out that billions of bailout dollars ended up in the coffers of Henry Paulson's old firm – Goldman Sachs. AIG Insurance had guaranteed banks' and brokerage houses' loans and investments that later had gone south, so AIG was the first company the government saved. AIG was on the verge of collapse and would have taken down other financial institutions that they had insured and whose losses they couldn't make good. Coincidentally, AIG was the insurance firm closely involved with Goldman Sachs.

BOOM – an $85 billion line of credit from the federal government to AIG! This was only the first of many financial bailouts to corporations that our government deemed "too big to fail."

As the months passed, executives at Goldman Sachs and AIG *continued* to receive multi-million-dollar bonuses, while Americans began to lose their jobs and any sense of security as a severe recession set in, and companies large and small went under.

Goldman Sachs' track record of being the No. 1 amoral corporation in America remained intact.

The financial crisis worse than imagined

No one knew just how bad the Great Recession might become. President Obama must have been a bit incredulous at his first detailed briefing, when Henry Paulson and his team outlined the true depth of the economic crisis.

Economists still argue over the underlying causes of the meltdown. Most of my conservative friends will make the case that President Obama has done a terrible job of managing the financial crisis and that his administration has only made things worse. They have many valid points, but as I write this, the economic story has yet to play out. It can take years to rebound from such a major setback.

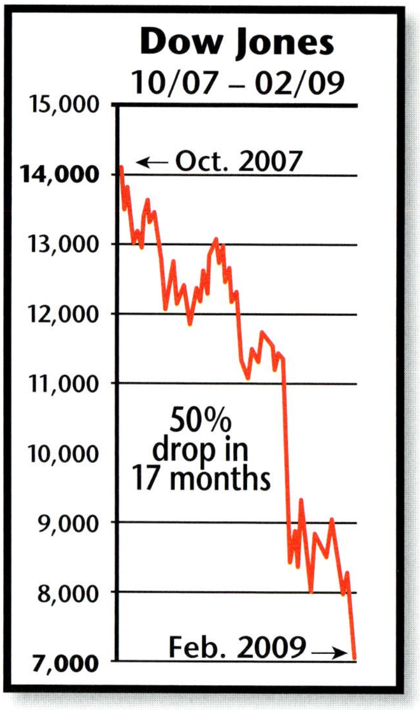

Of course the Fox News pundits began calling President Obama's economic recovery plan a failure only months after his inauguration. Karl Rove, the senior political analyst for Fox, wasted no time in labeling our new president a "radical socialist" who would quickly devastate the U.S. economy and never win a second term. Rove was wrong on both counts.

To keep this all in perspective, it's not as if the U.S. banking system has a sterling record. As The Wall Street Journal pointed out, the United States has suffered 16 banking crises during our 237-year history, while Canada has experienced zero – not one, even during the Great Depression. The story of our past troubles was detailed by Columbia University's Charles Calomiris and presented at the Atlanta Fed's 2013 Financial Markets Conference.

Obama fails to jail the crooks

What bothers me most about the Great Recession is that virtually none of the major players responsible have gone to jail – or even been punished in any way. A few of the notables include Countrywide CEO Angelo Mozilo, AIG CEO Joseph Cassano and Lehman Brothers CEO Richard Fuld, all of whom continue to skate free from the scene.

Countless articles have been written about these particular CEOs and other top executives and board members from their competitors. What these executives all have in common is that virtually all of them kept their fortunes intact and continue to live in mega-luxury. For whatever reason, the U.S. Justice Department failed to send any of these people to jail. Their amazing coat of Teflon may be connected to the fact that Wall Street employs 3,000 lobbyists and has spent $5 billion in political contributions over the last decade.

President Obama failed to keep his promise to jail the crooks. It was just one of many promises he has failed to keep. To date, there has been no significant change in the culture of Wall Street.

Several good books have been written about the financial meltdown, but none of them are as riveting as the documentary film *Inside Job*, which accurately presents the crime story resembling no other in history. The Academy Award-nominated movie by filmmaker Charles Ferguson is both informative and entertaining. No other book or movie does as good a job in presenting and explaining Wall Street's role in America's financial crisis and the global economy's near collapse, all in a manner that can be easily understood.

The film was produced in 2010 by Sony Pictures and is narrated by actor Matt Damon. There are many interviews with Wall Street's central players. Hearing the words directly from the miscreants is most revealing. Henry Paulson refused to be interviewed for the film.

Money-center banks reap record profits

In bailing out Wall Street, our government effectively put the burden and risk of underwriting the largest U.S. banks on the backs of American taxpayers. We now had public risk but very private profit. Meanwhile, the country's citizens watched their own personal equity in real estate and other assets diminish dramatically or vanish.

Tens of millions of people in America and around the world lost their jobs, homes, businesses and/or retirement savings. The American middle class was devastated, and yet the biggest banks are, once again, making staggering profits.

For example, Wells Fargo income has soared since the meltdown – their stock has risen from $12 per share in 2009 to over $50 per share when I checked in September 2014. The Wells Fargo bank executive I talked to was so proud – as if the bank's newfound success was a direct result of the bank's creativity and cleverness in merging with Wachovia. "We gained market share," he said. "In the end, the financial crisis will have a very positive outcome for Wells Fargo."

He was correct: Smaller community banks have been squeezed out, and now big banks rule. What the executive from Wells Fargo didn't say is that the banks became more profitable because their "spreads" became higher. The banks were able to borrow money from the government for almost nothing, but they passed on only a portion of this windfall to their own borrowers. In addition, bankers began adding new fees in every nook and cranny of their services.

The pundits on cable TV's CNBC business channel are almost giddy when talking about the remarkable rise in bank-share prices. The CNBC business channel has become a full-time promotion machine for Wall Street and free-market capitalism. It's no surprise that CNBC revenue is pumped up from all of those touchy-feely Wall Street brokerage-firm advertisements, all with some form of the same disingenuous message:

"We pledge to honor and protect our customers' assets."

The impact on America

My opening statement – concerning the scoundrels of Wall Street who continued to prosper after ruining the lives of millions of Americans – was not meant to be hyperbole. A report released in mid-2013 by the U.S. Federal Reserve Bank of Dallas lays out in detail some chilling, fact-based predictions: The 2007 to 2009 financial crisis will eventually cost the United States between $6 trillion and $14 trillion in lost economic output. Even worse, these financial losses will come in the form of declines in wages, home equity and the general economic security of the average American.

The Federal Reserve Bank of Dallas' report estimates the difference between actual and projected economic growth, and what growth would have been if the financial crisis had never occurred. The report's authors concede that there is no perfect method for calculating the impact of Wall Street's collapse on the American economy, and no sure way to know how our economy would have performed if the crisis had never happened. With that disclaimer, the report estimates that between 40% and 90% of one year's gross domestic product will be lost before growth "returns to trend" later this decade.

These predictions suggest that the long-term damage caused by the economic meltdown will mean a total loss (over time) of between $50,000 and $120,000 for every U.S. household. The reserve bank acknowledges that these figures are conservative, and that it is difficult to quantify the trauma caused by job losses and sustained or rising long-term rates of unemployment. The report also notes that the likelihood of high unemployment in coming years increases the possibility that these loss estimates may drastically understate the true cost of the economic debacle to American families.

The study concludes that the banking crisis strained the federal government's resources and capabilities – in part by adding to the national debt – and that the ability of both the government and the federal reserve to respond to future economic downturns has been impaired.

Shameless on Wall Street

There are certainly fine individuals in the financial services industry, but unfortunately many of those people worked in community and regional banks that were crushed or squeezed out during the unfolding of the financial meltdown. Bank consolidation has left us with fewer and bigger banks that wield enormous economic power. *In 1990,* the five largest U.S. financial companies controlled about 20% of banking industry assets. Today the five big banks own about 55%. More money and influence controlled by a handful of mega-banks doesn't paint a pretty picture for the future. It's my hope that Americans will choose to support their remaining community banks.

No remorse

It's safe to say that no apology will ever come from the Wall Street con men in their well-tailored suits. No visible remorse emanates from the banking community. Even after Wall Street and money-center banks caused the financial catastrophe, brokerage CEOs, bank presidents and their lieutenants failed to step forward and help the American people when they most needed help. The powerful and wealthy men in charge did not use the taxpayers' bailout money – or Fed funds that they could have borrowed at near-zero interest – to truly work with homeowners and businesses. Instead, they used various techniques to intimidate, harass and/or foreclose on borrowers.

The big banks' only concern was protecting their own bottom line. Many of their actions were not based on any sense of logic, fair play or even loyalty. The simple truth is that the money-center banks created and then manipulated the financial crisis in any way they could for their own financial gain.

Wall Street does not play on a level field. It never has.

Martin Scorsese's newest movie, The Wolf of Wall Street, was released in late 2013, starring Leonardo DiCaprio. The blockbuster film is the story of Jordan Belfort (DiCaprio), a Wall Street thief and con man who steals millions and leaves countless ruined lives in his wake. Scorsese leaves no stone unturned in a three-hour display of '80s greed and decadence.

It's a true story.

Belfort was convicted and served 22 months in prison. Yes, only 22 months – about the same amount of time an 18-year-old kid would serve for robbing a suburban liquor store with a pocket knife and running off with $300 and a carton of cigarettes.

Wall Street players don't need knives – greed is the common bond and weapon that propels their culture. Not much has changed since Gordon Gekko spouted the Wall Street mantra:

"Greed, for lack of a better word, is good. Greed is right. Greed works. Greed clarifies, cuts through, and captures the essence of the evolutionary spirit."

This latest Scorsese movie about Wall Street's culture comes on the heels of Oliver Stone's two movies, Wall Street and the follow-up film in 2010, Money Never Sleeps. And those two films followed a long line of movies about the nature of avarice, including the comedy Trading Places, starring Dan Aykroyd and Eddie Murphy. Trading Places was a huge hit more than 30 years ago, but it's even more relevant today.

The real titans of Wall Street are now smoother. The men wearing the monogrammed shirts with solid gold cufflinks cruise the corridors of our nation's capital as celebrities.

Karl Ichan is currently the richest Wall Street player, and he is followed by a band of heavy-weight players like Daniel Loeb, David Einhorn, Bill Ackman and others. Ichan used to be described as a "corporate raider" – one of the "barbarians at the gate" – but these days, Ichan and all the other Ichan wannabes have successfully re-branded themselves as shareholder activists. And men like Jamie Dimon – chairman and CEO of JPMorgan Chase – are now treated (by CNBC and our congressmen) like movie stars.

Every major business publication has consistently documented that three out of four stockbrokers can't match the average returns of the major stock indexes. You may be convinced that your stockbroker is a very smart person, but if he or she is actively managing your portfolio you are probably paying a heavy price. Over any extended period of time, only one in four stockbrokers can produce larger average profits than the broad-based index funds, which charge minimal fees.

During the past 50 years there have been several famous studies that analyzed stockbroker proficiency – and found it disappointing. Throughout the decades, dozens of articles have documented how monkeys throwing darts at the stock index page of The Wall Street Journal or using other "selection methods" have been quite successful. The monkeys beat the brokers' average return about 90% of the time, after brokerage fees were deducted.

The other day I overheard a local stockbroker making a pitch to a prospective investor, describing how over the past five years he had increased the value of a client's stock portfolio by 28%. That's very good – until you consider that the S&P 500 and Dow Index both increased by nearly 50% over the same time period. The stock market can be an excellent vehicle for long term investing – but it's prudent to keep a close eye on brokerage fees..

The typical customer has never been king on Wall Street. Incoming money from clients is simply added into a revenue stream from which to skim. The process starts the minute the customer meets with a broker. Wall Street has very smart lawyers, so the first requirement (even before you have the privilege of handing the firm your money) is your signature on a contract mandating that all disputes be resolved in arbitration administered by the Financial Industry Regulatory Authority, or FINRA. Every customer must sign their contract.

The game is played by their set of rules.

The idea of requiring all investors to arbitrate disputes before a tribunal appointed by the very industry being sued is immediately suspect because it deprives American citizens of their constitutional rights for a trial by a jury of their peers. FINRA has neither the appearance, nor the reality, of impartiality. Essentially, the contract the customer must sign was conceived by and for Wall Street. FINRA amounts to the securities industry sitting in judgment of itself – with predictable results.

If and when a customer loses his money to poor or even negligent management, he'll be subject to what amounts to a slow and biased system for any "financial justice" – or he can lick his wounds and walk away. Even given the level of Wall Street skullduggery during the past decade, the customer rarely "wins" in FINRA arbitration, and many cases are settled outside of FINRA, with non-disclosure clauses – so everything stays under the rug. The cost of the "clean hands appearance" is mere pocket change for the industry.

Big Banks Get Ugly

The operations of big brokerages and the big banks are now cut from the same cloth. In real life, money-center bankers operate like hard-nosed Las Vegas pit bosses. A couple of years ago, I had a discussion with a senior vice president from one of the major banks about what was happening behind the scene. I asked what the money-center banks were doing to help businessmen or homeowners who were falling behind on their interest payments.

"Not much," he said. "All the money-center banks are cracking down."

Then I asked him how the banks were treating borrowers who missed payments on commercial loans, and he didn't mince words. He looked me directly in the eye and said: "Our bank is doing anything the documents will allow us to do – and our lawyers wrote the loan documents. We have people tied up in more ways than they ever imagined."

The banker's statement was actually refreshing, because at least it was the truth.

Our banking system now operates in a world where oversight is increasingly conducted by outside consulting firms. There is a growing reliance on the part of government to depend more on private bank examiners paid by the banks. This cozy arrangement is a rising trend and is bound to bring its own set of problems based on the industry's track record.

Dirty players

Americans have found out that the big banks did more than just crack down on the middle class. Some of our leading banks were cutting corners in a most unethical fashion. The banks contracted with robo-signing foreclosure mills that routinely and illegally foreclosed on millions of American homes. When the big banks were caught in the scheme, they simply told the government, "So sorry, but we are not admitting to anything – deal with our team of attorneys."

What happened? A settlement was reached and the big banks paid a fine. On one hand, our Supreme Court has decided, "Corporations have the same rights and responsibilities as people" but somehow, when corporations break the laws, no people go to jail.

For money-center banks and most other mega-corporations, paying fines for unethical and/or criminal behavior is just a standard line item cost of doing business.

The syrupy TV advertisements that portray JPMorgan Chase, Bank of America or Citibank as caring so much about customers is the height of hypocrisy. You'd think their industry meltdown never happened.

My business partners and I watched Wells Fargo, our own bank, go through a crisis as its stock price plummeted during the fiasco. Wells Fargo quickly reshuffled executives with whom we'd had good relations for more than a decade. In the past five years, we've worked with four different executives – from three different regions – who have overseen our account. Executives at money-center banks now seem to constantly move around as banking has begun to resemble a game of musical chairs.

The crisis hit close to home. We continued to pay property taxes, mortgages and other governmental fees even when buildings sat empty. The recession has been difficult but manageable for my business partnerships, as we were able to meet each and every obligation. I had not worked such long hours since my 30s. I had no choice – in fact I felt fortunate, because we survived the downturn in real estate in decent shape.

Personally, I had stopped "investing" in the stock market about 15 years ago. After watching the disastrous stock market crash in 1987 and subsequent scandals, I had no desire to invest in "securities" that are constantly manipulated by third parties. Wall Street players have no real interest in a company or its workers – they only care about the movement of the share price.

From its high in 2007 to its lowest point in 2009, the Dow lost more than 50% of its value, and NASDAQ fell by more than 50%. Many investors faced margin calls while others sold

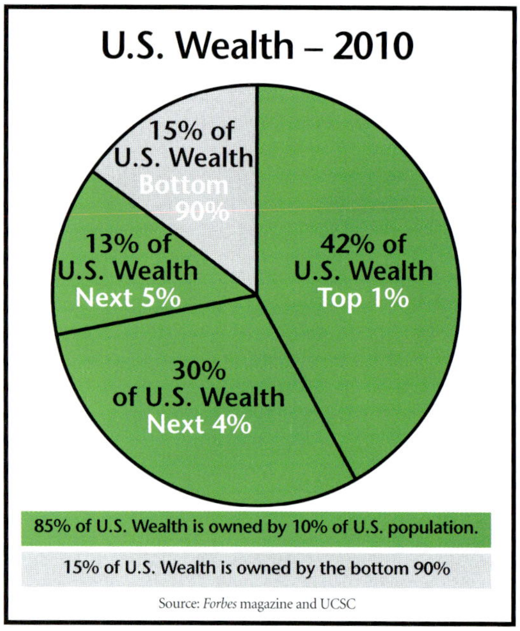

their stocks in desperation because they simply couldn't afford any further losses.

During the period from 2007 through 2010, real estate values in our area also declined significantly, depending upon the location and type of property.

Many of my lifelong friends, business associates and some of our tenants were unable to ride out the devastating impact of Wall Street's meltdown. During the past several years, we all have watched the hard work and dreams of our fellow Americans smash on the rocks of the Great Recession. Unemployment rose dramatically and foreclosures skyrocketed. It was the worst financial crisis in three generations.

Economic uncertainty has rocked my generation. The vast majority of boomers grew up in a time of financial prosperity, and most felt relatively secure until the most recent financial crises.

For members of the Pepsi Generation, economic disaster could not have come at a worse time in their lives.

This Too Shall Pass

America's cynicism meter is in the red zone. A sizable portion of the population has been disillusioned by the actions of our government and Wall Street. The approval rating of the U.S. Congress is now at rock bottom.

There have been several times in our history when America seemed in decline, and yet in hindsight we can see that the nation had every reason to be optimistic about its future. When my dad was my age, he used to watch the news and mutter, "The world is going to Hell in a hand basket."

I'm beginning to better understand my father's sentiment. Cynicism evidently creeps its way into the psyche of each American generation as it grows old. It's hard to stomach the government and deceitful corporations nipping constantly at your pocketbook. It's demoralizing to witness the senseless acts of terrorism that regularly fill our television screens. It's difficult to keep up with technology that is changing at an exponential pace.

We're living in an age in which everything changes rapidly, and yet we are still the same human animal that evolved gradually. For millions of years, we hunted and gathered our food and marked the changes in the seasons – slowly.

Changing gears and adjusting expectations

Every person in the Boomer Generation soon will need to face unknown chapters in their life, because no one can one avoid dealing with the aging process. The economic downturn has made it tougher for many to reconcile the realities of growing old while needing to postpone retirement.

Still, most boomers will have the opportunity to adjust their sails and redefine priorities to allow more focus on those things in life that bring affordable pleasure and fulfillment.

A life simplified can sometimes be more rewarding.

Boomers, like their children, are using technology to stay in constant touch with family and friends. The internet also allows unlimited exposure to reading, movies and education for a very moderate cost. Living arrangements and living spaces can be adjusted in a manner to bring family and friends together.

I expect that my generation will redefine what it means to be a senior citizen, and broaden the roles that old people can play – long before the boomer curtain falls.

Postscript on two Key Players

Henry Paulson

Phil Gramm

Henry Paulson: Near the end of 2013, Henry Paulson appeared on the cover of Bloomberg Businessweek. The occasion was the fifth anniversary of the Wall Street meltdown, and Paulson was presenting his version of events. He titled his article "The Crisis That Changed the World."

I wondered what Paulson would have to say – maybe detailing some important insights he'd gained from his role in the disaster or even expressing some remorse for the damaging events that had transpired during his watch. Instead, he chose to merely go through the motions, portraying himself and his colleagues as victims of one of those inevitable back-and-forth swings of capitalism.

Whoever is careless with the truth in small matters cannot be trusted with important matters.

– Albert Einstein

PICKPOCKETS BY DESIGN

AT ONE TIME or another we've all stared in confusion at our unintelligible monthly TV cable invoice, or frowned as we spotted a mysterious charge at the bottom of our bank statement. And the travelers among us have had the experience of standing at the airline counter when the agent introduces that "extra charge" – and we realize that there's no real choice but to agree, sign the credit card receipt and feel ripped off.

Internet companies routinely push "auto-ship" and "auto-renewal" policies that are deceitfully designed with fine print, buried and easy to miss. Try to cancel and you'll find yourself in a Catch-22 hell facing ridiculous penalties. They have rip-off down to a science.

I don't know when it happened, but many of our corporations suddenly turned into tricksters, using their sheer size and their customers' trust – or lack of attention – to pad their bottom line.

Corporations Take *Caveat Emptor* to a New Level

Sarah, our bookkeeper, recently came into my office to ask why a monthly statement from Bank of America showed an odd line item: **Late-fee/other charge: $30.** Since our mortgage payments were all on "auto-pay," Sarah wondered how there could be a late fee. Could I shed some light on the subject?

I had no idea, but I was curious, so I picked up the phone and called the special customer service number printed on the B of A statement. As Sarah can testify, the conversation went as follows, beginning with a recorded message:

"You have reached Bank of America's world-class customer service."

Next, a computer voice proceeded to offer a long list of menu options – none of which I needed.

After negotiating the computer-cue maze, I finally got through to a live person. The following conversation ensued:

B of A Service Agent: This is Bank of America's world-class service and I am Melanie. How may I help you?

I gave the security information Melanie requested and then was allowed to ask about the mysterious charge that Sarah had discovered on the bank statement.

Melanie (very nice)**:** Yes, I see that your mortgage is on auto-pay, so maybe it's not exactly a late fee – let me check my screen.

A few moments later she came back on the line.

Melanie: Mr. Branch, I see that the $30 charge relates to your mortgage, but that it was not a late fee.

CB: Exactly what kind of fee was it?

Melanie said she'd have to check another screen. I was put on hold for a couple of minutes, and then she returned with more detailed information.

Melanie: It was a fee related to a fax.

CB: What kind of fax and for what transaction?

Melanie: It is a suspended fax fee, from 2008.

CB: What happened in 2008?

Melanie: Our mortgage division contacted you to offer a program to extend your mortgage term. It was a special offer made to our best customers.

CB: What does that have to do with the fax charge?

Melanie: Our mortgage sales division requested a written payment history from our accounting division, and under the terms of your mortgage agreement we are allowed to charge $30 anytime a fax is requested.

CB: But I never requested any fax, or asked for any changes to the mortgage. And $30 for a fax charge seems ridiculous, and then trying to bill me five years after the fact might even be illegal.

I was starting to become annoyed.

Melanie: Mr. Branch, under the terms of our contract we are allowed to suspend such fees, and then apply them at a later date, at our option.

CB: Melanie, do you mind if I speak with your supervisor?

Now I was really irritated, but Melanie quickly responded.

Melanie: Mr. Branch, that won't be necessary. I'm looking at your history on the screen, and you have been a good customer, so I am going to waive the fee.

The conversation's tone began to cool down a bit. I asked if the billing I had received was standard practice, and if so whether other people had complained.

Melanie: Yours is not my first call on this matter.

CB: Melanie, could you please pass this message to the management? If Bank of America is going to claim that it provides "world-class service," it might be better if a real person actually answers the phone instead of a computer system. And tell them that world-class service does not mean ripping off their customers with sneaky five-year-old charges.

Melanie: Mr. Branch, we are required to open all conversations with the world-class service statement, as it is part of our script, but I can understand your sentiment.

I then apologized for being such a smart ass, and thanked Melanie for her time. ■

Breaking News

WSJ 4/1/13

Banking Industry Announces Rehab Program

Assimilated Press – Stunned by a 2013 Gallup poll indicating that only *1 in 50* Americans had "much confidence" in major U.S. banks, banking industry officials announced today that all CEOs will return to a "reputation rehabilitation center" at an undisclosed location in the Cayman Islands.

The news release on this most recent Bankers' Universal Rehab Program (BURP) sent an immediate shock wave through executive suites across the nation. One prominent banker, requesting anonymity, acknowledged that he would be entering treatment for the third time, then tearfully added, "Those Wall Street hipsters made it all sound so good – I was just recovering from the last fiasco in the '90s and they pulled me back in."

Informed that the latest surveys also indicate that the majority of Americans have "little or no trust" in money-center banks, the CEO quickly regained his composure and responded, defiantly, "We will *do anything* to regain America's trust!"

A source close to the breaking story traced the latest mandated banker rehab to chronic problems beginning in the early 1990s, when leaders in the retail banking industry attempted to follow their famous "free toaster" campaign by declaring to all new customers: **"Your checking account is free!"**

Americans quickly opened new accounts, but in time realized that banks had begun sneaking additional charges into every other aspect of their billing practices. The industry ignored complaints as a more lucrative market – "Derivatives" – offered windfall profits. It wasn't until 2007 that CEOs finally hit bottom and again reached out for help. Inspiration and renewed hope came in the form of TARP, the taxpayer-funded bailout. Once again CEOs pledged their commitment to banking sobriety.

Speaking yesterday to reporters, the president of the National Association of Repentant Bankers (NARB) acknowledged "past lapses in judgment" but assured Americans, "Those minor slip-ups are now ancient history." The NARB spokesman ended the press conference with this confident statement: "This land is filled with forgiving patriots. With our marketing experts and recent record profits, we can surely strive to make new promises and restore the nation's faith. Under our new program, there's no place for banking profits to go – but up!" 78

I only understand friendship or scorched earth.

– Roger Ailes
President, Fox News Channel

FOX NEWS

and 'The Liberal Media'

WHEN I WAS growing up in the '60s we had a choice of three TV channels – NBC, ABC or CBS – but around our house there were also stacks of magazines. My parents subscribed to *everything*: the local paper, The Wall Street Journal, Time, The New Yorker, Newsweek, National Geographic and a wide variety of specialty magazines like *P*sychology Today and Popular Science.

I still like the feel of a magazine in my hands and look forward to browsing each of the dozen different magazines that arrive in my mailbox every month.

When I was young, I spent far too many hours watching programs on the three national networks and PBS. As an older adult, I probably still waste too much time watching those same channels, but I also follow cable news on CNN, MSNBC and FOX.

Newspaper circulation has been declining for years, and many boomers now receive the bulk of their information from television. If you look at the Nielsen ratings or other media surveys, you'll find that much of the nation gathers its news from a variety of TV channels.

Over the last 15 years, however, one network has attracted a large and especially loyal U.S. audience: Many devoted Fox News viewers depend almost entirely on Fox for their news. In recent years, approximately 85% of cable, satellite and other service providers offer the Fox News Channel.

In the 1990s, Fox became the dominant U.S. cable news network and still holds that position.

Somehow, many conservatives have come to believe that Fox News is – as its motto claims – a "fair and balanced" source of information, unlike all the other news channels that Fox labels "the liberal media." Fox has done a great job in fostering this misguided notion among viewers, and remains "the most trusted news network," by a wide margin, among conservatives. No one was shocked when News Corp donated $1 million to the Republican Governors Association in 2010.

Over the years, Fox News has consistently denied any bias in its own reporting.

Even when it comes to science, Fox has its own unique perspective. In January 2014, much of the Midwest and East Coast was hit with crippling snowstorms. During the worst part of the cold snap, Fox and Friends host Steve Doocy (along with other Fox pundits) pointed out that the freezing storms should end any debate about "global warming." And in case any listener might question the sincerity of the proclamation, Fox presented a renowned expert – Donald Trump – to pontificate on the subject. Trump did not disappoint. The modest man with the mythical hair assured Americans that global warming was a "hoax" and another "liberal conspiracy to extort good money" from hard-working businessmen.

Frankly, it's embarrassing that Fox is the only news source for many of my fellow countrymen.

It should be self-evident to any objective viewer that Fox serves up a very limited menu of information – most of it presented in a manner meant to stir up emotion rather than civil discussion. It's also true that other cable stations – like MSNBC – have their own slant or bias, but none matches Fox News when it comes to generating more heat than light.

The Best Marketeers in the Business

Rupert Murdoch's news network is run by marketing people who truly understand their audience. Over the years, Fox has followed a very consistent agenda: emphasizing that our country's problems are somehow the fault of "liberals," while praising conservatives as responsible, God-fearing patriots. Fox has also consistently portrayed our current president as a failure on all issues large and small – an unshakable conclusion that Fox pundits began spouting within 90 days of Barack Obama's election.

Roger Ailes, who runs the Fox News Network, keeps the network on point. On many days, the talking points delivered by the various Fox anchors are so similar that it's hard to believe they are not carefully choreographed.

The seasoned veteran is a well-known ultra-conservative who left CNBC for Fox in 1996. He managed to bring along 80 NBC staffers, who then worked directly for him. Mr. Ailes, in turn, worked directly for Robert Murdoch, the Australian media mogul.

Fox's news chief has been active in conservative circles for a very long time – Ailes was a media advisor to Richard Nixon, campaign consultant to Reagan, and trusted political counselor to both Bush presidents.

Ailes has a reputation for taking no prisoners. He is famously quoted as saying: "I only understand friendship or scorched earth." One former top aide to Mr. Ailes described him as a cross between Don Rickles and Don Corleone. True to form, Ailes has a record of responding brutally to anyone who is gutsy enough to challenge his credibility. When journalist Bob Woodward revealed that Ailes was directly advising President George Bush after 911, Ailes publicly railed against Woodward.

It's not surprising that Fox presents a full line-up of talk-show hosts who reflect Ailes' conservative values and combative nature. It's hard to argue with success. Ailes' solid business plan pits Fox against all the other "liberal" networks and cable news channels. Fox has simply outmaneuvered competitors who all scramble to attract an audience from the political middle ground. In effect, Fox cornered the market on the conservative viewpoint. Ratings soared.

The left-of-center slice of the political pie was left for MSNBC, which has its own line-up of "left-wing-leaning" pundits, but when it comes to marketing and ratings, MSNBC is no match for Fox.

The television networks and cable channels are owned by huge corporations and are generally controlled by their boards of directors. Board members are mostly the kind of conservatives who hang out on large estates and country clubs – not exactly crunchy-granola left-wing socialists.

In truth, there's not much to uncover about "the liberal media" – it's not a sensational story. The owners of the so-called "liberal media" are mostly traditional businesspeople whose primary concern is making steady profits for themselves and their stockholders.

Who Are 'The Liberal Media' Vilified on Fox?

First, we have ABC, which is owned by Disney. We are all familiar with The Walt Disney Company – how much more American can a company be? The Disney news operation can hardly be called a hot-bed of left-wing radicals, especially with Diane Sawyer and Charles Gibson as its stars.

Next is NBC, a corporation that was owned by General Electric since the mid-'80s, until GE began a joint venture with NBC Universal (Comcast) in 2011. Recently NBC Universal has taken over ownership. Everyone knows GE – the corporation that manufactures so many of America's light bulbs, refrigerators, locomotives, jet engines and military equipment. Most reasonable people consider GE a mainstream American corporation. Boomer Brian Williams has been the NBC news anchor for 10 years and he personifies the American dream: A good Catholic boy who worked as a busboy and a volunteer fireman, and went on to become a world-famous journalist. Is Brian Williams the secret weapon of the liberal media?

Now let's look at CBS and Summer Redstone, its majority owner. Redstone might be suspect – he has often supported Democrats – but he also publicly supported George Bush for president in 2004, so it would be hard to call him a radical. Scott Pelley is the newest CBS anchor, following Katie Couric's long run – neither can be considered a "mouthpiece" for the left wing.

CNN is owned by Time Warner Corporation, which also owns HBO, Warner Brothers (movie division), and People, Sports Illustrated and Time, all solid American magazines – especially if you consider Sports Illustrated's yearly swimsuit issue. The women in bikinis are stunning, but they are not exactly left-wing propaganda mongers. Even as I write this, Comcast is making a play to take over Time Warner. CNN can be all over the board politically, and sometimes the network seems amateurish, but it's not exactly a haven for radicals.

The sad fact is that all of the big networks are controlled by old WASP-y men who focus on the bottom line, just as Rupert Murdoch and Roger Ailes do at Fox. They are all capitalists. Calling the other networks and their corporate owners "liberal" is just devoid of common sense. With all due deference to Bill O'Reilly and his "***culture warriors***," there are no liberal-media bogeymen trying to kill Christmas, brainwash our children, or "wage war" on religion.

Fox News – More Than Meets the Eye

It is somewhat ironic that Fox viewers feel that their network is the most wholesome and all-American of our available news sources. This reassuring image has been carefully crafted – it's no accident that the American flag constantly waves in the background during Fox newscasts.

In reality, Fox News Corporation is owned by a company controlled by Rupert Murdoch, who was born in Australia and raised in England. Mr. Murdoch heads an international media conglomerate consisting of several hundred companies in 50 different countries. His

News Corporation also controls more than 130 subsidiaries in nations identified as international tax havens by the U.S. Government Accountability Office, including companies in Panama, the Cayman Islands, the Channel Islands, and the Virgin Islands. It has been widely reported that Fox News Corporation's average annual tax rate is less than 15%. News Corps' brand of tax avoidance is not unique among large corporations, but the practice reeks of hypocrisy when compared to the patriotic rhetoric of Fox News commentators.

It's safe to say that Rupert Murdoch and his son, James Murdoch, are much more concerned with profit than any particular ideology or philosophy. For instance, the Murdochs invested $70 million in Vice Media through 21st Century Fox. Vice Media produces an edgy stream of "immersion style" stories that are essentially the antithesis of traditional journalism, and *sponsored* Denis Rodman's junket to North Korea to visit Supreme Leader Kim Jon Un. During this particular trip, Rodman took along NBA players and was promoting a basketball game with the North Korean national team. Vice Media and Rodman hosted a reception at Kim Jon Un's house.

Vice Media co-founder and CEO Shane Smith summed up his own philosophy as follows:

"We are not trying to say anything in a paradigmatic 'left' or 'right' way, because ... I think both sides are horrific. And it doesn't matter anyway. Money runs America; money runs everywhere."

Shane Smith and the Murdochs make interesting bedfellows.

It is also interesting to note that Rupert Murdoch did not become an American citizen until his mid-50s, for legal and business reasons. U.S. law requires that anyone who owns substantial domestic media outlets be a citizen – Murdoch's U.S. citizenship allowed him to control a worldwide media empire. Some years ago, he purchased *The Wall Street Journal*, one of America's oldest and most influential newspapers. Murdoch's conservative influence on the *WSJ* has steadily become more apparent. It could be argued that Murdoch is among the most powerful men in the world. During the past 15 years, Fox News has helped to foster, shape and guide the most conservative wing of the Republican Party.

Murdoch's Juggernaut May Be Losing Steam

In 2012, Murdock testified under oath in the United Kingdom about his "personal knowledge" of his companies' illegal hacking of private and government voicemails. Maybe the 80-year-old was "forgetful" that day, or maybe the widespread phone-hacking practice simply "escaped his attention," but in any event he claimed to have "no knowledge" of illegal activities. Just the same, he later resigned as a director of News International, amid joint investigations by the British government and the FBI into possible bribery and/or corruption. As I write this, Murdoch has been in the news again, trying to buy a major rival, Time Warner, with a bid of $75 billion. I'm skeptical that he'll succeed in his takeover attempt, but his appetite for control of all media is mind-boggling.

Roger Ailes, 74, is beginning to slow down – both Ailes and Bill O'Reilly, who is Fox's biggest star – are starting to resemble "angry old men" who have passed the high point of their careers and are increasingly out of touch with contemporary America.

Fox shareholder Saudi Prince Al Waleed bin Talal

If the ongoing criminal investigations land Murdoch in trouble, he may have to rely more on the second-largest shareholder of Fox News: Saudi Prince Al Waleed bin Talal. The ties between the two men run deep: The prince owns some 55 million shares in Murdoch's news corporation, and Murdoch owns almost 20% of Rotana, the prince's privately held Arab media conglomerate.

Al Waleed bin Talal's company is headquartered in Bahrain, an island nation in the Persian Gulf. Rotana operates a number of free-to-air television channels, owns the largest record label in the Arab world, and controls more than 40% of the region's movie production and distribution.

Whatever Murdoch's ultimate fate, Fox should never be short of funding. Prince Al Waleed bin Talal is the richest man in the Middle East and worth more than $30 billion. He is also the controversial Saudi prince who published this statement only days after 9/11:

"At times like these, we must address some of the issues that led to such a criminal attack. I believe the government of the United States should reexamine its policies in the Middle East and adopt a more balanced stance toward the Palestinian cause."

Simultaneously, the prince gave a $10 million check to Rudy Giuliani, who was then the mayor of New York. "America's mayor" returned the gift intended for his city. It was hard for Giuliani, or anyone else, to find much loyalty to America in the Saudi prince's statement about 9/11.

Al Waleed bin Talal is also a major shareholder in the SRMG, the largest media company in the Middle East, and is generally considered the most influential Arab in the world.

Unusual shareholders

Suffice to say, Murdoch and Prince Al Waleed bin Talal are not exactly Norman Rockwell material, and make an odd couple as Fox's largest shareholders. Roger Ailes continues to be a truly gifted marketeer and runs a tight ship, so the Fox News Channel should remain a strong force in carefully targeted news and conservative politics for the foreseeable future. The "most fair and balanced news in America" now runs deep in the boomer psyche. ■

Rupert Murdoch

Prince Al Waleed bin Talal

Roger Ailes, President, Fox News

More Heat Than Light

This predominately boomer family of pundits (average age 57) comprises individuals who are outspoken and command a huge audience. Their collective messages (via television, radio, the internet and print) reach more than 50 million Americans weekly. To a person, this homogeneous group emphasizes a "non-elitist" message and claims to understand what's right for "the average American." Using the word "average" may be a bit of a stretch since each of these superstar pundits hardly lives on an average income. While Limbaugh and O'Reilly earn over $20 million, the *average* annual compensation to each member in this group is easily north of $2 million. It's safe to say that in the past decade this bunch has "raised the heat" on political discourse in America. These fine folk are true believers, and, moreover, they are well compensated to keep their ratings high and the pot boiling. *Hard to argue with success!*

PATRIOTS
Riding High Horses

CONVENTIONAL wisdom has it that "each generation grows more conservative with age." Judging by boomer viewership of the political pundits shown at left, my generation confirms the adage.

During the past 15 years, a small group of broadcast personalities has emerged as the "most watched," and arguably the most influential, in America. Each of these media stars wears patriotism on their sleeve. The group is generally united in their view that America has an intrinsic claim to the world's highest moral ground, which often includes "a Christian interpretation" of the U.S. Constitution. Good, bad or indifferent, this group has a significant influence on the political and social views of our nation.

The following is a quick review of these patriot-pundits, who collectively have the ear of more than 50 million Americans each week.

Ditto-Head Patriotism

In 1988, The Rush Limbaugh Show became nationally syndicated. The colorful Mr. Limbaugh stars on the highest-rated talk show in the United States., his huge radio audience is almost entirely white and about 80% male. Clear Channel extended the show from 2008 through 2016 by offering Mr. Limbaugh a $400 million contract.

Mr. Limbaugh calls his followers "ditto-heads." The radio host and his sizable band of followers regularly bubble over with indignation about America's rightful place in the world. Some of Mr. Limbaugh's comments are often provocative, but mainstream Republican politicians dare not challenge Limbaugh because he's proven to be a very powerful force on the conservative political scene.

Other popular commentators who seem to share a similar world view include Bill O'Reilly, Sean Hannity, Sarah Palin, Ann Coulter, Larry Kudlow, Michael Savage, Glenn Beck and Alex Jones. All of these media celebrities have their own large number of devotees, and carefully bathe their followers in patriotic rhetoric extolling America's exceptionalism.

O'Reilly's Connection to the Holy Spirit

The top pundit at Fox News is Bill O'Reilly. He's in a league of his own. Fox News' biggest star routinely commands the highest market share among shows on cable TV channels. He claims that all of his work is part of God's plan to "use my special gifts in a positive fashion." In a 60 Minutes interview with Norah O'Donnell, he related how he "woke up in the middle of the night and received a message directly from the Holy Spirit," telling him to write his latest book, Killing Jesus.

Mr. O'Reilly often decries "the liberal media," and has remarked that "Fox News is good for America." He styles himself a "moderate conservative," and in fact he may be moderate if you compare his views with those of two fellow Fox pundits, Sean Hannity and Ann Coulter.

Anyone who has watched O'Reilly over time knows that he can be heavy-handed or a downright bully. He often interrupts, talking over his guests even though they have been invited to participate. Sometimes he simply tells his participants to "Shut up."

Like Fox's other pundits, Mr. O'Reilly makes no attempt to mask his disdain of the incumbent U.S. president. O'Reilly has dubbed his devoted TV and radio audience "culture warriors" and continually warns them about the dangers of Obama's ongoing socialist agenda.

The man who controls what he calls the "No Spin Zone" also spouted this gem: "My advice to all homosexuals, whether they're in the Boy Scouts, or in the Army or in high school: Shut up, don't tell anybody what you do – your life will be a lot easier."

Fox "News" Pummels Our President 24/7/365

Other Fox commentators follow in O'Reilly's footsteps: The handsome **Sean Hannity** has similar views to O'Reilly's, but Hannity is openly mean-spirited, displaying his utter disgust for President Obama on his daily broadcast. **Sarah Palin**, the darling of the Tea Party, was re-signed by Fox. The network and Palin have reconciled previous differences and now she's back in Fox formation.

Ann Coulter is another Fox regular who doesn't mince words. After 9/11 but before President Bush's invasion of Iraq, Coulter published this declaration: "We know who the homicidal maniacs are. They are the ones cheering and dancing right now. We should invade their countries, kill their leaders and convert them to Christianity." During the Iraq War, she claimed, "President Bush will go down in history as one of America's greatest presidents." Ms. Coulter is also a strong proponent of the "more guns, less crime" point of view, and suggests that more Americans should carry concealed weapons.

Ironically, on the topic of women's involvement in politics, Ms. Coulter seems to agree with Rush Limbaugh, who for years referred to "liberal women" as femi-Nazis. From Ms. Coulter comes this charming sentiment: "It would be much better if women did not vote. That is simply a fact. In every presidential election since 1950 – except Goldwater in 1964 – the Republicans would have won, if only men had voted. If we took away women's right to vote, we'd never have to worry about another Democrat president."

Business and Politics

CNBC (the Comcast/NBC "business channel") is broadcast into 85% of American homes with cable TV and has a worldwide viewing audience of about 400 million. Over the last 20 years, the channel has become increasingly influential in analyzing and passing judgment on trends in U.S. business and the American economy.

Larry Kudlow, Rick Santelli and a boomer crew of conservative stock-market analysts operate under the banner of "First in Business, Worldwide." As a group, they generally espouse, above all else, free-market capitalism. Kudlow and Santelli are openly scornful toward "anything liberal." It's no surprise that CNBC is 100% pro-business – almost all of its commentators and guests have Wall Street backgrounds and incessantly deliver their "businessman's perspective."

In 2007, Rupert Murdoch indicated that CNBC was not business friendly enough. Accordingly, he launched the Fox Business Network and promised it would be more pro-business. In keeping with that promise, Fox features **Neil Cavuto, Stuart Varney** and other anchors who are unabashedly ultra-conservative. Varney's been a main staple on Fox for more than a decade, and recently raised a few eyebrows when he criticized Pope Francis for questioning "trickle-down economics." Mr. Varney also indicated that it would be wrong to raise the minimum wage because of "moral reasons," since many workers who currently earn $7.25 per hour may not "deserve" a higher wage. The fact that $7.25 per hour is not a "livable wage" appears to be irrelevant.

The Successful Fringe

Michael Savage, a nationally syndicated radio personality, spews his vitriol at anything connected to Democrats. Born Michael Weiner, he changed his name and created The Savage Nation daily talk show. By 2009 he commanded upward of 10 million listeners on 375 radio stations across the United States. Mr. Savage also gained America's attention with his book Liberalism Is a Mental Disorder. If you listen to his broadcasts, you know he means what he's written. He refers to his philosophy as "conservative nationalism."

Former Fox News host **Glenn Beck** is a man who has often encouraged his viewers and radio listeners to buy gold and "survival seeds." For several years, Beck was Fox's darling – until he told a national audience that President Obama "has a deep-seated hatred for white people and their culture." Fox News had to reduce the advertising rates on Beck's show, as he became a little too wacky and embarrassing for some Fox sponsors.

The parting of Glenn Beck and Fox was not exactly amicable, but Beck then turned his focus to his radio show. The Associated Press reported that Beck signed a five-year, $100 million contract with Premiere Networks. With more than 400 stations carrying his radio program, Beck still has the ear of a sizable following.

In 2013, Mr. Beck proposed building ***Independence USA,*** his own Ayn Rand-inspired utopian city. Beck estimated he could construct the project for approximately $2 billion dollars. However, as I write this, Beck has yet to find that his idealized free market is beating a path to his door.

The prize for the most intense talk show host should go to **Alex Jones**. Jones describes himself as both a conservative and a libertarian and on many issues agrees with Ron Paul, his long-time friend.

Once an unsuccessful Republican candidate for Texas state representative, Jones entered the winner's circle with the Alex Jones Radio Show and was syndicated on more than 100 radio stations. He now has an estimated audience of more than two million listeners.

But Mr. Jones shines brightest on the internet – his online presence is greater than Rush Limbaugh's and Glenn Beck's combined. His most popular websites are Infowars.com and PrisonPlanet.com, but his YouTube channel also does well, so far receiving a total of about 300 million views.

After 9/11, Jones began to speculate that our own government had probably been part of a conspiracy that planned and carried out the 9/11 terrorist attacks, and today he remains the leading marketeer of general right-wing paranoia. For example, he has headed a drive to have Piers Morgan deported because Morgan openly supports gun control. Jones had a meltdown on Morgan's CNN show, claiming Obama was some sort of foreigner out to "take our guns and enslave us."

Alex Jones's Infowars.com website may appear a bit creepy to the average web viewer, but the site's online store is a dream come true for survivalists. This week's specials include a "survival seed vault" and "Tyrant Obama" T-shirts. Seriously.

A Night Karl Rove Would Like To Forget

For more than a decade, **Karl Rove** had been considered "the architect" of conservative strategy. As a Fox News commentator (and George Bush's former key political advisor), he assured his national TV audience that Obama would lose the 2012 presidential election, primarily because Obama was "so out of touch with America." During the 2012 Republican presidential primaries, Mr. Rove claimed that any of the better candidates could beat President Obama, and after Romney won the nomination, Rove confidently predicted that Republicans would regain the White House.

It is interesting to note that – as the senior political analyst for Fox News – Rove failed to discuss the "FiveThirtyEight" polling in the run-up to the 2012 election. Rove knew that this poll had produced the most accurate forecast of the 2008 election results. As the chief strategist in Republican politics, Rove was well aware in the weeks before the 2012 election that this reliable poll was trending heavily toward Obama, giving him a two-to-one chance of winning.

On election night, Rove remained in denial as he collided with a reality he couldn't spin. He sat at his Fox News desk, staring white-faced into the camera like a shell-shocked Pillsbury doughboy. Even after the Fox number-crunchers called Ohio for Obama early on, Rove remained defiant until the end.

Rove's financial supporters who backed his super-PAC to the tune of $300 million were probably more than a little irritated. But win or lose, it was always going to be a great payday for Karl Rove.

Some of my conservative friends told me they were depressed in the days after the election, because they felt Rove and Fox News had misled them about Romney's "almost certain victory," and because they had developed a strong disdain for America's re-elected president.

I could sympathize – the election defeat would be especially hard for Fox loyalists who watched only Fox, where their favorite and most trusted pundits gave them the news and also warned them that the president was at the very least un-American, and more likely a radical socialist.

After the election, Rove seemed to disappear from Fox for a short time and in his absence received some flak for his political "mis-analyses." Rove seemed to be going through a bad spell, as he had at least twice before in his long career as a very successful and durable political operator.

Rove's former buddy and fundraiser, the lobbyist Jack Abramoff, was sent to prison in 2006 for his role in the K-Street scandal, convicted on charges that included fraud and illegal channeling of campaign funds. Abramoff had implicated Rove and Rove's senior advisor, Susan Ralston. Ralston resigned, shielding Rove from the heat. Another bad spell occurred when attorney Scooter Libby seemed to take the heat for Rove, when Libby was convicted of a felony in the Valerie Plame scandal. Rove has always had a good coat of Teflon.

In recent years you might say that Rove has evolved into the proverbial Texan with a big hat and no cattle, a "political expert" who has been consistently irrelevant for eight years running. And yet Karl Rove always seems to bounce back, which must be why Fox News continues to pay him a boatload of cash. Fox regulars still praise him as the "high priest" of the Republican Party, and Rove remains the "deep thinker" on Rupert Murdoch's network.

In 2013, Fox seemed to be going back to the future with Karl Rove and Sarah Palin.

Reactionary Rhetoric Unlikely To Soften

When I hear most of these conservative media figures turn to the subject of religion, their words reveal that they give little thought to the facts that Christians represent only about a third of the world's religious followers, or that a significant group of Americans don't share their interpretation about what it means to have "Christian values."

There seems to be no end to ultra-conservatives in our country who cherish the days when the old white men went completely unchallenged and had total control of the nation's steering wheel.

The conservative pundits wax on nostalgically about our Founding Fathers, or the glory days of Ronald Reagan's America. Many seem to want to return to an era that never truly existed. And even if it did, it would hardly be relevant in today's world.

Perhaps it is time for the grumpy old men in my generation (on both sides of the aisle) to loosen their grip on the steering wheel. ■

You have to know the past
to understand the present.

– **Carl Sagan**
Cosmologist

U.S. History – Not a Disney Story

I'M EXTREMELY PROUD of our country and would be the first to say that America is one of the best places in the world to live. Americans enjoy tremendous personal freedom, and their civil rights are guaranteed and protected by law. In some countries, I might end up in jail for some of the things I've said in these pages. That's why my favorite holiday has always been the Fourth of July.

Our Declaration of Independence (1776) is a truly inspired document that can bring tears to your eyes, especially when you hear the following section from the preamble read aloud:

"We hold these truths to be self-evident, that all men are created equal, that they are endowed by their Creator with certain unalienable Rights, that among these are Life, Liberty and the pursuit of Happiness."

The U.S. Constitution was ratified a decade later, followed by the first 10 Bill of Rights and 17 amendments, including those that ended slavery and gave women the right to vote.

There are also about 25 "landmark decisions" by the Supreme Court that can substantially change the interpretation of existing law. Landmark decisions have radically affected American life, from segregation to sex-based discrimination to gun control.

There are those who point out that America is actually a "constitutional republic" and not a true democracy, but I've chosen to use the term "democracy" because it is generally accepted when describing our form of government.

In any event, most constitutional scholars agree that the U.S. Constitution is a "living document," and the principles that it sets out in these documents are the foundation of America's democratic form of government and the American way of life, even though we live in a world none of our Founding Fathers could have foreseen.

History is always evolving. Winton Churchill's famous quote that "History is written by the victors" rings true. The political and religious leaders who controlled the printing of books (including the Bible) and those who later controlled the media, generally presented history to be more palatable or more consistent with their own ideology. In 2014, the Texas Board of Education approved "updated textbooks" that include more emphasis on the influence of Moses on the U.S. Constitution.

Growing Pains

America is a great and admirable experiment – no other major country in the world has, from its founding, embraced the spirit of democracy so strongly as central to its national character.

Yet, while there have been many triumphs in our short history as a nation, we've also had our share of regrettable chapters:

- Our ancestors – in the name of God – put men and women to death who they believed were witches.
- Our leaders sent soldiers to disperse or even wipe out countless Native Americans whose ancestors had inhabited this land long before any Europeans arrived. Our government later confined generations of Native American tribes to reservations in desolate regions, far from their ancestral homes.
- For a long time our forefathers found it acceptable to own other human beings. Our government allowed African-Americans to be kept in bondage because slavery seemed a pragmatic and profitable avenue to economic success and the development of an open continent. People may argue about the underlying causes of the Civil War, but no one can deny that a huge portion of America's pre-1861 GNP was based on an economic model dependent upon slave labor.
- During World War II the U.S. government placed Japanese-American citizens in internment camps and confiscated their possessions without due process. Released at the end of the war, these internees and their descendants waited five decades to receive any compensation.
- American women had to fight for their right to vote, which wasn't granted until passage of the 19th Amendment to the Constitution in 1919.

Civil Rights an evolving struggle

In 1958, a black man by the name of James Wilson was convicted by an all-white jury for stealing $1.95 from Estelle Barker, a 74-year old white woman, and sentenced to death. The Alabama Supreme Court upheld the conviction. Wilson was electrocuted.

I was 9 years old at the time and I remember it being discussed in my home.

Seems like it was only yesterday that Jackie Robinson was allowed to play Major League baseball and Americans began to integrate our public schools. I can still remember sitting beside my dad as we watched – on live TV – Martin Luther King Jr.'s famous 1963 "I Have a Dream" speech, delivered from the Lincoln Memorial's steps in our nation's Capitol. I also remember watching scenes of

National Guard troops holding back crowds of screaming white people so a few black children could enter a school.

It's not hard to understand why these memories remain painful for many Americans. If those scenes are still vivid in my mind, they're surely much more deeply etched in the minds of African-Americans who suffered racism firsthand.

Even in 2014, I heard comments here in California and in Texas that lead me to believe that many of my fellow citizens haven't adjusted to the growing ethnic diversity of modern America.

I often hear people suggest that black Americans should just get over their sensitivity to racism, and it makes me wonder how these same people might feel if their ancestors had been brought to America in chains and sold into slavery.

Not long ago, I was having breakfast with Jim Agee, who was sitting at the table shopping for a restored hot rod on his iPad, when he suddenly said:

"Hey, listen to this – here's a guy on eBay with a restored '67 Chevy Nova. It's in cherry condition, but the car only has the 283 engine and not the 327. The seller has an active blog about the car, and some guy just wrote and asked why he thinks the car has not sold sooner and if the smaller 283 engine is the issue. Here's how the seller responded –"

(The word-for-word exchange, on eBay, between the potential buyer and the seller, dated 1/4/2014)

> **Question:** I've been looking for the right car for a year and keep seeing your car come back every few months, I would have tried to buy already with a true 327, curious why this car hasn't sold. C. Thornton
>
> **Answer:** Reason it hasn't sold is because some dumb asses voted in a Muslim president and his job is to bankrupt this nation. Some say he's not doing a good job, but he is doing a good job for our enemies. The economy is shot. If it was in Bush's time I would have gotten my original asking price of $35,000. This is a killer car always in one family and never any rust. Drives new. Thanks

In recent years I still see pickup trucks in the South with Confederate flag decals on the rear windows. Apparently some of our fellow citizens haven't yet dealt with the outcome of the Civil War, which the Confederacy lost almost 150 years ago. When I've asked about the decals, I've been told that they're merely a show of "Southern pride." But that's not consistent with the comments I hear as a white boy in the midst of other white boys.

Whether in Texas, California or other states – old attitudes die hard.

U.S. leaders: exceptional, but human

America's revered founders were a small group of brilliant and exceptional men. However, when we take off the Disneyesque filter, we see that some of them were no less manipulative than many of our modern-day politicians. Some of the signers of the Declaration of Independence owned slaves, frolicked outside the confines of their marriages, and were no strangers to playing hardball politics.

In a parallel way, many of our 20th century presidents weren't exactly role models for "family values."

Franklin D. Roosevelt and Dwight Eisenhower (both married) had lengthy affairs with other women. President Kennedy was a practiced womanizer who had numerous affairs, including a long-running secret relationship with a college girl who waited for him in hotel rooms when he traveled. President Johnson reportedly fathered a child outside his marriage. His former press secretary commented in his biography of Johnson, "LBJ has the instincts of a Turkish sultan in Istanbul." President Clinton tarnished the image of the presidency and lessened his effectiveness as a leader – the price he paid for oral sex with a young female staffer, acts he vehemently claimed were not sex.

President Nixon was not a philanderer, but he was a mean-spirited S.O.B. who ordered his political team to break into Democratic headquarters to gather campaign information. He continually lied about his involvement in the Watergate scandal and finally left the White House in disgrace to escape impeachment. Even the beloved President Reagan had his flaws: He refused to mention the word "AIDS" because he thought the epidemic was a gay disease and therefore not worthy of his public attention.

Frenemies

Over the decades our government has consistently cozied up to repellent dictators anytime our leaders imagined it was in our best political, military or economic interest.

We can all remember the photo of Donald Rumsfeld shaking hands with Saddam Hussein during the Reagan era. Rumsfeld facilitated the Iraqi strongman's access to both chemical and biological weapons for Saddam's war against Iran.

Ronald Reagan famously invited Afghan Mujahideen leaders into the Oval Office in 1983 and it was Reagan who stated their case, with the network cameras rolling: "These men are the moral equivalent of our Founding Fathers." Reagan's positive appraisal seems out of focus – as soon as the Soviets left Afghanistan, the Mujahideen leaders began infighting. They certainly never shared our American values and soon were confronted by, or integrated into, the organization we now know as the Taliban.

The Iran-Contra affair of the mid-'80s – when we secretly sold rockets to Iran to fund the Contras in Nicaragua's civil war – was another sad episode in our history. Marine Lieutenant Colonel Oliver North was indicted on 16 felony counts and convicted on three.

During the televised Senate hearings, North admitted that he had previously committed perjury when he testified before a congressional committee. The charges against North included other illegal activities. North worked for years to technically clear his name and resurrect his reputation. These days he occasionally appears on Fox News as a political commentator and military analyst.

Strange, how the world turns.

Since 1960 our nation has engaged in a string of questionable conflicts in regions ranging from Cuba to Central America to Vietnam and Cambodia. America is the world's largest provider of weapons of war. We sell arms to anyone we think can wage war against our enemies, at least in the short term. Our military/industrial complex is a well-oiled money-making machine that profits most during wartime.

Gaps and All – America Stands Tall

Notwithstanding the above, it would be unfair to judge America by the gaps between our ideals and our actions. You can't define America by her mistakes or poor judgment because they aren't a true reflection of the totality of our past, including the many heroic and honorable actions we've taken on as a nation, often against great odds. Anyone can point out similar (and worse) inconsistencies in the history of any nation.

It's difficult to keep in touch with the past because America's collective consciousness is re-booted and adjusted on a 24-hour news cycle.

It's tough to keep a balanced perspective on current events.

Certainly when we consider America's more recent history of foreign policy, it seems clear that our military engagements have had limited success and resulted in unintended consequences. In the 50 years I've been watching, our national priorities have continually driven us towards military conflict rather than patient diplomacy.

President Eisenhower's 1960 warning about the ever-growing power of the military/industrial complex was prophetic, and has become our reality.

It's a dilemma that boomers will pass on to the next generation. ■

Top: Hovering U.S. Army helicopters pour machine-gun fire into a tree line to cover the advance of South Vietnamese ground troops in an attack near the Cambodian border in 1965.

Bottom left: Our troops were young – the average age of our infantry was 22.

Bottom right: The war ended on April 30, 1975, when Saigon was evacuated of American civilian personnel and tens of thousands of South Vietnamese civilians associated with the Southern regime. It was the largest helicopter evacuation in history.

The Vietnam War

UP THROUGH the ninth grade, everything in my little world seemed to be "life as usual" in America, but during my high school years, it started to change. America's involvement in Vietnam escalated and the conflict became front and center as I started to see my friends and even some families divide into two opposing camps about the war.

In the late '60s and early '70s, it was not uncommon during the course of a conversation to learn whether the person you were talking to was "for" or "against" the war. Discussions about Vietnam quickly became divisive. As the fighting overseas heated up and American and Vietnamese casualties mounted, battles often raged between college students and their conservative parents. Across America, lines were drawn and sides were taken. All through high school I listened to others, watched and read about the war.

The War Changes America

By the late 1960s, while the Vietnam War continued to escalate, a significant portion of college students began to spend more of their time at anti-establishment venues like rock concerts, where it was easy to escape with like-minded spirits. The West Coast was a hotbed of youthful counterculture activities culminating in 1967's "Summer of Love." The epicenter of what the media called "a national movement" was located in the famous Haight-Ashbury district of San Francisco.

The country was beginning to tear itself in half. Many young people were demanding peace and wanted no part of the war, but most Americans still seemed to be fine with guns and butter. Ironically, two common threads often connecting some college students and soldiers in Vietnam were the drugs in their bloodstreams and the rock music that filled their ears.

I attended many counterculture gatherings, especially rock concerts, but I had no real interest in experimenting with drugs or becoming a hippie. I also had no interest in joining the armed forces and shipping off to a foreign country to fight a war that I didn't understand. I was still a kid, torn by what I saw and read, and bothered by the growing hostility in my own country, which was now often a conflict between generations.

A controversial involvement

It was a strange time. While many of the boys my own age were going off to war, many others like me stayed home, receiving college deferments and going about their normal lives. My friends and I sat in the college cafeteria with our girlfriends, sipping milkshakes. Young men who didn't have money or the high school grades to attend college soon found themselves conscripted into the military and sent to the jungles of Vietnam. There, many suffered life-altering physical and emotional wounds or lost their lives.

America's involvement in Vietnam had its beginnings in the mid-1950s after the French lost a civil war in their former colony, French Indochina. The wisdom of our subsequent involvement has been debated for years, and remains controversial.

By the late 1960s, America had some 550,000 soldiers stationed in Vietnam. The U.S. justification for increased military involvement was also hotly debated. President Johnson used two incidents of North Vietnamese attacks on U.S. forces to push through the Gulf of Tonkin Resolution (1964), which led to our full involvement in what had, up to then, been a civil war. Some of our top military leaders – and former President Eisenhower – joined concerned U.S. senators in warning about the perils of the States engaging in a prolonged conflict in the jungles of Southeast Asia – but to no avail.

The war ended officially in 1975, when the U.S. evacuated our embassy in Saigon. All of the remaining American civilians and tens of thousands of South Vietnamese civilians left, leaving behind a tragic state of affairs.

Before the United States even left Vietnam, many of my friends who had fought there came home to a country where many of the kids their own age – as well as growing numbers of older Americans – were actively protesting the war. The returning veterans were not greeted with the respect they deserved. These were men who had risked their lives on behalf of our country. Nineteen- and 20-year-old boys had gone to fight, many of them voluntarily enlisting but many others drafted, with little choice in the matter. The dubious war had turned into a gut-wrenching quagmire.

The protests to the war grew in the spring of 1970 as Nixon launched the bombing and the invasion of Cambodia, and American colleges erupted in protest, especially after National Guard troops shot and killed student protesters at Kent State University in Ohio. That summer, after my first year in college, the government held a national draft lottery drawing on network television in an effort to make the draft seem more equitable.

I sat in a room with a group of college buddies as we watched the dates called off. Some were "lucky" and some were not. I happened to receive a draft number that ensured I'd never be called into service. On one day, with one lottery drawing, my life changed. I was spared having to fight in the war of my generation – I felt both guilty and sad when I thought of young men who would go off to war due to – literally – the luck of the draw.

Forty Years Later

The war is still a sensitive issue with many boomers. In the '60s, most soldiers and civilians knew only what our government told them. And like most wars, the real story morphed into a more palatable tale over time, in keeping with patriotic and/or political purposes. But the Vietnam War did not reflect well on our government, even though our soldiers did their dangerous jobs bravely, under terrible conditions.

Decades after the war in Vietnam had come to a close, the U.S. military declassified many official documents from the '60s and '70s. In 2007, our National Security Agency (NSA) concluded that the North Vietnamese "turning-point incident" in the Gulf of Tonkin that our government used to justify going to war never actually took place. This did not come as a big surprise to the millions of Americans who had protested the war.

From my personal perspective, I saw the Vietnam War tear into the fabric of our country. From 1965 to 1973, I saw what it did to my friends who went off to fight, and what it did to my friends who stayed home and were enraged by our government's escalation of the war.

As part of the research for the novel I was writing for my Cal Poly English class in 1969, I made it a point to talk with men who were actually serving in Vietnam. Most of the soldiers that I talked to during my stay in Thailand were on R&R leave in Bangkok, and I engaged them in conversation in the bars and waiting rooms of massage parlors. There was an ever-growing sex trade in Bangkok, all set up to service American soldiers during their short breaks from the war in Vietnam. A section of the city offered block after block of bars and sex shows. I was 19 and the scene was somewhat shocking. It was an unexpected eye-opener, because the U.S. media had essentially ignored the Southeast Asian sex trade, which had become an institutionalized part of the war.

Visit to Saigon

When I visited Saigon after leaving Thailand, I quickly realized that it was not Bangkok. It was a war zone, and the MPs and soldiers were all armed. I was still determined to gather information for my book, so I approached some of the soldiers who looked about my age. They were generally willing to talk, but very few were inclined to discuss the politics of the war. They did describe openly some of the horrific scenes they had witnessed, the craziness of the war and drug use. Most of them knew the exact count of days before they could come home.

When I arrived at my "hotel" in downtown Saigon, I was advised by the Vietnamese man at the front counter to place my passport and traveler's checks in the hotel safe. I was nervous because it was a small dive-hotel, and the man at the counter barely spoke English. He said my passport would not be safe in my room, so I did as he requested. On the day I left, I paid for the room and asked for my passport. The hotel clerk acted like he had no idea what I was talking about. I asked to see the manager, and another man came through the door behind the counter. He was younger, had the same story, and told me to leave. I started to get angry – until a third man came through the door and I thought better of it.

There was an American MP on nearly every street in downtown Saigon, so I figured I'd better go find one and ask for help. The first MP I found wanted nothing to do with me, and told me to go to the American embassy. I walked another block and spotted another MP, and asked him for help. I showed him my Stanford Research Institute ID and explained what had happened to my passport.

"Yeah," he said, "I know those people."

We went back to the hotel and the MP told me to stand in the corner of the tiny lobby while he stepped to the front counter. The MP began speaking in Vietnamese to the clerk, the same man I had complained to only minutes earlier, before his associates became involved. Now those two men appeared again. I had no idea what was being said, but the conversation quickly became heated. There was a pause, and suddenly the MP banged his rifle on the counter, cocked his weapon and motioned for two of the men to stand against the wall as the third man disappeared.

It was tense. We all stood in silence for less than a minute and the third man came back and placed my passport and traveler's checks on the counter. The MP grabbed the items and told me to walk out the front door, as he backed out and followed me. We walked at a fast pace down the street and the MP hailed a cab, gave me my passport and checks, and told the cab driver to take me straight to the airport.

I waited for hours at the airport – my original flight had been canceled. I managed to buy a seat on a flight to Hong Kong, for what seemed a very high price. The small plane was packed with Vietnamese carrying their clothes and other possessions in cloth bags that spilled into the center aisle. I peed in a bottle during the flight. No one spoke English – not even the pilot when he made announcements over the intercom.

I felt ashamed of myself, because it hit me that I was a naïve college kid who had no business being in Saigon, and no one from my family even knew where I was. By the time the plane landed in Hong Kong, I'd had time to reflect on just how badly I had screwed up.

Overview

The Vietnam War was costly in every sense of the word.

- Our nation spent more than $140 billion ($650 billion, adjusted for inflation) before the conflict was over.
- Approximately eight million men served in the U.S. military during the course of the war in Vietnam.
- There are varying estimates about the total loss of life, but we know that 58,000 young Americans died, and another 300,000 were wounded. Thousands of our soldiers returned with post-traumatic stress disorder, or illnesses stemming from exposure to Agent Orange, for which they didn't receive the medical care they deserved.
- No one knows for sure, but it is estimated that one million North Vietnam soldiers died. Estimates of Vietnamese civilian deaths range from between one and two million.

It seems to me that a long list of old men – mostly politicians with various axes to grind – misled our country about the nature and progress of the Vietnam conflict. These old men sent millions of our young men off to fight a questionable war for more than a decade. ■

Another Kind of Casualty

Most of us still vividly remember a special childhood friend, the one we trusted with our youthful secrets, who was outside our family circle and without judgment understood and accepted our personal flaws.

Larry Leslie was that friend to me.

I admired Larry. He was always smarter, stronger and better-looking. When we hiked in Big Sur, he could climb much faster, but he always slowed down and waited for me along the trail, without saying a word. We were best friends from about ages 9 until 17. I always figured Larry would grow up to be a famous athlete, or a professional race car driver like his dad.

Larry's 1967 Carmel High School yearbook photo

Larry's actual fate turned out to be a heart-breaker and remains a mystery to me.

I lost track of Larry after we lived together in Monterey the summer before I started college. One day he phoned to let me know that he was going to enlist in the military, but he didn't say much else. He didn't call again or write, but a couple of years later I found out from a mutual friend that he had been shipped off to Vietnam.

After that I only talked with Larry once, by phone, after he came home from his first tour of duty. The person on the other end of the line had changed from the boy I knew. I barely recognized his voice. Larry talked in disjointed phrases, about "the killing," about "gooks," and about how no one understood "the real story." He was not friendly and didn't seem inclined to chat about old times. He ended our brief conversation by saying that he was "going back" and that he'd look me up when he returned to "the world."

A few years passed, until one day I ran into a young woman in Carmel, a girl Larry and I had known in 10th grade. In the course of a short conversation, I learned that Larry had died the year before, after returning from Vietnam.

Our talk grew awkward. The woman seemed reluctant to share much about his death, other than to say it was a tragedy. Perhaps she was uncertain of the details, or simply wanted to spare me some unpleasant truth. Afterward, I didn't have the heart to call Larry's parents, who had divorced. I didn't know Larry's brother very well, and so after all those years I did not expect to hear from anyone in his family. I had to let it go.

It's now 45 years later. I know that my friend did not die in Vietnam, but the war tragically altered the course of his life. To my knowledge, you will not find the name "Larry Leslie" on any war memorial. Larry was a young man who served our country and returned home to America and somehow fell between the cracks, long before his time. ■

Iraq War 2003-2012

The Shock and Awe air campaign began on March 21, 2003. The spectacular bombardment was watched on worldwide television. The first night of bombing was part of a broader attack that sent 1,000 strike sorties against targets into the Iraq cities of Baghdad, Kirkuk and Mosul.

Over 2,000 guided missiles were dropped during the first four days of bombing, averaging 500 missiles every 24 hours.
Source: U.S. Air Force Magazine

Left: President and Commander-in-Chief George W. Bush, on the deck of the *U.S.S. Abraham Lincoln*

President Bush:
"Major combat operations in Iraq have ended. In the battle of Iraq, the United States and our allies have prevailed."
From his speech delivered under a "Mission Accomplished" banner on the *U.S.S. Lincoln* aircraft carrier, May 2, 2003

The Iraq War

I HAVE ALWAYS been proud of the men and women who have served and who continue to serve in America's military forces. We have freedom because of those who gave their lives in the past to honor their country.

As I grow older, my sense of gratitude grows deeper for all the young men and women who chose to enlist in our military services to risk their lives to defend our country.

In our democratic system of government, it's our civilian leaders who determine when and where to use military force. It's always been "the older men" – the politicians – who decide when and where to send our younger men into harm's way. The war in Iraq is "officially" over – but I was struck by the comments of one American citizen who offered a unique perspective about our nation's decision to fight the Iraq war.

On a plane flight to Houston in 2012, I sat next to an articulate young man who looked to be in his mid-20s. Our polite exchanges soon turned into a long conversation during which I discovered that he was born in Iraq but had become a U.S. citizen in his early teenage years.

I gathered that he was from an affluent family who had emigrated from Iraq sometime in the late '90s, several years before the conflict. He had graduated from a university on the East Coast, and was on his way to Houston to visit his sister. Toward the end of our conversation, I asked him what he thought about the Iraq War.

He seemed to be taken aback by the question, and I could see that he was hesitant to answer. At first he spoke in an almost apologetic fashion, but then grew more comfortable as he shared his reflections about the war. In summary, here's what he told me:

The young man explained that he thought it would be difficult for Americans to put themselves in Iraqi shoes, because over the past 10 years 100,000 Iraqi civilians had died and much of the population had been traumatized. He said the Iraqi children were the most affected. Everyone who his family knew in Iraq had personally suffered the loss of someone – a friend, a family member, a sweetheart or a business associate.

His father had told him many times that most Iraqi people hated Saddam Hussein, but he remembered that day-to-day life in Iraq was generally peaceful when he was growing up – it was safe to walk down the street and shop at the neighborhood market.

His father had told him that Hussein never cared about religion, but kept the different religious factions from causing trouble. He told me he was concerned because today there was a new generation of young men in Iraq who disliked America, blaming the U.S. for the current problems in their country. He said he was always puzzled about why America had invaded and felt that the invasion had ended up strengthening Iran's increased influence on Iraq, which he felt posed an additional threat and uncertainty. He emphasized that the fighting between Sunnis and Shiites has gone on for centuries and would probably resume as soon as the U.S. pulled out. He paused and then sighed: "the U.S. invasion of Iraq was a tragedy for all concerned." The young man was reluctant to discuss details about his personal life, except to say he doubted that he would ever again return to Iraq. He mentioned that his sister was very happy living in Houston and they were both proud to be U.S. citizens.

In Their Own Words

Cheney Rumsfeld
Nixon administration, 1971

Cheney Rumsfeld
Bush administration, 2004

Vice President Dick Cheney: "Simply stated, there is no doubt that Saddam Hussein now has weapons of mass destruction. ...Every analysis said this war itself would cost about $80 billion. Recovery of Baghdad, perhaps of Iraq, about $10 billion per year. We should expect as American citizens that this would cost at least $100 billion for a two-year involvement. We will be greeted as liberators ... I think it will go relatively quickly, in weeks, rather than months." *(From an interview on 8/26/2002; and on* Meet the Press *3/16/2003, only days prior to the invasion of Iraq)*

Secretary of Defense Donald Rumsfeld: "I can't tell you if the use of force in Iraq today would last five days, or five weeks, or five months, but it certainly isn't going to last any longer than that." *(From an interview on 11/14/2002, with Steve Croft on CBS)*

Deputy Defense Secretary Paul Wolfowitz: "There's a lot of money to pay for this ... the oil revenues of that country could bring between $50 billion and $100 billion over the course of the next two or three years.... We're dealing with a country that can really finance its own reconstruction, and relatively soon." *(From an interview on 3/27/2003)*

The Iraq War "officially ended" nine years later in 2012. The killing and conflict continue.

The Aftermath

Approximate casualties as of September 2013

U.S. servicemen deployed to date	2 million to 2.5 million (Iraq and Afghanistan wars)
U.S. servicemen multi-deployment	400,000 men (3 tours of duty or more)
U.S. servicemen killed in Iraq	4,409 as of May 29, 2012 (U.S. Dept. of Defense)
U.S. servicemen wounded in Iraq	31,928 as of May 29, 2012 (U.S. Dept. of Defense)
U.S. servicemen with PTSD	450,000 (20% to 25% of returning servicemen)
Iraqi security forces deaths	16,623 Iraqi military and police killed (estimated)
Iraqi civilian deaths	110,000 to 250,000 (depending on the source)
Iraqi civilian injuries	200,000 to 300,000 (depending on the source)

Financial costs

The **estimated cost of the Iraq War** by the Bush administration: **$100 billion**.

The **actual cost** of the Iraq War to date: **$1 trillion**

The **long-term costs:** Depending upon the source, the cost of the Iraq war will be anywhere from 15 to 20 times greater than predicted. The Congressional Budget Office (CBO) report published in October 2007 estimated that the wars in Iraq and Afghanistan would cost taxpayers a total of $2.4 trillion by 2017, of which $1.9 trillion is attributable to spending on Iraq.

The U.S. President's Commission on WMD – March 31, 2005

"We conclude that the intelligence community was dead wrong in almost all of its pre-war judgments about Iraq's weapons of mass destruction."

I've always found it difficult to fathom why Cheney, Rumsfeld, Rove and President Bush were so motivated to invade Iraq. Saddam Hussein (as bad as he was) had virtually nothing to do with the attack on 9/11. The Bush Administration knew that 15 of the 19 men who highjacked the planes were Saudis, and they knew that Osama bin Laden and al-Qaeda were not controlled by Saddam Hussein. And yet they promoted the "weapons of mass destruction story" even as they simultaneously ignored all mounting evidence that did not support their claims.

Tragically, over 3,000 innocent Americans died on 9/11, and subsequently, 30 to 40 times as many innocent civilian Iraqis died as a result of the U.S. invasion. The initial and ongoing economic cost has been crippling. The continuing stain of the U.S. being associated with "systematic torture" in several prisoner interment camps, is heartbreaking. When our country invaded Iraq, we assumed the responsibility of taking control of a country whose citizens historically viewed America with suspicion and/or hatred. Cheney's prediction that we would be "greeted as liberators" reflected the man's pure arrogance.

In his book, World Order, Henry Kissinger makes the point that Bush, Cheney, Rumsfeld and Rove essentially "pursued their own crusade" – which ignored history as well as then-present realities. That's not to say that Kissinger or any administration official has had any good answers for "bringing peace to the Middle East," or that President Obama will (or can) avoid a bloody war with ISIS or the next group of terrorists. I hope that our government goes slowly, as any progress will likely only come in very small steps. ■

A Few of My 21st Century Heroes

SOME of the individuals I've greatly admired and who have captivated my attention through the years are listed below, in alphabetical order, followed by a few of my local, Central Coast favorites.

Madeleine Albright

Madeline Albright's life exemplifies the promise of America. A brilliant woman, she became the highest-ranking female government official in American history and the first to serve as secretary of state, confirmed by the Senate in 1997 by a vote of 99-0.

Albright's parents were forced into exile by Hitler and emigrated to the United States just prior to 1940. Her grandparents perished in the Holocaust. Albright grew up in Colorado, became a U.S. citizen in 1957, attended Wellesley College in Massachusetts on a scholarship and later received a Ph.D. from Columbia University in New York. She is a wife, a mother of three daughters and speaks four languages.

All secretaries of state have their detractors – sometimes harsh critics who second-guess their difficult decisions. However, I always found Madeline Albright's public statements on foreign policy issues carefully researched, reasoned and clearly expressed. No one can deny that she was one of the most dedicated and articulate leaders our country has known. She is currently a professor of international relations at Georgetown University in Washington, D.C., and was recently awarded the Presidential Medal of Freedom.

Muhammad Ali

Muhammad Ali is an American original who transformed himself from "Cassius Clay" into one of the most famous and admired sports – and cultural – heroes in the past 100 years. He was crowned Sportsman of the Century by Sports Illustrated and awarded Sports Personality of the Century by the BBC. Ali is the first and only World Heavyweight Champion to regain the title twice. Our nation watched him win a gold medal for America in the 1960 Summer Olympics in Rome. As the years progressed, any Ali championship fight was a national event. But what I most admire about Ali happened outside of the ring.

This is a man who showed the world his deep convictions about religious freedom, racial justice and the importance of defending moral principles. Because of his sincere religious beliefs and his opposition to the war in Vietnam, Ali resisted the military draft but didn't take the expedient route of leaving the country. He allowed himself to be arrested and gave up the best three years of his career after he was stripped of his title and forbidden to fight. Ali spent four years in court before being vindicated by the U.S. Supreme Court and allowed to return to the ring.

When he developed Parkinson's disease, he showed remarkable grace. There is no question that Ali was a controversial figure in his time, but America inevitably re-embraced Ali and continues to honor him. He lit the Olympic Flame at the Atlanta Olympics in 1996. The purity of his spirit is undeniable.

Bill and Melinda Gates

This world-famous couple possess unimaginable wealth and devote themselves to helping humanity in a calm, selfless and intelligent manner. The Bill and Melinda Gates Foundation is so well run that even Warren Buffet pledged nearly his entire fortune, deciding the foundation was the most effective way for him to distribute his great wealth for the good of humanity. The foundation currently has *over* $35 billion at its disposal and billions more in the form of future pledges from Bill and Melinda Gates, Buffet and others.

The Gates Foundation focuses its efforts on enhancing health care, reducing extreme poverty, expanding educational opportunities and providing wider access to information technology. The organization operates both domestically and internationally, and employs more than a thousand people who oversee programs to help people all over the world.

Bill and Melinda Gates are among America's most effective ambassadors: gifted organizers who, by their actions, have encouraged other billionaires to follow their example.

Billionaires Club Members: The Giving Pledge

There are only two requirements for those who wish to join this club and take the "Giving Pledge:" Members must be worth at least a billion dollars, and they must promise to give away 50% of their wealth during the course of their lives, or at their deaths, to philanthropic organizations that serve humanity. Buffet has personally solicited many fellow billionaires, and as of 2014, 125 club members had pledged an estimated $500 billion.

Billionaires Club members are diverse in both age and background and include George Lucas, Paul Allen, Elon Musk, Ted Turner and Mark Zuckerberg – to name a few. What is most exciting about the club is that these individuals are mostly self-made entrepreneurs who have decided to become involved and engaged. There is no requirement to give to any specific cause, but these extremely bright people have committed their time and immense wealth to tackle some of the most difficult issues facing mankind, including many of the very complex problems that governments are unwilling or unable to address effectively.

A complete list of Billionaires Club members can be found at thegivingpledge.org. YouTube also offers a short video of PBS' Charlie Rose interviewing a small group of club members. A breath of fresh air, it's definitely worth a watch.

What is important and most encouraging is that this growing group of billionaires just may be the beginning of a shift in the mindset of our nation's mega-rich. Perhaps Buffet and Gates have started a trend that may continue to grow and reach a tipping point. If, instead of keeping wealth to create family dynasties, it becomes a common practice to give away excess wealth, it will be a welcome change. Maybe the ostentatious display of extreme riches will become passé. For those in the Billionaires Club, it appears that the continued accumulation of excess billions has ceased to be fulfilling, or central to their legacy. Their commitment and generosity is a powerful statement and bodes well for the future of all of us.

Charles Osgood and Charles Kuralt

These two soft-spoken men have brought CBS' Sunday Morning into American homes for the past 34 years. Kuralt co-founded the very positive and intelligent program in 1979, when it was welcomed by viewers as an exception to the media's cynical offerings emphasizing negative news. Sunday Morning has shone an uplifting light on our country and its people, featuring stories that have been both informative and inspiring.

Charles Kuralt was a first-rate journalist attracted to the fascinating, creative and admirable lives of regular Americans, featured in his "On the Road" segments on Walter Cronkite's CBS newscasts. Kuralt had also served as a combat reporter in Vietnam in the '60s. He died in 1997, at the age of 63.

Since then, the kind, friendly and amusing Charles Osgood has continued as host.

Nelson Mandela

I've always been in awe of this man, who passed away at 95 in early December 2013 and was rightfully honored and mourned by the entire world. Much has been written about Nelson Mandela, who was held by the South African apartheid government in three different prisons for 27 years. Somehow, Mandela maintained both his amazing mental capacity and his calm, compassionate demeanor. When he was finally released from prison in 1990, he led his nation in a long struggle to replace the apartheid regime with a multi-racial democracy. He served as president of South Africa from 1994 to 1999. His life serves as a testament to the power of human courage and wisdom that can confront and eventually transform man's inhumanity to man. Mandela has been called the most important figure of the 20th century.

In the weeks following his death, I read and listened to many heartfelt remembrances of Nelson Mandela, but a comment by Andrew Young, the close associate of Martin Luther King and a former U.S. ambassador to the United Nations, made the most lasting impression: "The legacy of Mandela is forgiveness and reconciliation."

Elon Musk

Elon Musk first came to my attention as the co-founder of PayPal, the internet billing and payment service, which was sold to eBay in 2002 for $1.5 billion. I didn't know much about Musk until a few years ago, when I started reading about the Tesla Model S sedan in various car magazines.

Tesla Motors is Musk's new car company, which sells a sedan that looks like a Maserati – but runs on batteries. Mr. Musk is the Tesla "product architect," and his masterful design is both elegant and functional.

Musk was born in South Africa, the son of a South African father and a Canadian mother. He moved to California to obtain a Ph.D. in physics at Stanford, but soon dropped out to pursue his business interests, and later became a naturalized American citizen.

Musk is a genius who is both tenacious and fearless. He took on the major automotive manufacturers and succeeded, by obsessively believing in the design of a remarkable new automobile and by resurrecting a defunct automotive plant in Fremont, California, for pennies on the dollar.

Against all odds, Tesla is a roaring success. The Fremont plant began production in 2010 and now employs 3,000 people. Tesla sales for 2013 were projected to top $2 billion. The plant, operating according to Musk's manufacturing strategy, will enable Tesla to build more than 400,000 cars annually – 15 to 20 times their current output.

As if creating PayPal and Tesla Motors wasn't enough, Musk has put together SpaceX, the first private company to deliver cargo to the Space Station. SpaceX now has billion-dollar contracts with NASA and private companies. More importantly, SpaceX has helped re-ignite America's interest in space exploration.

Musk also released plans in late 2013 for the "Hyperloop," a proposed ultra-high speed ground transportation system between Los Angeles and San Francisco. In addition, he is providing both ideas and funding to SolarCity, the nation's leading provider of domestic solar energy.

Many people compare Musk to Steve Jobs. Both men followed their extraordinary convictions, and managed to "disrupt" traditional industries. They intuitively understood the "global ecosystems" their products were specifically designed for. They constantly broke new ground. Jobs didn't just help invent the iPod – he combined it with iTunes – and re-invented the entire music business.

But although Jobs was a truly gifted visionary, he was not an engineer or an inventor in the way Musk is. Musk holds degrees in both economics and physics – he's a genius on another level.

Like Jobs, Musk doesn't tolerate "naysayers" and has been involved in his share of controversies, but his conflicts pale when compared to his accomplishments. Musk is only 43. His creations have given him both credibility and great wealth, which is estimated in the neighborhood of $8 billion. I admire that he's also generous: In 2012, Musk became a member of the Billionaires Club.

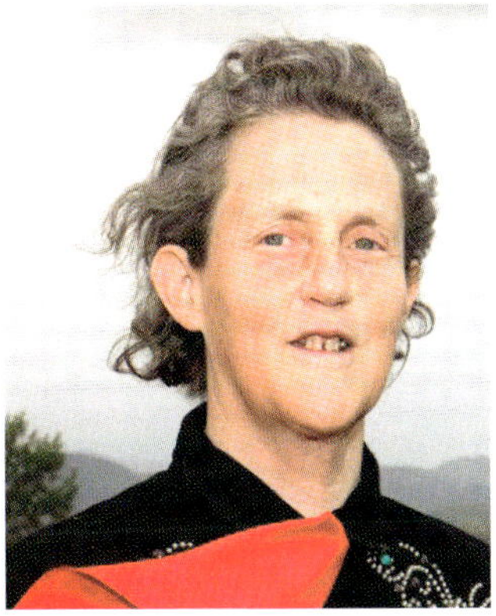

Temple Grandin

The bestselling author and doctor of animal science – is a truly unique American boomer. As a professor at Colorado State University in Fort Collins, she became famous for her work on the humane treatment of livestock. Grandin is autistic and earlier she'd invented the "hug box," a full-body pressure device that autistic children and adults can use to help calm themselves. She is internationally known as an "autism activist," and is considered by Time magazine to be one of the "100 most influential people in the world."

Grandin's personal story of struggle and accomplishment is extraordinary, but most Americans were unaware of her achievements until the release of the 2010 HBO-produced biopic, starring Claire Danes. The movie was nominated for 15 Emmys, and won several awards, including Outstanding Movie Made for Television. Danes took home a Golden Globe for Best Performance by An Actress in a Motion Picture for Television. Read one of Temple Grandin's books, or see the movie – it's quite a story!

Tim Russert

A journalist whose informed curiosity and intelligent, probing questions helped educate and inform America, Tim Russert brought a level-headed decency to his craft, exemplified by his steadiness in engaging powerful political figures for 16 years on Meet the Press. Russert began anchoring the news interview show on NBC in 1991 and remained there as an important and honest questioner of America's political, social, military and economic leaders until his death in 2008.

Russert's gentle demeanor encouraged his guests to speak freely and deeply about issues of the day, in contrast to the confrontational format that produces today's typical media sound bites.

Tim Russert authored a bestselling book, Wisdom of Our Fathers. You can glimpse Mr. Russert's presence in the style and mannerisms of his son, Luke Russert, who has followed in his father's footsteps as an NBC political analyst.

Sonia Sotomayor

The Supreme Court is perhaps America's finest and most powerful institution, and I pay close attention whenever there's a new justice nominated by the president. When Justice Sotomayor was appointed by President Obama in 2009, I didn't know much about her life, but over the past several years I've read more about her and listened to several of her lengthy and impressive interviews with journalists. I've come to have an appreciation and deep respect for this remarkable person. She's a boomer and an amazing woman who has shown America what a hard-working individual can achieve in a society that offers an equal opportunity for success.

The Sotomayor family came to the United States from Puerto Rico during World War II. Sonia Sotomayor was born in 1954 in the Bronx and spent her early years living in a tenement, but later grew up in a racially mixed housing project. Sotomayor's father barely spoke English, had left school early to work as a machinist, struggled with alcoholism and died when she was 9. Her mother worked as a nurse, but Sotomayor has stated many times that it was her grandmother who was her true inspiration.

As a child, Sotomayor was diagnosed with diabetes and at 7 began taking daily insulin injections. She has said that at a young age she knew that her physical life would be somewhat limited, but that she always watched Perry Mason on television and by the time she was 10, she was determined to become an attorney. She excelled in school and took advantage of every learning opportunity.

Sotomayor earned a scholarship to Princeton University, where she was a straight-A student. In 1976, she entered Yale Law School on a scholarship and became an editor of the Yale Law Journal. In 1991, she was nominated by President George H.W. Bush to the U.S. District Court in New York and was confirmed in 1992. President Clinton nominated Sotomayor to the U.S. Court of Appeals Second District, where she served from 1998 to 2009.

When I hear Justice Sotomayor discuss a subject, I always sense that she's very comfortable in her own skin: a straightforward person without pretensions who's in touch with the lives of everyday working Americans. Her life experience, her obvious empathy for others and her brilliant intellect bring a refreshing perspective to our Supreme Court.

Malala Yousafzai

Malala Yousafzai started her public life with her blog – at the age of 12. She wrote under a pseudonym for the BBC, detailing her life as a girl in Pakistan under Taliban rule. She wrote about how the Taliban were trying to ban education for girls, and later how they began attacking and blowing up girls' schools.

Despite the risk, Malala openly continued her support for equal access to education. The New York Times produced a documentary about Malala's life and work, and soon she was nominated by Desmond Tutu for the International Children's Peace Price. The world had begun to take notice of this remarkably brave schoolgirl.

At 14, Malala had blossomed into an articulate young woman who was a beacon of light for young women in Pakistan and across the world. Then, in her 15th year, a Taliban gunman shot Malala in the head and neck while she was returning home on a school bus. The world was stunned and rallied to her support. Malala almost died, but after several surgeries in England and a lengthy recovery she began, once again, to speak.

By 16, Malala had returned to the public eye as the embodiment of courage and hope. She has won numerous international awards and was recognized by *Time* as one of the 100 most influential people in the world. In 2014, she was the youngest person to receive the Nobel Peace Prize.

It's hard to watch one of her recent interviews on YouTube and not smile – or shed tears – at the wisdom and strength of her message.

Local Heroes

The Central California Coast *Achievers*

My hat is off to "The Achievers," who at one time or another have called the Central Coast home. The imagination and hard work of approximately 30 local inventors, designers, engineers and other creative individuals have helped advance our state and our nation.

Vic Hickey led a General Motors team that designed the suspension for NASA's Lunar Rover. Burt Rutan designed the White Knight and SpaceShipOne, the tandem craft for his privately funded space mission. Mike Spangler helped pioneer and build recumbent bicycles. Tom Spalding Sr. founded Spalding Ignitions and with his son, Tom (my former business partner), developed the high tech video equipment used at auto racing events.

A tribute to these remarkable people and others can be found in The Achievers, a book created in a group effort led by Tod Rafferty and Brian P. Lawler, and funded by the local community. Mr. Lawler is a well-known photographer, a writer and professor at Cal Poly. He is the author of several books on the graphic arts industry and a regular contributor to CreativePro.com. A copy of The Achievers can obtained from Amazon.com.

Mission Plaza, San Luis Obispo

Ken Schwartz

Ken was mayor of San Luis Obispo from 1969 until 1979, and a city councilman from 1998 to 2004. We were lucky to have such a gifted leader at such a critical time for our city. In the late 1960s San Luis Obispo's downtown was a mess. There was a high vacancy rate – some of the major stores on Higuera Street stood empty. San Luis Obispo could have easily gone the way of many small towns and ended up with a hodgepodge of structures in opposing styles and asphalt parking lots at its center. Even worse, key parts of the historic downtown could have been replaced by a "modern" mall.

Ken was an architecture professor at Cal Poly and had watched the town grow since the early '50s. During the '60s, he became the driving force behind the approval of a master plan for the city, which preserved the character of the town and incorporated several strategically located multi-level parking structures. Ken envisioned a "pedestrian-friendly city" with Mission Plaza and Santa Rosa Creek as focal points. His plan was controversial in the business community, which had always demanded more conventional parking lots, but he persevered and diplomatically guided our city with his remarkable long-term vision. Ken also instituted an urban tree program and a thoughtful signage ordinance that helped preserve the early Spanish California flavor of San Luis Obispo.

Myron Graham

Myron was the owner of an art supply store on Monterey Street and one of the strongest proponents of "cultural programs and projects" in and around San Luis Obispo. It was always a treat to visit his store and to engage Myron in conversation about the town he so loved. He served as a city councilman for eight years, and was a tireless promoter of The Little Theater, The Art Center, The SLO Symphony and Cuesta, our local community college. Myron was the councilman who spoke up at critical times in support of Mayor Schwartz, helping convince the rest of the council to accept construction of the Mission Plaza. As a member of the Rotary Club, Myron worked constantly to encourage young people to become involved in the arts. Myron died at 99, in 2012.

Cliff Chapman

I first met Cliff in the early '70s, when he owned and operated Marshall's Jewelers, across the street from Tom Spalding's and my first stereo shop on Higuera. Cliff came to our store to introduce himself and we became friends. Over many years, Cliff worked behind the scenes with numerous organizations to help raise millions of dollars for various worthy charities in our community. His ocean-front estate in Shell Beach continually hosted a wide variety of philanthropic events. Cliff donated the estate to the City of Pismo Beach before he died at 82, in 2012.

Botso Korisheli

A dear friend by the name of Liz Scott Graham called one day raving about a film that documents the life of Botso Korisheli – a celebrated county citizen. I have long admired Liz, so I listened thoughtfully to her enthusiastic review. She said the film was heartwarming and inspirational and insisted I see it, and arrived at my office with a ticket. I had no knowledge about Botso other than the man was a pianist and a well-known music teacher in Morro Bay. The documentary was eight years in the making. It's beautifully written, uplifting and due to be released in 2015. The film is aptly titled, Botso: The Passion of Music and the Power of Art. Botso, now in his 90s, has been a blessing in our community for the past 50 years. See the film with your kids. ***The New York Times*** review: "Botso is an enchanting film... Mr. Korisheli's humanity is magnetic, and no more beautiful case could be made for the psychological healing power of making music." **BotsoTheMovie.com**

The pessimist complains about the wind –
The optimist expects it to change –
The realist adjusts the sails.

WILLIAM ARTHUR WARD
Fountains of Faith

Adjusting the Sails

THE DAY I BEGAN writing this book, my fingers flew across the keyboard. A few months later, I had a draft. The words had come easily because most of what I wrote about had been banging around in my head for years.

The title *American Made* simply reflects who I am: born and socialized in the USA. The book itself was written, produced and manufactured in America, by Americans.

When I contemplated what I might reflect on when it came to my personal observations about our culture, I tried to concentrate on "American-made" topics. In other words, my essays (on health care, Wall Street, education) are about "home-grown" concerns and not challenges imposed by other nations.

I'd watched these issues arise and grow over several decades.

After some additional research and editing, I sent my first draft to my older brothers and to a few close friends. I asked for reactions and suggestions, and the comments flowed freely.

The philosophical feedback can be summarized as follows:

Cliff, what lessons did your childhood adventures teach you? Is hyperactivity still a problem? What did you learn from your business experiences? Who are your personal heroes? There were references to your marriage struggles, but no details or insights – why not?

You glossed over your period of drug addiction. In terms of the experiences you've described, do you have any conclusions about what they might mean to others, or words of advice to impart?

Where's the dénouement in your journey? No closing thoughts?

As I read the various comments, I felt my mother's ghost, hovering.

• • •

The comments from my brothers and friends seemed relevant and on-point and a response was in order. I carefully considered their questions as I sat at my keyboard, and then thought: *I've already said too much.*

It didn't seem to me that writing in more detail about any discomfort I may have suffered (or caused) because of self-inflicted mistakes would serve much purpose. The problems that I'd experienced in my life appeared mundane and minor when compared to the difficulties others had endured.

I'd shared my perspective about our evolving American society. It's obvious that I'm not a fan of preemptive wars or Fox News.

Setting aside the above cop-outs, here are answers to some of the questions and a few thoughts about what I've learned – so far.

My Own Life

I came to the conclusion years ago that I was very fortunate to have been born in a time of peace and into the arms of loving and affluent parents. For whatever reason, I've had more than my share of luck and the blessing of unconditional love from my family. My mother once said that her greatest joy in life came from seeing how much her husband and sons all loved each other.

My parents emphasized to their children that the world is not necessarily "a fair place," and that life can indeed appear to be a random series of strange and conflicting events. My dad said I was free "to pray every night" for something good to happen, or scream outside at the top of my lungs – but the universe was a busy place, and it might not have time to notice one kid in Carmel Valley, California.

In my lifetime, I've seen little evidence that the wheel of karma is well-balanced and turns evenly for everyone. That said, it's also been my experience that when I've treated people in an uncaring or mean-spirited fashion, I was destined for a fall. When I treat people well, they usually respond in kind. For the most part, I like to think that you reap what you sow, but of course history is full of evidence to the contrary.

There were times growing up when I felt sorry for myself. When my life didn't go as planned, my father always encouraged me to let go of what might have been, because "living with self-pity will eventually rot your guts." He suggested that I try to remember and appreciate the good things I already possessed. And he always asked me "What have you learned?" from a setback or disappointment, a question I usually found irritating and not easy to answer.

My mother told me that "carrying around hostility" was not a positive trait, and that if I held on to negative thoughts and feelings they would quickly tarnish my spirit. My parents tried to "reason" with their children, and engaged us in lively discussions – even with other adults who often joined us at family dinners. To my amazement, I found many adults more interesting than kids my own age.

At 65, I see the world spinning exponentially faster

Futurist Marshall McLuhan began his adult years in the late 1930s by courting with letters a young woman he had only met briefly. His missives were sorely lacking in the romance department, but he persisted, and after a dozen long letters, he convinced the woman to accept his marriage proposal. McLuhan's patient attention and obvious intellect eventually captured her heart. They were married and raised a family of six children.

Three decades later, the very same man penned a book titled The Message is the Medium, in which he predicted that "the new electronic media" – he was writing about the impact of television – would become an extension of our central nervous system and forever change both the world and the way we thought and lived.

McLuhan had insight: Today, only 50-odd years down the road, kids are more in touch with their smart phones than with nature. Few young people have ever sat down and written a letter. Teenage thumbs obsessively send thousands of instant texts per year – while driving. The new generation communicates in quick bursts of coded shorthand, but these same multi-tasking, tech-savvy youngsters know frightfully little about their own heritage as Americans. Learning about our "founding fathers" must seem awfully boring – because any event or person more than a decade past appears to them as irrelevant – "so ancient history."

As the internet keeps trending – instantly spreading the same words and images around the globe – we will quickly face a future in which a sizable portion of the civilized world will truly live in a "global village," influenced by one "global messenger."

What messenger?

The 24-hour news cycle. The incessant babble on Twitter, the narcissism of Facebook, the endless parade of TV reality shows, and crime dramas.

Last week I sat at a wonderful dinner party, and during the table conversation many of the younger guests were so addicted to their technology that they couldn't manage to sit through an evening of human conversation without compulsively checking the screen on their smart phones.

As if they were afraid of missing a call from the White House.

It's unclear what this behavior portends, but it's not likely to nurture the human spirit. A large portion of millennials would prefer to lose all of their hair if given a choice between going bald and permanently losing their personal computers. They dwell in the twilight zone of the internet, and their social identity and self-esteem often reside squarely on their Facebook page, where many eagerly share their most intimate lives with both friends and strangers.

And boomers?

We will soon go the way of the dinosaurs, relics of a bygone era.

I swore I'd never be like my parents – but more and more I hear the voice of my father, his words from decades ago echoing inside my head.

Today, privacy – one of the most precious gifts of human freedom – has nearly vanished. Our government and corporations can explore every nook and cranny of our personal lives. It's an unsettling reality, as it runs contrary to core American values.

And yet, we still live in a remarkable country, and my generation possesses both the resources and the power to help make a difference.

I've certainly witnessed my own family and a long list of my boomer friends live productive and creative lives. The people I came to know in the '60s possess a wide variety of political views, but their Postscripts in the Scrapbook section reflect a group of hard-working Americans who followed their dreams. As far as I'm concerned, boomers still rock.

The question is: What legacy do we want to leave?

Substance Abuse

Given the unpleasant stories and images that stream across our televisions, smart phones and laptops, it should come as no surprise that humans feel compelled to self-medicate in some form or fashion. Whether the drug of choice is alcohol, prescription painkillers, cocaine, weed, or nicotine – the need and the product are ubiquitous.

Unfortunately, once people become addicted, they always face the terrible odds that their lives will be mired in misery. The truth about taking any powerful drug is this: For every hour that a stimulant or narcotic makes a person feel good, there will be multiple hours of feeling not so good after the drug wears off. The bad hours soon turn into days, weeks and years. My own story was no different from anyone else's who becomes hooked on a dangerous substance – I had only three real choices: stop, end up in jail, or die young.

I decided to choose the only sane option and quit. If anyone would like to know the details of that arduous episode, it's in the book I wrote 30 years ago, available through Amazon.com.

Hyperactivity

As long as I can remember, my toes were already twitching when my eyes popped open in the morning. I was born in overdrive. I was often scolded by teachers to "Sit still and be quiet!" Until I was 16, that was virtually an impossible task for me. Hyperactivity is difficult for both the child and the parents. My mother chose not to treat my condition with drug therapy, but every case is unique.

For me, the good news was that hyperactivity meant getting lots of stuff done. The not-so-good news is that my normal state of being is busy. To this day, I often cannot relax until I "wear myself out." My mother said that when I was a boy, I'd run around the yard making noise, and then suddenly become quiet. She told me that any silence worried her, so she'd go find me – I'd often be napping under a tree.

Then I'd pop up and start the process all over again.

It's easy to take offense at hyperactive people, because they can often appear distracted, bored, rude or aloof. In my case, there may be some truth to those observations. For the most part, I'm just preoccupied – focused on some idea in my own private world. I can pass a close acquaintance on the street and not return his or her friendly wave because I'm simply oblivious, caught up in my own internal dialogue. My wife will point out such impolite behavior, but I can't even remember seeing or hearing the friend who hailed me. It's a problem. When I'm reading a book, magazine or newspaper, I become so involved that my wife has to shout at me to get my attention: Guaranteed grief.

I have a hyperactive nature, but I do not have an "attention deficit," as I am able to concentrate intensely on one subject for long periods of time.

Every hyperactive person has his or her own story, and I don't have any advice when it comes to modern-day treatments for ADHD. Over the years, I have noticed that medical professionals and the pharmaceutical industry have turned treating ADHD into a rapidly growing industry. After a doctor makes the diagnosis, a common practice is to prescribe psychoactive drugs. In 1990, approximately 585,000 American children were taking psychoactive medication. That figure is now 3.5 million. A six-fold increase poses some serious questions.

ADHD treatment remains a controversial subject. In the current Dictionary of Mental Disorders (DSM-V), the guides to diagnosis of ADHD have been further refined, although not much has changed in terms of treatment.

The syndrome manifests in a variety of symptoms and can't be successfully handled with a one-size-fits-all diagnosis or treatment. The Center for Disease Control (CDC) reports that 15% of American high school boys have been diagnosed with ADHD. Some researchers speculate that ADHD is related to diet, upbringing or even today's social and physical environment.

Words of Advice

The only words of advice I have are simple, although they're not always easy to follow: Be honest. Love your family and friends and others as much as you can. Listen to the ideas and experiences of others. Learn the facts and avoid quick judgments. Pay close attention to diet and exercise. Find something you truly like to do and work hard at it. Don't always wait to see what life will bring – sometimes take a few steps, look around, then sprint to the moon.

Pay your bills. Admit when you are wrong and take personal responsibility for your actions. Stay engaged in life. Practice random acts of kindness. Wear sunscreen and floss regularly.

Women, Love and Marriage

I know very little about women, except for some sketchy concepts I've cobbled together, over time, about American women. I am aware that most of the women I know are very intelligent and alert and rapidly gaining the respect and admiration they've always deserved.

As an American man, I have to admit that I do resent one notion that many women seem to foster – the idea that men should be married, that there's something amiss if a man reaches his fourth decade and has yet to "settle down."

Not every man is designed for matrimony. Sometimes, men just don't see a problem – so they can't understand why they're presented with a "solution."

On the other hand, it's taken me decades to learn that, if you are married, it's often best simply to do what the woman wants. I reluctantly confess that the adage has merit. Life is smoother when you finally learn the surprising fact that your wife is … always right.

Some episodes of my life are best left to private memory. My past marriages are just that – personal and past. Not all relationships are destined to last a lifetime. It's obvious (and sad) that boomers will not celebrate as many 50-year anniversaries as our parents' and grandparents' generations did. Divorce is now mainstream in America, with more than 50% of all marriages failing.

I often find it perplexing, and sometimes embarrassing, to look back and realize how many times I screwed up – made life-altering mistakes – especially when I remember how sure I was when I made the original decision.

It's difficult to see yourself, or the world, clearly in present time.

Lifestyle

During my adult life, I've never achieved a balanced level of health for any long period of time, because I've never overcome my neurotic relationship with food and exercise. I've been periodically proactive about my health, but those times never seem to last much longer than a year.

Like many people who have difficulty controlling their weight, I use food as a crutch. When I'm down, I nurture myself with something warm or sweet. If I feel hyperactive, I'll eat a juicy hamburger to slow down. When I'm stressed, or joyous, I'll reward myself with frozen yogurt and the world instantly takes on a brighter shade. I rationalize my behavior and bask in self-acceptance, confident that tomorrow I'll begin a more sensible approach.

This is not a strategy that I'd recommend to anyone.

On a more positive note, I can pass on the information that I've received, in my earlier years, at every health spa I've visited across the country.

The basic message is not startling or new:

Good health means finding a reasonable balance among mind, body and spirit. As much as possible, nourishment should come from fresh food – heavy on the vegetables, fruits and whole grains, and light on any meat. Exercise frequently. It doesn't matter if you walk, swim, dance or practice yoga – it's all good. Sex is a wonderful and healthy activity, so enjoy it often. Learn a practical method of relieving stress, whether it's through meditation, prayer, yoga, or any other constructive activity that brings a sense of peace. If you indulge in mind-altering substances, stick with natural products like wine or marijuana – in moderation.

Good health should be a common-sense practice, but for me it somehow remains an elusive goal.

One boomer's lament

My friend Jim Agee brought a music CD to my recent attention – it's titled Hold the River Back and it's the latest album by Doug Groshart, a talented local recording artist. Recently, a group of us went down to the town square to join a crowd attending his concert. One particular song he wrote lamented growing older and one particular lyric haunted me through the night:

The hardest thing I've ever done is growing old while I still feel young –

Groshart's sentiment is seeping its way into the psyche of boomers, who are finding it more difficult to keep up with the rapidly changing world. At 65, I am not so compelled to muster the energy – or possess the will – to hold back the relentless tide of aging. Some boomers may fight tooth and nail to "stay young" but personally, I have no interest in remaining in the game one season too many.

Spirituality

As I was growing up, I always associated "spirituality" with church. Most community churches are wonderful places and often act as the heart and soul of small towns across America.

As I grew older, I began to appreciate and admire churches that help the hungry, the homeless and those who are simply too old or sick to help themselves. Many churches get down into the trenches, where government is so often both inefficient and ineffective.

I've never been a regular churchgoer, but I certainly believe in God, as I intuitively feel there is more to this universe than meets the eye. I'm not a fan of organized dogma but I'm always thankful that I live in a country where people have such religious freedom.

Groundhog Day with Bill Murray is one of my favorite movies because it conveys with humor how a person's attitude toward life can affect reality. I'm continually aware that my own reality is often a reflection of my state of mind – especially when I become preoccupied with self, or my thoughts or feelings are unduly negative. If I shift my focus and allow myself to begin to see the world through someone else's eyes, my perceptions usually change and allow me to move forward in a more positive direction.

Most spiritual teachers stress the importance of a balanced and thoughtful approach to life. From my perspective, there are many paths to personal growth, peace and self-acceptance. For me, spirituality has come to mean treating yourself and others in a loving fashion.

A Long, Bumpy Road for Mankind

Sadly, there are billions of my fellow humans who do not have any sense of security, let alone the luxury of time to write a nostalgic book about themselves, their family, friends, and experiences.

Millions on our planet continue to live under the same desperate conditions as their ancestors endured. Much of the world remains undernourished, uneducated and immersed in fear and distrust of more affluent cultures. In many countries, women are still regarded as second-class citizens and find themselves at the mercy of men.

Is it any wonder that a fog of anxiety and distrust hangs over our planet?

Since time immemorial there has been overwhelming evidence that humans are a flawed and dangerous species. The particular group who "found" America and later conquered the West proved to be an aggressive bunch. A Native American Indian chief once commented:

The people who came to take over the land had tense faces and a cruel demeanor. They were always seeking something. What were they seeking? They are an uneasy and restless people. We don't know what they want. We think they are mad.

The chief had a point. If you flash forward to modern times, it's not hard to see that America has grown just a tad discombobulated. After all, we've created a society whose major exports to other nations include firearms and heavy armaments, violent movies, alcohol, drugs, tobacco, pornography and manic video games for children. Americans have an insatiable appetite for pharmaceutical painkillers, tranquilizers, illegal narcotics, sugar, fat, meat, guns and mindless reality shows. As I've already noted, our country has the highest percentage of people in prison of any country on Earth, and we fight war after war in foreign lands. Thomas Friedman recently made the point in his essay that "It's not that hard to hijack the United States into a war." America no longer possesses the same level of global influence or dominance, and thus we have far less control over world events – every action can bring unforseen consequences.

Of course America is certainly not alone in its misdeeds and failures. Most other industrialized nations have very serious problems of their own. If you watch any TV nightly news program you know what horrible turmoil currently lurks on many foreign shores.

Global anxiety and the growing divide

We all share the same planet – billions of human beings, all going about our daily lives. Abraham Maslow, the famous psychologist who laid out the "hierarchy of needs," explained that it's in our DNA to seek security, sustenance and a fair share of love.

We're lucky that most Americans still live fairly high on Maslow's pyramid, at least in comparison with the rest of the world. It's my personal opinion that Americans are privileged to reside in the best country on the planet. And yet, our own culture's accelerating rate of change is challenging the very fabric of the human nervous system, and, perhaps, our very existence.

The Future and the White Light

Humanity has some work to do. Humans have always been preoccupied with imposing their will on each other, as well as on other species. Since the day a caveman first sharpened a stick, we've been in relentless pursuit of more efficient methods to kill our fellow humans.

How fast we have traveled from bows and arrows to nuclear bombs.

Our world is further complicated by the fact that human beings have always had the innate desire to get "buzzed" – drinking, smoking, snorting and injecting any substance that is, at least temporally, pleasurable.

This remains a sticky wicket for mankind.

Environmentalists speculate that our biggest challenge may come via unintended consequences – we are the only "intelligent" creatures who have seriously degraded the Earth's environment. Our planet displays the ruins of many former great civilizations that believed they would be eternal, but succumbed to warfare, plague, famine or natural catastrophe.

According to scientists, a super volcano in Yellowstone National Park or an asteroid may yet change the course and destiny of the world.

On the other hand, it's hard to deny that we could be facing future events that might resemble any number of sci-fi movie plots, or an esoteric episode of Star Trek. If and when such a scenario unfolds – and whether we're threatened by monsters from within or without – I sincerely hope that the good guys win.

Many in my generation are confident that a Biblical event is coming down the road and will be our salvation. It's a possibility. How great it would be to see all my loved ones in Heaven!

Notwithstanding a cataclysmic disaster or man's own powerful defects, I am hopeful for our nation and the future of mankind. Perhaps some evolving combination of advanced technology, humane government and benign spiritual inspiration will curtail man's destructive tendencies.

At this stage in my life, I feel blessed to have my family and good friends and (knock on wood) my health. And as a boomer (and thanks to my dad's generation) I am optimistic, in spite of world turmoil.

I want to believe that Superman, the hero who was sent to Earth by his parents from a dying planet, got it right with his guiding principle:

Truth, justice and the American way.

Acknowledgments

When I started writing, I called Elaine Sullivan. We've known each other for more than 40 years and I knew she would provide honest insights and candid suggestions. She remembered much of our business history in San Luis Obispo and had saved many items from the '70s and '80s. The boxes of memorabilia saved by my mother provided the rest of the material, some of which I had not seen before.

Writing can be a lonely exercise. There is only room for one set of hands on the keyboard and (for me) the activity requires a quiet working space. The process can be frustrating. Sometimes I'd read what I had written only a few days before and cringe.

One night I stared at the ceiling in a funk, wondering, What the hell was I thinking when I decided to write a vanity book? Who would want to read my personal ramblings?

Writing about "personal stuff" means private disclosures, opening closed doors, and the possibility of ending up naked in front of strangers. At 65, that prospect can be disconcerting, but encouragement came from family and friends and bolstered my spirit.

My brothers, Greg and Tony, helped with their critiques and provided important details about family stories. We had some heartwarming conversations as we compared firsthand accounts of our early lives together. As I noted in the opening pages, I was less than an attentive husband as I put together this book and I am grateful for Lynette's support. My stepson, Tyler, pitched in by reviewing what I had written and had excellent criticisms and constructive suggestions.

I would have been in sad shape without the help of editors Nels and Vicki Hanson. They took a personal interest in the material and gave thoughtful and steady guidance.

As for the design and layout, I'm thankful that Ashala Lawler agreed to take on the project. I had worked with her husband, Brian, in the past, and both he and Ashala are well-known for their professional expertise.

I'm also very grateful for Terry J. San Filippo's contributions. She organized, scanned and cataloged all the photographs and other materials. Terry was extremely organized, offered insightful suggestions and, most of all, was fun to work with.

This book was truly a collaborative effort. Thanks to one and all.

Row crops in southern San Luis Obispo County

Final Note

The personal material in ***American Made*** came from my own recollections, yet I did my best to consult with third parties who had direct knowledge of our shared history. I may have missed some details, but I believe all the essentials are correct.

I apologize in advance if I did not give proper credit where credit is due.

It was my intent to be as accurate as possible about people and events. Facts and figures that appear in the essays have been checked and verified by others. Multiple sources of information can produce a range of differing statistics about the same subject, but I've tried to select data that seemed a fair average of what I felt were the most objective analyses.

Because my book is truly "One Boomer's Reflections," I decided it was unnecessary to include extensive footnotes or a detailed bibliography. If you find errors, please feel free to bring any mistakes to my attention. You can write me at 755 Santa Rosa Street, Suite 310, San Luis Obispo, CA 93401, or email: AmericanMadeStory.com

Morro Rock, Morro Bay, California

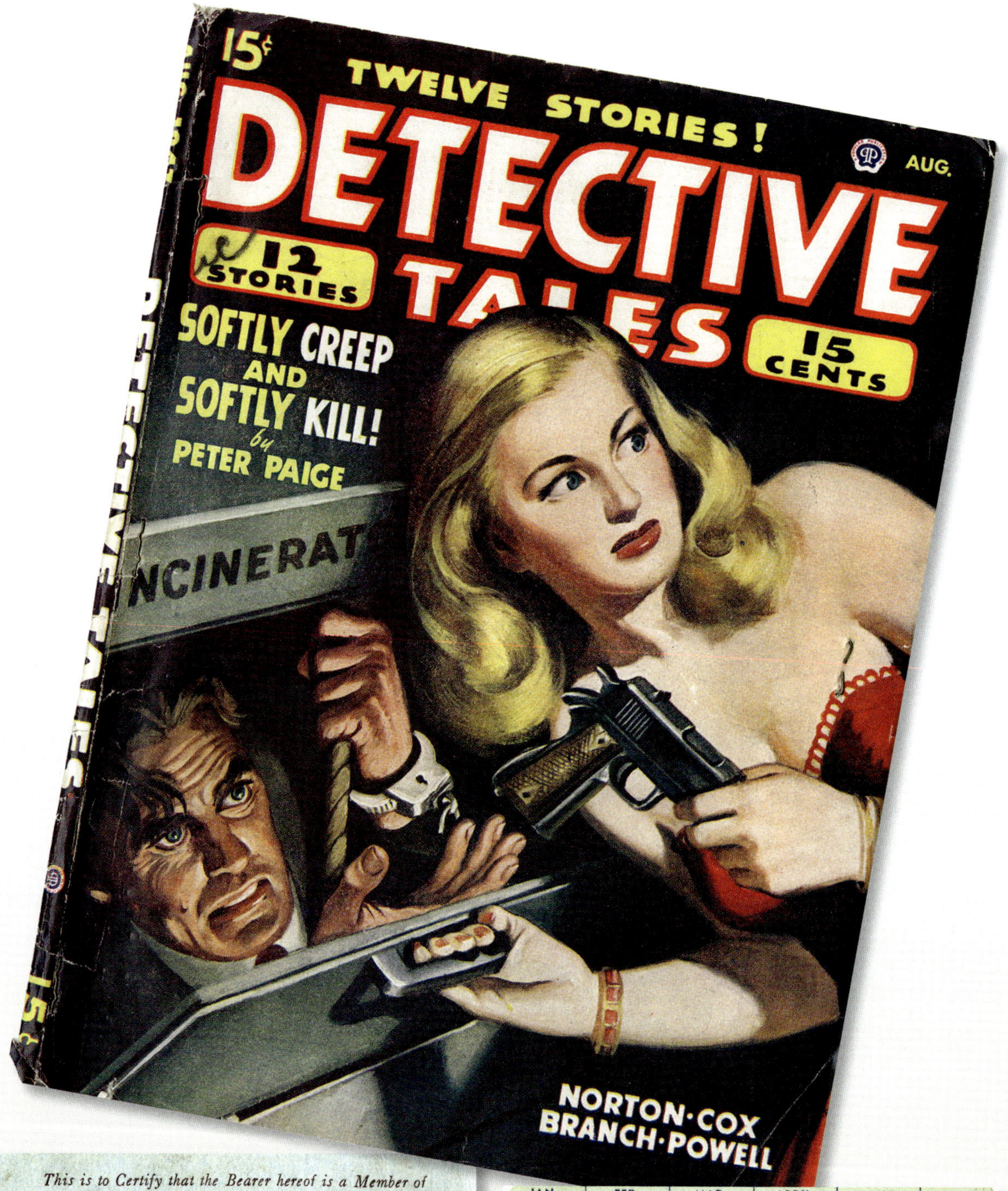

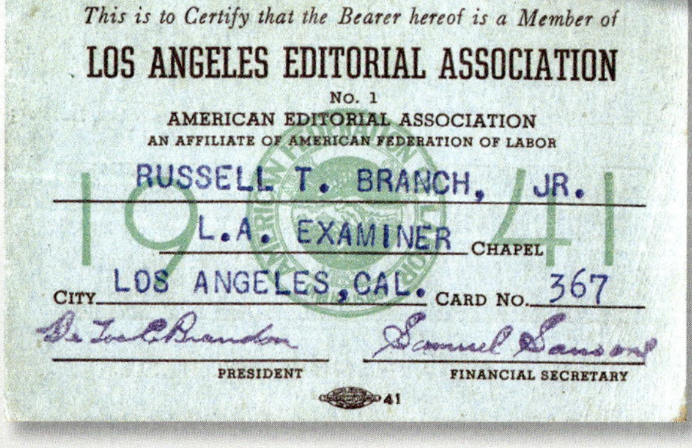
This is to Certify that the Bearer hereof is a Member of

LOS ANGELES EDITORIAL ASSOCIATION

No. 1

AMERICAN EDITORIAL ASSOCIATION

AN AFFILIATE OF AMERICAN FEDERATION OF LABOR

RUSSELL T. BRANCH, JR.

1941

L.A. EXAMINER CHAPEL

CITY LOS ANGELES, CAL. CARD NO. 367

PRESIDENT FINANCIAL SECRETARY

1941

JAN.	FEB.	MAR.	APRIL	MAY	JUNE
RB	RB	RB			

SCREEN READERS' GUILD

1943

NAME Russell Branch

DATE ISSUED January 1943

Treas. Pres.

JULY	AUG.	SEPT.	OCT.	NOV.	DEC.

1943

DAD TOLD US STORIES

When Greg and I were young boys, my dad would delight us with elaborate bedtime stories. I always wondered how he could make up his stories so quickly and in such detail. In all the years growing up, I never heard my father mention that he had written "detective stories." Yet I found a stack of pulp fiction magazines in one of the boxes left by my mother. My dad's name appeared on several magazine covers as a featured writer. Most of the stories were written while Greg was still a baby during 1946 and 1947, so my guess is that in later years we heard versions of the tales he had already written for pulp fiction magazines. One of Dad's stories was titled ***Death Rides a Motorcycle***, and it was no coincidence that the hero-detective-racer rode both Vincent and Aerial Motorcycles – exactly the same models owned by my father.

My grandfather had graduated from MIT and had hoped that his son would follow in his footsteps and become an engineer. Instead, my father chose to enroll at Cornell University in New York. To the further consternation of his parents, my dad later dropped out of Cornell to pursue a career in writing and chose to follow a young woman he had met on the East Coast (my mother) back to her home on the "much less traditional" West Coast.

My father worked for ***Time*** magazine and later as a story analyst for Colombia Pictures, before he spent many years as an editor for Stanford Research Institute.

Top left: Russ at the beach

Top right: Russ with his pipe, as a young writer

Bottom: Russ with Cliff (left) and Greg on a family camping trip

Before WWII, my father worked for *Time* magazine and later as a story analyst for Colombia Pictures, prior to enlisting in the Merchant Marine. After the war, he spent the majority of his writing career working as an editor for the Stanford Research Institute.

Columbia Motion Pictures, 1942

Note

MILKMAN, KEEP THOSE BULLETS QUIET!

Maybe some day I'll be able to tell my children about how Daddy became involved in the Case of the Philandering Milkman. At the moment, though, I'm too busy trying to collect my twenty-five fish a day from a dead client—and living long enough to pin a murder on a killer whose description fits me like a custom-made shroud!

CHAPTER ONE

Mayhem in the A.M.

I SHOULD have gone to the beach. . . . It was one of those soft, warm, dreamy afternoons. Even through the smoky haze of downtown L. A. it was a beautiful afternoon, and it would have been just that much nicer at the beach.

To hell with the office, I told myself. Are you your own boss, or are you? Did you just collect a fat fee, or did you?

I decided the answer was yes. But I also decided I was a fool if I thought that check

The voice was calm, dispassionate, almost friendly. "We're warning you, chum. It's too big for you. Stay out of it and stay healthy."

82

Aug. 1947

Thrilling Novelette of Movieland Murder

83

Betty Branch

Betty Branch died in 2011 at the age of 92. My mother graduated in 1936 from Beverly Hills High School and followed her mother's example by graduating from Stanford University. Betty was selected as a college editor for Mademoiselle magazine and it was at a meeting of Mademoiselle's college editors in New York that she met my dad, a young aspiring copywriter for Time/Life. My dad had been selected to escort her to the Mademoiselle Ball – they met, and that was it. Pretty good love story.

My mother was fearless in advancing the role of women in our society, long before it was fashionable, as summarized in Bill Morem's tribute on the opposite page. Morem's column best describes my mom.

Betty on her horse, Brownee, 1930

Betty at the *Stanford Daily*, 1939

Russell and Betty on their wedding day, 1940

Russ Branch died in 1992 at the age of 76. At that time my father had been married to my mother for 52 years. In their later years, they lived in San Luis Obispo.

My dad was somewhat shy and had a gentle spirit. He was extremely well-read, and was not afraid to say what he thought, especially when he felt that expressing a needed clarification or opposing opinion was warranted. My father was thoroughly devoted to my mom and affectionate to his sons, teaching us by his example.

He was a writer and professional editor, and as a young man had dropped out of Cornell University – against his parents' wishes – to pursue his own dreams. My dad said that working as a volunteer for our local literacy council brought him great satisfaction. He said that each time someone learned to read, there were always heartfelt tears of joy.

THE TRIBUNE Newspaper of the Central Coast

Dec. 2011

From an article by Bill Morem

About Betty Branch:

If you've been on the Central Coast for any length of time, odds are good that you've heard of Betty, most probably with the adjective "dynamo" appended to her name. Although our paths never crossed, she earned her fair share of ink before dying Dec. 21 at the age of 92 – 92 well-spent and compassionate years.

Her life began Oct. 21, 1919, in Brentwood, a suburb of L.A. that was so rural at the time that Betty rode her horse down a dirt path that ran parallel to Wilshire Boulevard.

As it turned out, she was a writer from the get-go, holding down the editor's job of the school paper at Beverly Hills High, where she graduated in 1936. She went on to Stanford and worked on the *Stanford Daily,* where she caught the eye of *Mademoiselle* magazine editors who selected her as a college editor for their publication.

It was through *Mademoiselle* and a meeting of college editors that she met her future husband, Russ, who was an editor with Time/Life. During their 52 years together, before his death in 1992, he and Betty co-founded the *Canyon Crier* newspaper, which covered Laurel Canyon and the Hollywood Hills. Later, Betty would own, publish and edit the Carmel Valley *Outlook* newspaper, while Russ would go on to be a senior editor for the Stanford Research Institute.

In addition to running newspapers and raising three boys – Tony, Greg and Cliff – Betty returned to Stanford for a master's in education, which led her to guidance counseling at UCSB and later marriage and family counseling. Following a four-year stint in Thailand involving a classified project through the Stanford Research Institute overseen by the State Department, the couple moved to San Luis Obispo.

Now, any of the aforementioned professions and avocations would be a résumé buster for most folks, but Betty's sense of social duty further blossomed on the Central Coast. For example, she co-founded the San Luis Obispo Women's Resource Center and Grandmother's House; was a director for the Family Services Agency; set up a reading program for inmates at the County Jail; and, right around the dawn of personal computers, founded "Computer Rooters," a program that helped seniors navigate the burgeoning technology.

In 1990, Cuesta College and The Community Foundation presented Betty a Woman of Distinction award for her work for the Progress for Women. In sum, her life was just about as purpose-driven as they come. And in that light, perhaps my New Year's resolution should be one of becoming the person my pug thinks I am. Because, in the final tally, Betty Branch set an incredibly high bar for positive action, obliterating stereotypes while relentlessly moving empathy forward. In short, she broke the mold.

Life with Greg Branch and Motorcycles

Greg on the road at 17

The open field where my brother Greg and I rode our motorcycles as young lads now lies under the Mid-Carmel Valley Shopping Center, but our house and "motorcycle garage" still remain.

Growing up, Greg took apart everything to see how it worked, and could fix almost anything. He kept all of our family's motorcycles in good working order and it came as no surprise when he became a mechanical engineer.

Two days after graduation from high school, Greg started a cross-country journey on his Triumph Tiger 500 motorcycle. He was only 17, and my mother made him promise to call home each Sunday, so she could keep track of him on his trip. She waited each week for his call. Once, Greg called from a phone booth in Mississippi, and during his conversation with my mother he was surrounded by police. A nearby shopkeeper thought Greg looked suspicious and called the cops. It probably didn't help that he was riding a foreign motorcycle with California license plates. After all, he could have been a civil rights agitator – it was 1965. Greg talked his way out of the situation, but he didn't stick around Mississippi.

On his tour of America, Greg took many odd jobs and visited our relatives who lived in other states. He was gone four months, and rode about 12,000 miles. I didn't say much to Greg about his amazing odyssey when he came home, but he was definitely my hero and as fine an older brother as anyone could hope for.

In the '60s, people like Greg and I were called "motorcycle nuts," and over the years we owned both road and street bikes from most of the European, Japanese and Canadian manufacturers – about 40 different bikes between the two of us.

When I settled in San Luis Obispo, I'd compete each year in the Hi Mountain Enduro race near Pozo in the backwoods of the county. The Cal Poly Penguins Motorcycle Club hosted the event and about 300 riders from all over California would enter. In 1973 – almost 40 years ago – I took second place in the OPEN B class competition. I still have the rusting trophy in my garage – it's the only trophy I ever won.

My last street motorcycle was a BMW RS1200, which I sold just before I married Lynette Branch. She was aware that my motorcycle riding had landed me in the hospital a few times and she made it perfectly clear that if – at my age – I ever brought home a motorcycle, I'd have to find another wife.

On a BSA, 1972

Riding in a race,
early '80s

Jumping off sand dunes in Pismo Beach on a Yamaha 360 – a fool, for not wearing a helmet.

My café racer – a custom Triumph:
Wish I still had it

With Dick Blake in Pozo, early '70s:
Dick rode Husqvarna and Bultacos,
I rode Yamahas and Can-Ams.

Just before starting the Hi Mountain Enduro – the only trophy I ever won.

Tom Spalding – From Go-Karts to Jets

Tom Spalding left California Cooperage during its very early stages to pursue his interest in auto racing. It may seem odd that Tom jumped from stereos and hot tubs to auto racing, but given the background of his father, it was no surprise. Here I've gathered some old photos and stitched together facts about Tom's dad, and I've also included an excerpt from an article about Tom's stint as a professional race car driver.

As you'll see from the next few pages, Tom has worn many different hats and helmets. My friend and old partner is soft-spoken and humble – a low-key guy who happens to excel at almost everything he does. In January 2014, he flew me over to Vegas for the Consumer Electronics Show (see page 340). As I listened to Tom discuss the nuances of the latest generation of electronic devices with various engineers, I realized he is still well-versed on cutting-edge technology. If it sounds like I'm bragging about my old partner – I am.

Tom's mother, **Patricia Spalding**, was also a great help in the early days, working as my assistant and providing some "adult influence" at California Cooperage. Patricia had her own entrepreneurial spirit and started **Spalding Labs** in the late '70s. She actively ran the company for 30 years, until she turned the enterprise over to Tom.

From college through the beginning of California Cooperage, Tom and I were inseparable. We rode our dirt bikes together, shared a ski boat and spent time at Nacimiento Lake. For several years we owned the Trout Farm Ranch in Tassajara Canyon, near Santa Margarita. We used to ride our dirt bikes from the Trout Farm up into the hills and catch the railroad tracks over Cuesta Grade down into the city of San Luis Obispo to Warehouse Sound Company. It was always thrilling to ride through the dark, curving train tunnel in the mountain – at one point you couldn't see daylight at the other end – in those days the little headlight on a dirt bike was not much better than a flashlight.

In 1999, Tom sold Ergo, the computer company I joined in late 1989. He had moved back the year before to Silicon Valley in California and was one of the founders of 2Wire, a successful internet DSL company that AT&T eventually purchased. Tom now owns and runs Spalding Labs in Reno, Nevada. Check out bugbiz.Spalding-labs.com to see how he has merged high tech and horses with that business.

Truth is, Tom was always "the brains" behind our businesses, and he's one of the smartest guys I've ever had the pleasure to call a friend.

Tom Spalding Sr. ("Senior"), Tom's father, was one of the original Southern California Hot Rodders. In 1940, at the age of 20, Tom Sr. and his brother Bill built a **Streamliner** – the second such car built at that time. The Spalding Streamliner hit an amazing (for that time) 127 mph at Muroc Dry Lake, now home of Edwards Air Force Base. They also sold high performance cams and ignitions before and following WWII. In 1948, Tom Sr. and Bill built a **Track Roadster** that was featured in the very first issue of Hot Rod magazine – the roadster is shown at the Bonneville Salt Flats in 1949. Tom Sr. is in the center and Bill is on the right.

In 1958, Tom Spalding Sr. gave Tom and his brother Pat a "Go-Kart" for Christmas. Given Tom Sr.'s racing background, the "stock" go kart was soon modified to the point where it ended up on the cover of Rod and Custom magazine – quite an accolade for a go-kart. Tom Jr., at age 14, is seen sitting in a twin-cylinder racing kart, one of a series of custom karts. In the process, Tom Sr. started a business that produced and sold state-of-the-art racing kart parts, and Tom Jr. began to hone his racing skills.

Tom Sr.'s main business was building speed equipment for all kinds of racing cars. His "Flamethrower" ignitions in the '50s and '60s were state-of-the-art. He also designed the first high performance electronic ignition ("BDI"), which he introduced in the late '60s. The winning race cars in the Indianapolis 500 were equipped with **Spalding Ignitions** in 1968, 1972, '73, '74, '75 and '76. For a number of years roughly 90% of race cars on the starting grid at Indy were equipped with a Spalding BDI ignition.

Spalding Ignition "BDI" circa 1967

Track Roadster, Bonneville Salt Flats, 1949

Spalding Streamliner, 1940

Tom Sr., standing, brother Bill in car

Tom Jr., 14

SPALDING RACING

For the 1979 Can Am season, Tom's race team built the first "ground effects" Can Am car. The concept was pioneered the year before on Mario Andretti's World Championship winning Lotus Formula One car. The Can Am was the highest level of road racing in the United States and a stepping stone to Formula One in Europe. Of the Can Am drivers of Tom's era, two went on to be Formula One World Champions and one won the Indy 500.

A New York Times article describes Tom's new concept of a live driver's-eye view. Tom's Can Am car was the test bed for his **Racevision** technology. He pioneered the first live, in-car camera system, which debuted in CBS's 1979 Daytona 500 broadcast. It garnered the highest ratings ever for a motor sports broadcast to that time. The system transmitted a video signal to

a circling helicopter, the technique still used to this day. Racevision cameras were the first live cameras at the 1980 Indy 500 in Al Unser's car and in a Formula One car at Watkins Glen. Tom won an Emmy for his Racevision technology at Daytona in 1979. Starting in the '80s, Tom focused so intently on the television side of racing, he ended up hiring a driver to drive his own car. This was, much to the relief of his mother, the end of his own racing career.

Sports Section

The New York Times

VOL.CXXVIII.... No.44,293 —NEW YORK, SUNDAY, JULY 29, 1979—

New Racevision System Puts an 'Eye' in the Cockpit

By PHIL PASH

Racevision camera mounted on Can Am car. Tom Spalding hopes it will revolutionize television coverage of auto racing

"Tom Spalding's Racevision camera mounted on Can Am car may revolutionize television coverage of auto racing."

Racevision: The driver's-eye view

Tom racing at Road Atlanta, Can Am Series, 1978

Excerpt from a 1979 race program:

Tom Spalding is one of the sport's newer drivers and he is an interesting man. His father is a well-known automotive designer, so Spalding grew up with a natural interest in cars. Tom also has a background in electrical engineering.

Lately, he has been working on a high technology television camera that transmits live pictures and sound from a race car at speed, which was used by CBS for coverage of the Daytona 500. With profits from The Warehouse Company, Spalding started racing in 1977.

He recorded a remarkable first season, generally finishing in the top six, including a win and two seconds. Unlike most first-year amateurs, Spalding started in the big leagues, as his wins were in the Trans Am.

Tom, Trans Am Series, 1977

In 1978, he was third overall at the Sebring 12 Hours, and also started racing in the Can Am series with the Schkee Lola and drove it in six Can Am races. This year, he'll have an all-new car designed by ex-Dan Gurney engineers Roman Slobodynskyj and Gary Wheeler. Like the Schkee, Spalding's new car is at the very limits of technology.

Spalding was SCCA Pro Racing Rookie of the Year and third overall in the 1977 Trans Am Championship.

Tom's "Spirit" ground effects Can Am car

First live camera in a Can Am car, racing at Elkhart Lake, Wisconsin

Tom Spalding

PictureTel

The racing video work led to other video technologies, and in 1984 Tom was one of the founders of PicTel (later PictureTel), which was the first company to create a practical video telephone – a pioneer in video conferencing. While video conferencing is common today with FaceTime and Skype, transmitting video in 1984 was a breakthrough. As CFO, Tom was responsible for the company's IPO. His wife, Barbara, who worked with Tom at PicTel, is shown on the monitor.

2Wire

In 1998, Tom again teamed up with one of his PictureTel partners as one of the co-founders of 2Wire. Their new company produced a "DSL broadband residential gateway" that transmitted voice, video and internet over a standard phone line. This device became the standard product provided by AT&T, British Telecom and TelMex. Over 80 million units were sold and at one point perhaps 30% of broadband customers in those markets had a 2Wire box – they're still in use today. AT&T eventually purchased the company. If you happen to look at your "WiFi connection" and see a 2Wire unit, it's one of Tom's.

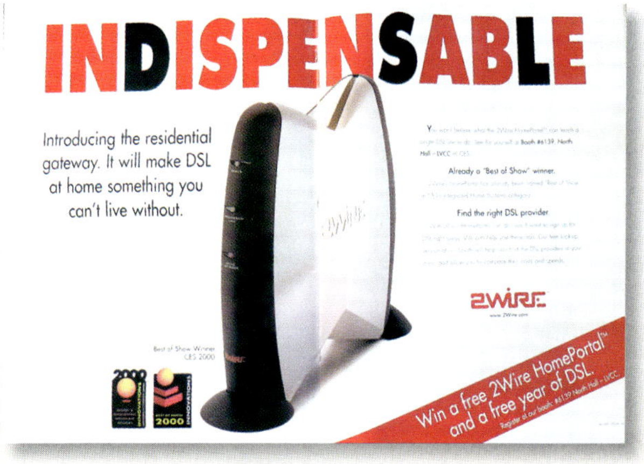

Frequent Flyer

The old guy still likes speed. Tom mostly flies his Cirrus aircraft, but also flies a twin-engine Eclipse jet. During the past several years, Tom has logged over 200,000 air miles, visiting Spalding Lab customers in nearly every state. Tom and his wife, Barbara, currently reside in Nevada, but the Spaldings still have family on the Central Coast. If you want to check out his aerial photos – go to flygy.spalding.com

They went easy on us.

Cliff and Tom in mayor's office, mid-'70s

In the mid-'70s there were a few SLO city administrators who were already upset with Tom and me even before the Warehouse Sound concert. Late one night, we ventured into City Hall with a photographer when no one was present. Tom and I sat down at the mayor's desk (as a spoof) for the photo. Then we decided to use the photo in a national advertisement and when the ad appeared, an irate city official called me on the carpet. Ultimately, the city official decided not to prosecute because I explained that the door had been "left open" and we did not touch anything. I'm not sure that SLO Mayor Schwartz even cared – because he never said a word about it.

However, the police did call a couple days after our rock concert and asked me to drop by. I went to the police station, sat in a chair, and waited for quite a while. One of the ranking officers then motioned me into a small office, shut the door and asked me to sit down. He came over, leaned into my face, and stared directly into my eyes.

"Who the hell do you guys think you are? You ever pull another stunt like that and you'll end up in jail. You understand?"

I tried to be cool. Before the concert, I had worried that we might get into trouble, so I had pre-planned an excuse. I started to mumble something, but the officer instantly threw his hand up in the air in a manner indicating it might be wise for me to keep my mouth shut.

"Are we clear?" he demanded.

Very respectfully, I replied, "Yes, sir" and he told me I could go. That was it.

In 2014 the police might have been less forgiving. Young people today don't get much slack.

Tom Spalding

The Spalding Family

Tom Spalding's parents are among the finest people I've ever met. Tom Sr., who passed away in 2001, was a serious master craftsman, always hard at work "inventing something." In addition to his motor racing accomplishments, he fabricated many components used in Tom Jr.'s "in-car camera systems" for RaceVision. His impressive shop looked like a hospital operating room: clean, organized and fully stocked with the best tools and machines. Whenever I went over to the Spaldings' home, Mr. Spalding always patiently answered my questions about the latest project he was designing and building.

1981: Tom's wife Barbara, Tom, Patricia holding grandson Nick, brother Patrick and Carol, Tom Sr.

Patricia, Tom Sr.'s loving wife, now 92, remains wise, charming and tactful. I was touched by her recent call to tell me that she had read, and enjoyed, *American Made*. I was lucky enough to have Patricia as my executive assistant in the '70s, when I was still in my twenties, and she provided a mature adult presence.

Barbara Spalding (Tom's wife) deserves much of the credit for the success of their various Spalding enterprises, as she has been a co-participant in each venture since his racing days. Tom is the first to say that her influence for the past 35 years has been an integral part of their shared success.

Tom Jr.'s brother, Patrick Spalding, trained as both an engineer and biologist. He designed and manufactured an array of products, including biomedical research equipment that flew on the Space Shuttle, and a tiny balloon to stop cranial bleeding.

When Patrick turned 35, he enrolled in medical school and became a leading OB/GYN in SLO County, delivering over 4,000 babies to date. Carol Spalding, Patrick's wife, worked for my former partner, John King, for some years (it's a small town) and now manages her husband's medical practice. Patrick and Carol have watched a whole lot of children grow up in our community – including four of their own.

Spalding Labs

In 1977, Patricia and Patrick founded Spalding Labs. Together they raised Arabian horses, and as all horse owners know, flies were a big problem. At the time, Patrick was at UCLA and learned of new research in biological insect control then under way at UC Riverside. As part of his master's program, Patrick raised his first batch of Fly Predators® that he and Patricia used on their horses. This new approach completely eliminated their fly problem. It was birth control for flies – so to speak.

During the '70s, ecological consciousness was in its infancy and pest control with beneficial insects was considered outside the box – pesticides were still the accepted "smart" method for controlling flies. Traditional horsemen were initially skeptical, believing that putting out bugs to kill bugs was a crazy idea. "We were considered on the lunatic fringe," recalls Tom Jr., who did the company's ads. Spalding Labs began as a small, kitchen-table family business selling Fly Predators® via the mail. The business grew steadily for 25 years, and in 2001 Patricia turned the business over to Tom.

Tom Spalding, 2014

Spalding Cow·Vac

Under Tom's guidance, Spalding Labs has emerged as the nation's leading supplier of equine and dairy fly control. Spalding Labs' Fly Predators® are sold directly to customers (Spalding-Labs.com) and through thousands of feed stores, veterinary clinics and mail order companies. Spalding Labs now has a product for the good health of nearly every domesticated animal – from the family dog to horses, cows and chickens – and those in zoos and fairgrounds. Spalding Labs even sells a Cow·Vac, which vacuums flies off cows on their way to milking. The Cow·Vac's production designer was Patrick's son, Zac, a mechanical engineer who is currently enrolled in medical school.

Radio.Spalding-Labs.com

Tom's love of music is now reflected in his Flying SL Ranch Radio streaming cowboy music station (radio.spalding-labs.com) and Spalding Labs' sponsorship of Michael Martin Murphey's nationwide concert tours (murph.spalding-labs.com).

Tom and I have now been "partners" for 45 years, in all kinds of ventures. The year 1969 was a very lucky year for me – I was in the right place at the right time when I met Tom.

Dr. Robert Miller with Scooter, 2012

Coming Up Next

Zara

Tom has always been a storyteller - from the early days at Warehouse Sound Company, and particularly as seen through his RaceVision in-car cameras and Fast Company TV shows. He still is the creative force behind every catalog, advertisement and the website. A visit to Spalding-Labs.com is a treat. You'll find over 100 great videos, including one starring their animated Fly Predators® character, "Zara." Go to zarah.Spalding-labs.com

It came as no surprise when, a year ago, Tom sent me a movie script for a feature film based on the life of Dr. Robert Miller, a world famous veterinarian and best-selling author. Miller has treated an unprecedented array of wild and domestic animals. He was also one of the early proponents of what is now called "Natural Horsemanship" or "Light Hands Horsemanship" – the non-coercive training of horses. He is best known for his scientific explanation and promotion of "Imprint Training" that bonds newborn foals to humans.

Dr. Robert Miller, with patient, 1960s

Equus Rising – The Movie

Equus Rising is a movie based on the three decades of Dr. Miller's life and work unraveling the mysteries of behavior between horse and man, which has had a worldwide impact.

The story begins with Dr. Miller facing a life-changing career decision that could risk his livelihood. At the same time he is given only seven days to save an abused horse named Emma, about to be put down for being "impossible to handle." Coincidentally, a bitter young journalist (Jennifer) arrives to conduct an interview for a national magazine. Dr. Miller convinces the young reporter (who is also at the end of her rope and knows nothing about horses) to help him with calming Emma. Over a very short period of time, Dr. Miller applies his unique methods of communication to connect and bond with Emma – which also holds the key to healing Jennifer's troubled heart.

As the story unfolds, we watch Jennifer and Dr. Miller work together, and we see flashes of Dr. Miller's extraordinary life. As a young veterinarian, he moves to California and finds himself in the midst of wild animal parks and movie animal trainers. Suddenly he is treating sick lions on his dining room table, elephants appear at his front door and escaped orangutans roam the neighborhood.

Through Dr. Miller's experiences, and his application of the scientific principles of Natural Horsemanship, we learn some of life's most meaningful lessons, such as how each of us can affect the quality of our lives and those around us through understanding, patience and the real power of kindness.

If horses had heroes, they would look to Dr. Robert M. Miller.

Flying drone with camera

Inset: Hand-held remote control

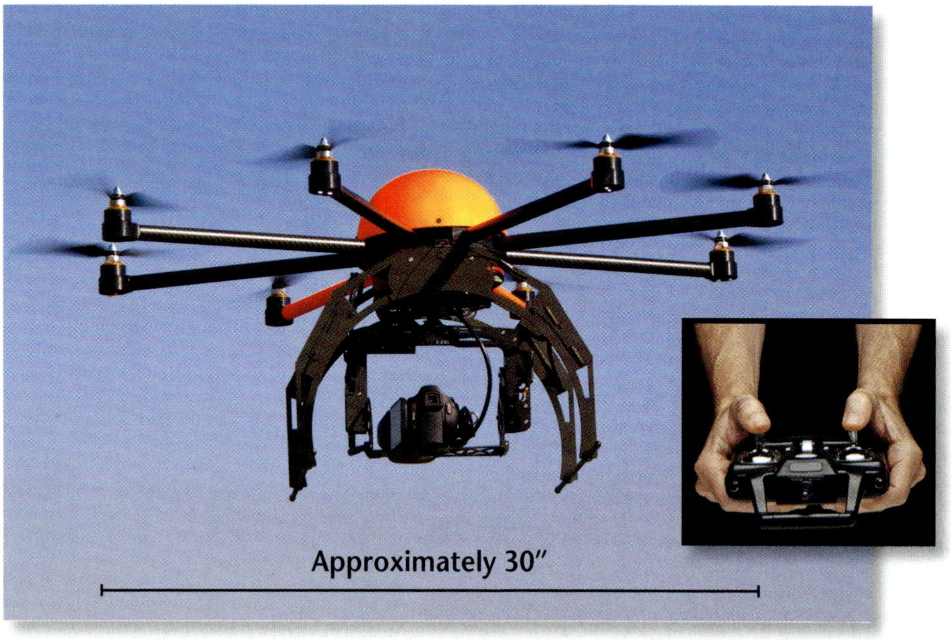

Old Friends – New Show

One day in November, I called Tom Spalding to ask a few questions about the newest video technology. Tom quickly shared his expertise, then added, almost as an afterthought, "Hey, I'm headed to Vegas to attend CES in January. I'll fly into San Luis and pick you up."

"Great," I said. "Just tell me the day and time. I'll be at the airport with bells on."

It was not our first tech date. Tom and I attended the Consumer Electronics Show (CES) in the '70s and early '80s, when it was held every year in Chicago. We'd make an annual pilgrimage to see all the new offerings in the audio business. The show was held in the main hall at the McCormick Place Convention Center, in a space of about 300,000 square feet. Around 200 exhibitors would share their latest creations. Then, in the late '90s, CES moved to Las Vegas.

Tom landed at the San Luis Obispo airport in his Cirrus SR22. It's his third Cirrus – he's a seasoned pilot and I had no qualms about putting my life in his hands. The SR22 is a small but very fast single-engine prop plane. We cruised over Nevada at 16,000 feet, our ground speed 220 mph. We each wore a nasal cannula for oxygen.

The airplane is monitored and operated by two 14-inch tandem flat screens that serve as the main flight instruments. A smorgasbord of information flows across both screens – detailed data about the plane, the weather and the surrounding territory – a far cry from the analog days.

Tom also flies an Eclipse twin-engine jet and years ago ordered a new Cirrus jet that might arrive sometime in 2016. Tom is 192nd on the customer waiting list, so he's not holding his breath. He signed the papers for the Cirrus in 2009 – apparently there is no shortage of buyers for personal jets.

Over the years, Tom had continued to attend CES, but it had been a while since I'd made the trip. The event is presented for people "in the business" and isn't open to the general public, but it's not difficult to obtain tickets.

The Las Vegas CES can be an overwhelming multimedia experience of sight and sound. It now occupies several buildings at the convention center, where 150,000 visitors converge to see, show and talk about the newest industry products. The consumer electronic displays are spread out over more than 2 million square feet of booths and exhibits by the 3,000 exhibitors who demonstrate and describe their electronic innovations. A few days are needed to tour all the displays. All the familiar brands – Sony, Pioneer, Samsung, Kenwood, JBL, Sennheiser, Altec Lansing – still exhibit, but the vast majority of companies exhibited at the show did not exist before 1995.

I hadn't been to Las Vegas for a few years. With the economy on the rebound, new construction is under way. Otherwise, the desert oasis appeared to be the same frenetic city that never sleeps. I thought there were more sidewalk barkers pushing "escort" cards in your face, or guys asking if you were interested in "party favors" (drugs for tourists). Vegas has always been a strange concoction brewed in the middle of the desert. Not exactly home sweet home.

The CES was terrific and highlighted an obvious trend: Business is digital and every consumer, from children to boomers and beyond, is a digital consumer.

I walked into the huge LG booth and donned a complimentary pair of 3D glasses, watched a massive video display (80 feet wide and 20 feet high) play ultra-high-def animation with surround sound. I ducked when an imaginary tiger leaped off the screen. The new ultra-HD video is an incremental step forward over current technology.

It was interesting to see a lot of "old guys" at the show. I felt right at home. Much like our nation's businesses, CES was largely a mature man's domain. The majority of people who run or manage these companies are 40 to 60 years old and the ratio of men to women (at the show) was nearly 4 to 1.

Here's a quick rundown on "new technology:"

Wearable technology: Every type and configuration of high tech wristwatches, rings, glasses and "wearable" cameras were on display. These devices can now keep track of everything going on in your body and in your environment.

A great example of this wearable technology is GoPro. They are the company who made the wearable camera famous. Their booth was over the top, featuring a racing Ferrari, a racing motorcycle and a $1.5 million Pagani sports car, all outfitted with GoPro cameras. Other companies also sell GoPro-type cameras, but Nick Woodman, the surfer who started GoPro, is one of the best marketeers on the planet. GoPro sales have doubled every year since 2004. If you would like to know more, head over to their website: GoPro.com

Remote control devices: Welcome to a new generation of high tech robotic vacuum cleaners, window washers and mini-helicopters. The robotic window washer is a great idea for high windows (irobot.com) but my favorite device was the Flying Eyes model mini-copter by Uneec Technology (FlyingEyes.com).

I was sitting at the display counter, looking at the Flying Eyes mini-copter and wondering if

I dare touch the remarkable machine. Flying Eyes is not a toy – it's a small drone designed primarily for aerial photography. I ended up checking it out up close and personal. No one seemed to care. The miniature helicopter is designed to carry a payload of up to 6 pounds.

At this exhibit I happened to be sitting next to a young man with a chiseled face and a ripped physique. He was wearing a huge diamond watch. I struck up a polite conversation, commenting that the drone was "one cool machine." The man looked amused and replied: "Good for shooting a video."

We exchanged a few pleasantries. I had no idea who the guy was, but he was beautifully dressed in casual attire. Suddenly Uneec Technology staff members came up and asked if they could take the man's photo, with him sitting next to their drone.

It was about that time that I noticed that the man seemed to have an entourage. A small group stood about 8 feet away, and then a woman broke from the group and rushed up to the Uneec staff: "No, please, no photos." She actually placed her hand about 12 inches in front of the man's face.

The man was the famous hip-hop artist and mogul 50 Cent. As soon as the photographer showed up, the rap star shrugged at me, stood up and walked away. His abrupt departure dashed any chance to ask him if I could be a back-up dancer in his next video.

Music/audio programing: "Streaming music" in radio formats from Pandora, YouTube, iTunes Radio, and Spotify are rapidly evolving to challenge traditional radio. Today, Pandora is essentially the largest "radio station" in the nation, and their "playlist generator" tailors your streaming music to your personal taste. When Pandora went public in 2011, they had 800,000 tracks from more than 80,000 artists, and around 75 million users.

Dr. Dre and Jimmy Iovine (chairmen of Universal Music Group) launched the Beats Music streaming service in 2013, convinced that their "more sophisticated mix" would win over a loyal group of music lovers. Apple just snapped up Beats for $3 billion (not a bad payday) so Apple foresees a big future in the streaming music business. Currently, Beats has over 500,000 paying subscribers. By 2018 the industry expects the "industry subscriber base" to reach 150 million.

Ultra-HD TV: The newest iteration of high definition television features ultra-high def in "4K." The very thin monitors are curved and come in varying sizes, up to a 108-inch model. Yes, a 108-inch screen. 4K sets have four times the pixel count of the current 1080 pixel sets. The stylish flat-screen television that so many of us bought just a couple of years ago will soon look "dated." The curved 4K screens will hit the stores in mid-2014.

Bitcoin: There was a buzz at CES about "Bitcoin," the "international digital currency" recently covered in several national business publications. In place of traditional currency, Bitcoin can be used as a peer-to-peer payment system. Bitcoin claimed about $10 billion in transactions in 2013 and has grown in 2014 despite Bitcoin falling about 50% against the U.S. dollar. People have opened over 40 million Bitcoin accounts, and it's accepted at progressive companies such as Overstock.com, Dish Network and Dell. Bitcoin is the product of developer Satosi Nakamoto (a pseudonym), who introduced Bitcoin in 2009 as "cryptocurrency" to control the creation and transfer of digital money. I spent an hour at the Bitcoin booth, and I still don't quite understand how it works, or if it will succeed as a new, long-term currency form. Bitcoin "experts" speak in esoteric phrases about the lack of intrinsic value of traditional currency, versus the benefits of Bitcoin. There will be a digital currency in the coming years – I'm just not sure the new medium of exchange will be Bitcoin. It will be interesting to see how the U.S. government will react if and when Bitcoin gets substantial momentum as an alternate currency.

Other CES highlights

- A thermal imaging camera for your iPhone is now only $300. Think of the possibilities.
- A wide array of new high tech security systems and control devices are available to better aid you in your car and home. Now you can start your car, turn on any appliance, or check your home security from anywhere with your iPhone.
- "Driverless technology" is no longer a pipe dream. Both Audi and BMW showed off their new technology, but since lawmakers need to agree on legislation, this won't be available anytime soon.

New technology *not* shown at CES

A **"quantum computer"** called The D-Wave 2 has been developed and manufactured by D-Wave in Burnaby, British Columbia, and it may prove to be revolutionary.

The D-Wave computer combines digital computation with quantum physics and has the potential to solve problems that would take today's fastest computer a century to compute. The D-Wave's unit operates from within a 10-foot black box that maintains the temperature at just above 0° Fahrenheit. The manufacturer is backed by a mega-venture investment firm from Silicon Valley; Amazon founder Jeff Bezos; and Q-Tel, an investment arm of our government.

Cliff and Tom

Current customers include defense contractor Lockheed Martin and unnamed U.S. intelligence agencies. D-Wave is confident that its computer will change how we find cures for human diseases, conduct our everyday business on Earth and explore the universe beyond our planet. Skeptics claim the D-Wave 2 is overrated and will have limited use. As I write this, the D-Wave 2 runs about $10 million a pop.

We've come a long way from caves.

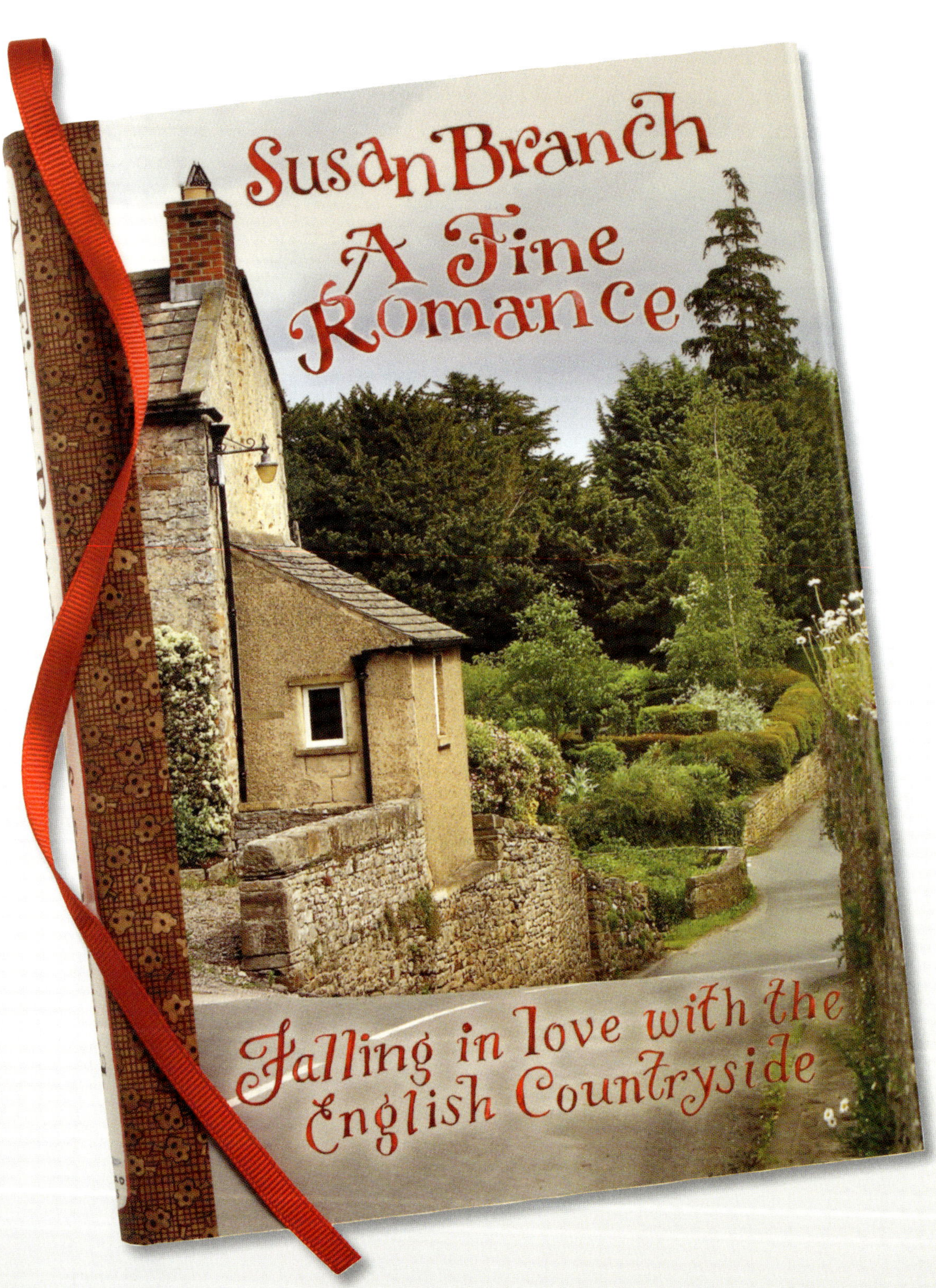
Susan Branch
A Fine Romance
Falling in love with the English Countryside

A Fine Friendship

Although Susan Branch is my ex-wife and has lived for years on the East Coast, we have remained good friends for the past three decades. The stormy seas of our younger years have long settled into calm waters.

My wife, Lynette, has become friends with Susan and Joe Hall (the love of Sue's life) and the four of us occasionally get together for dinner when they come west to stay in their house, just down the road from us. Sue and Joe just celebrated 25 years together with a trip to England. Sue's a best-selling author, and she wrote a book about their adventure: *A Fine Romance: Falling in Love With the English Countryside.*

As *American Made* goes to press, Sue's newest book (shown on opposite page) is selling well in both America and in England and is currently No. 1 on Amazon's list of British travel books with a five-star rating. It's also available in bookstores and directly from her website.

If I seem to brag a little about Sue, it's because I admire her spirit and prolific talent. She is a nationally renowned writer, designer and artist. At last count, she has sold well over *four million* books, along with millions of calendars, greeting cards, and the many offerings from her line of fabrics and chinaware.

Nearly 90,000 devoted fans read Sue's monthly email newsletter, *Willard,* named for her maternal grandfather. She also maintains a popular interactive blog, and the comments from readers are fun to read. Go to: **SusanBranch.com**

Susan announced the 10th Anniversary Edition of *Autumn* in October, 2014. The book, a reprint from 2004, is her first from Spring Street Publishing Imprint, Susan's new publication house.

Susan Branch

The other day on the phone, Sue mentioned that she is "several hundred pages" into writing a novel, a prequel to *A Fine Romance*. Susan's newest work is fiction, but much of the story is drawn from her early years in San Luis Obispo, when she was married to yours truly. She says it's a "thinly disguised memoir" – based on her 18 diaries.

I may have been the inspiration Sue needed to move cross country to Martha's Vineyard. And that's what scares me. I admit I'm a bit nervous about her writing about our former life together in '70s California. I have the same awkward feeling seeing Lynette and Sue chatting up a storm when we spend an evening catching up.

San Luis Obispo is a small coastal community with its own generous share of California stories. Susan tells me I shouldn't be too worried, though it would not surprise me if her new book is in *Bridget Jones' Diary* style. She insists that the real names of her characters have been changed to protect the innocent.

But what about the guilty? Sue doesn't have a mean-spirited bone in her body, but all her good friends know she can be wickedly funny. It was the '70s, after all, and many of us boomers were moving fast and (like many young husbands) my matrimonial brain wasn't yet fully developed.

If you are not familiar with Susan Branch's work, you're in for a treat. Sue keeps her head, hand and heart connected directly to the page. Her books are a return to a now-distant, more innocent time, with all the copy in her own handwriting, so you feel that you're reading a letter from a friend.

Watch for her new book – it's due out in mid-2015.

Susan's inspirational handwritten watercolor books from the "Heart of the Home" are about home, family, food and the little things that make life sweet.

Jim Smith, Family and Friends

Jim, 1970

Jim Smith and I have now been business partners for 43 years. Jim was a practicing attorney from the mid-'60s through the '90s and oversaw the evolution of his legal firm from Grundel, Fredman and Smith to Burke, Smith, Helenius, Hayes and Tardiff. Jim also became one of the major shareholders and chairman of First Bank of San Luis Obispo, and helped orchestrate the sale to Santa Barbara Bank and Trust. In four decades as partners, Jim and I have never had a serious fight, and have supported one another through financial ups and downs and personal transitions.

Everyone who knows Jim Smith knows how much he loves sports, especially the Chicago Cubs. He's been a *lifelong* fan. Jim is a guy who travels from San Luis Obispo to Chicago just to catch an "important" Cubs series.

Jim graduated from the University of Wisconsin, so when the Badgers played the UCLA Bruins in the 1999 Rose Bowl, Jim and I made the trip down to Pasadena to watch the game. It was a game for the ages, and Wisconsin won 38 to 31. The game ended, Jim was elated, but we were on the UCLA side of the stadium. Jim suddenly decided he needed to be on the Wisconsin side so he could sing the "Badger Song" along with his fellow alumni. We fought our way through the crowd like crazy men to reach the other side of the field in time for Jim to join in the singing. As the song ended, Jim turned to me with tears in his eyes and said: "It's going to be just like this when the Cubs win the World Series."

The Smiths and the Kings have always been extended family. When I returned home from Sausalito, I lived for a time in the Kings' guest studio and after a divorce I lived in the Smiths' guest room. **Kevin Smith** (Jim's son) and I shared a house for a year or so in the late '90s and remain great friends. During that time, Kevin met (and later married) **Carolyn Johnson,** who was the local news reporter on KSBY TV. Not long after they were married, Carolyn was offered a position with ABC News in San Francisco, and she and Kevin moved to the Bay Area. Kevin continued his legal practice, and Carolyn was the lead anchor for ABC (KGO) for many years. In 2014, the Smiths moved to Studio City with their two children after Carolyn was offered the position of co-anchor for NBC in Southern California. **Kelly Smith,** Jim's daughter, is also an attorney and lives in San Luis Obispo with her daughter, Grace.

Mr. Cool with his new 240Z, 1971

River rafting trip in the late '70s

Beverly and Jim with Bandit, early '80s

Kevin with his son, Griffin, 2013

Grace Smith and her mom, Kelly Smith, 2013

Logan with her mom, Carolyn, Stanley and Grandpa Jim, 2013

First Bank of San Luis Obispo: Chairman Smith with fellow bank officers Reese Davies and David Booker, mid-'80s

Kevin, Cliff and Jim, early '90s

John King, Jim Smith and Brendan McAdams

Left to right: I snapped this photo of Ben, Jim and John in Greece during the mid-'70s.
Below: John, Jim and I on a ski trip in Colorado in the '80s

John King, Jim Smith and Dr. Brendan McAdams were already in their 30s when I was 21 and they took me under their wing. They had previously been involved as investors in our retail stores and in Warehouse Sound Company, and we developed friendships that remain to this day.

John King has an engineering background from his years at Cal Poly in the '60s. His son, JG King also attended Cal Poly and went on to receive his MBA at Pepperdine University. JG developed the AJ Spurs chain of steak houses, and later sold it to work with John at King Enterprises. Together, the two oversee an organization of 600 people who operate King Venture hotels, restaurants and a myriad of other commercial projects in Southern, Central and Northern California. John King is the true definition of a "job creator."

In the '70s, John King truly worked around the clock, and when he finally went on a vacation to the Virgin Islands, it was not more than a week before I received a phone call. John told me he had turned over a check for $100,000 from our partnership account, because we had just entered into escrow to buy a beach resort in St. Thomas, and he said we needed to cover the check. I thought he was kidding, but he wasn't. I scrambled with Jim Smith to deposit the funds – that day.

Once, some years ago, I called John's son, JG, to check to see if John had closed escrow on a property they were selling. JG responded dryly: "Yes, skid marks."

I didn't understand at first. "Skid marks?"

"Yes," said JG. "He's off to buy another property."

My neighbors in the early '70s: John King and his son, JG. On vacation with John and his wife, Carole, in Hawaii, late '70s

In the early years, Jim Smith and I were originally partners with John King, and Rob Rossi later came into the picture. Rob and John began working together, and split off from Jim and me to form new partnerships, including the Rossi-King Organization (RKO) and Rossi-King Enterprises. As the years continued, John and Rob began to focus more on individual projects.

John and Rob are two of the most prolific entrepreneurs on the Central Coast. While John focused on acquiring hotels, restaurants and a variety of other commercial real estate, Rob became involved in numerous commercial projects, including Central Coast golf courses, several wineries and development of the Santa Margarita Ranch. In addition, John and Rob are still partners in several downtown San Luis Obispo properties. I've known JG since he was about 8, and now he's about 50. John and Carole had their 50th wedding anniversary in 2013.

Left, Brendan McAdams: Ben is still a practicing physician, and he and his wife, Pat McAdams, are still partners in some of our real estate ventures. Ben is also a tireless fundraiser for non-profit projects. Over the decades, I've watched Ben donate his time to a number of good causes, and he has quietly helped raise millions of dollars for many community projects.

With the Smiths, Pat and Ben McAdams and other friends, rafting the Rouge River, Oregon

Lynn and Chris Helenius

David Riordan - Multimedia Man

David Riordan lives and works in Boulder, Colorado. We starting working together in the '70s, and have collaborated on many projects over the years, including production of a music CD called *Wilderness America* to raise money to help the Emily Polk and Sierra Club save the pygmy oaks in Los Osos, California.

David Riordan

David lived in Northern California, but we stayed in touch and occasionally I would travel to Marin County during the years he was married to Jane Bay. Jane worked as a righthand executive for George Lucas, and one night the phone rang. Mr. Lucas had invited us over for dinner at his new house in San Rafael. Actually, it was more of a mansion. We sat at a small table in the kitchen, eating tacos. Mr. Lucas was totally down to earth and charming. I hung on his every word through dinner, because the man who produced both *American Graffiti* and *Star Wars* was one of my heroes. At one point during the meal, a huge bear-like dog wandered into the kitchen and up to the table. I looked at the dog and said: "Wookie?" and Mr. Lucas laughed and confirmed. The house was more traditional than I expected, yet was also warm and casually elegant with all kinds of original art from famous artists.

The next day Jane took us on a tour of Skywalker Ranch in Lucas Valley, not far from San Rafael. The ranch development encompassed several hundred acres and housed the administrative offices and post-production facilities for Lucas Films. Mr. Lucas had brought in skilled craftsmen from all over the country to work on the facilities and the attention to detail and the scope of the facilities were inspiring. His own office was like the inside of a boat, and was filled with meticulously detailed models from *Star Wars*. As someone who was interested in construction, it was wonderful to have a glimpse at what this person had planned and constructed with exquisite execution.

David and I openly and actively discussed politics since our college days, but as I matured into a pragmatic businessman, I learned that publicly expressing personal political opinions could be problematic. Just the same, I believed that the U.S. invasion of Iraq was a mistake and I knew that David had similar feelings.

TwoVoters.com DVD, 2008

In 2006, I wrote and placed a "personal letter" as a national ad in *USA TODAY*, questioning the course of the Iraq War. There seemed to be no end in sight to the quagmire.

When John McCain chose Sarah Palin as his running mate in 2008, I was motivated to act. David and I decided to collaborate on a project called TwoVoters.com. We wrote and produced a DVD and set up an interactive website. We placed full-page ads in *Newsweek* and other national publications to help drive website traffic. The campaign caused quite a stir. Our various videos went viral and were seen by millions of Americans. We did not have any formal affiliation with the Democratic Party and I paid for the campaign out of my own pocket. My main motivation in launching the TwoVoters campaign was primarily based on my opposition to the war in Iraq. As it turned out, Obama certainly did not need any help to win in 2008. The

David and I worked together on *Medicine Wheel,* his solo album for Capitol Records, which was recorded in LA at Capitol studios. In later years, we also collaborated on several other projects, including *Wilderness America* (to help raise money to preserve open space) and four other Warehouse Sound Co. albums, in connection with a promotion of Capital recording artists.

election was not even close, but just the same I was proud of our efforts and it was great to work with David. All TwoVoter materials disclosed our names and backgrounds.

My sudden flurry of political activity did not sit well with my wife, or with some of my conservative friends, but it soon became water under the bridge. Life moved on. I have not been involved in politics since 2008. From my vantage point, any remaining political civility has dried up and most of the political discourse has become inflammatory and divisive. I don't fit well in any of the camps.

David has always held cutting-edge and creative jobs, so I have learned a lot from our collaboration during our long friendship. He spent many years in Southern California and became the vice president of production for Time Warner Interactive, then the creative director of Interplay Entertainment, and the senior producer for Philips Media. David later became the creative director of Disney Interactive, developing the website for *Toy Story*. He's an award-winning musician, a music producer, and a lecturer at the UCLA Media Program as well as the USC Film School.

Currently, David is VP of media development at Integral Life, and a list of his past projects can be found on Wikipedia. We've always remained close friends, and I'm sure we will collaborate *on something* – once again.

Left to right: Cliff, David and Doug Johnson at the annual motorcycle convention held in Indianapolis, Indiana, in the late '70s. David's company had designed an "inflatable theatre" (in the background) for showing convention audiences a multimedia presentation that the three of us produced, documenting the history of the Windjammer.

Richard Blake

Dick and Cliff
at the Avila Bay Club, late '90s

Richard Blake expanded Blake Printery and started a new company in the 1970s called Poor Richard's Press. A few years ago Poor Richard's became PRP Companies, after Dick sold the larger portion of his printing operation to a national enterprise and retired. The PRP offices are still located on Beebee Street. Now Dick spends free hours on the shooting range, perfecting his marksmanship with his .45 pistol. Dick tinkers with business, but spends most of his time with his wife, Arlene. They still live in San Luis Obispo, but whenever I call Dick's cell phone he's never home – he's in Colorado, or Alaska or somewhere overseas. We once flew in his helicopter from San Luis Obispo to Colorado, a memorable flight that included a tour in and around the Grand Canyon.

In our younger years, when we lived next to each other, Dick installed a helipad in the open area between our houses. The master bathroom of my house had a shower with a large but private window facing an unpopulated mountainside. One morning, while I was in the shower – I was shampooing my hair and my eyes were shut – I got an uneasy feeling as the window started to rattle. I rinsed off and there was Dick, at eye level, hovering in his chopper. He grinned, waved, backed straight up, and took off. We had a lot of fun together in our youth, but always made it our practice to stay within the limits of all laws that we felt were applicable.

Dick with Lucy, after we landed near San Luis Bay. The pooch has her own set of headphones and loves to fly. The helicopter is a model MD-500-E.

Elaine Sullivan

Elaine Sullivan joined Warehouse Sound in 1971, at the time Tom Spalding and I were launching our mail-order stereo business. Elaine was a recent Cal Poly graduate and before long became our vice president of operations, overseeing much of our day-to-day business. Elaine was a no-nonsense executive who demanded professionalism from our staff as well as from our vendors. In those days she was married to Mike Diskin, our CFO, and together she and Mike helped build our company. After a divorce, Elaine left California Cooperage during its early stages of development to return to college to earn a nursing degree. After becoming an RN, she spent several years in the Bay Area as a critical care and ER nurse.

In the late 1980s, Elaine decided to return to the business world and moved to Martha's Vineyard. There she built the famous Black Dog merchandising business, created a website and award-winning catalog, and established a number of retail stores. She also produced the bestselling *Black Dog Summer on the Vineyard* cookbook. Black Dog became even more well-known during the Clinton sex scandal, when President Clinton bought gifts for Monica Lewinsky at the Black Dog store on Martha's Vineyard. *The Boston Globe* reported that Elaine told a pesky *Good Morning America* staffer to "Get a life," to the amusement of islanders who witnessed the incident. Elaine made the papers again when her marketing strategy for Black Dog was favorably reviewed in *The Wall Street Journal.*

After 9/11, Elaine returned to California and now lives on the Central Coast, where she serves as director of marketing for International, Graduate and Extended Education at Cal Poly. As part of her marketing responsibilities for Cal Poly on an international platform, Elaine has worked closely with Peregrine media, shepherding the production of a video to showcase Cal Poly to both international and out-of-state students and their parents. YouTube: *Cal Poly Preparation for a Connected World.* The video is terrific – makes me proud to be a Mustang.

Elaine greets President Bill Clinton on his visit to Black Dog Restaurant in Vineyard's Haven, late '90s

Elaine with her thoroughbred Doc, circa 1977

Chris Whittle

Cliff and Chris sailing in St. Croix

Chris Whittle continued in the publishing business and developed Whittle Communications, which published *Esquire* magazine as well as other specialty publications. In the early '90s, Time Warner acquired Whittle Communications.

In the following years, Chris moved on to other projects – he was the creative force behind Edison Charter Schools. Mr. Whittle ruffled some feathers as CEO of Edison in his attempt to accelerate the evolution of the American educational system – it's never easy to challenge the U.S. academic establishment. I think that he has finally found his calling with *Avenues* school, located in Manhattan. He calls the venture his "last big rodeo."

Chris, 2013

Avenues has been called "a world school" – plans for future locations in London, Paris, Beijing and elsewhere are in the works. Chris' new school incorporates a refreshing educational philosophy and cutting-edge technology. He and his partners raised $75 million to build Avenues, and the facility is state-of-the-art, offering classes from kindergarten through high school. It's an educational system that Apple might have designed and built if it were in the education business. I talked to Chris shortly after the original effort in Manhattan was completed, and I asked how he managed to raise such a huge sum of money to build what I called "a new-age school for the children of the international mega-rich." His reply: "We hope to set some new standards in education – we hope to lead the way."

This new approach to education may be expensive for the schools' backers and for students' parents, but so is a Mercedes. As Mercedes often points out, the benefits of R&D technology and road testing of the most expensive Mercedes cars eventually appear in their less expensive models. In its first year, Avenues has been receiving good press. I talked with Chris again after the school opened, and he was pleased with their progress. At the time of this writing, there is already a waiting list for admittance. For more on Avenues, Google: Chris Whittle, *New York* magazine or visit **Avenues.org**

Cliff, Chris, Gary Hare and David Riordan, meeting about marketing strategy for California Cooperage, circa 1980

Bruce James and Steve Puglisi

Bruce James
and President George W. Bush

Bruce James is another "older guy" who helped me in my early years, and we have remained friends ever since. Bruce owned ***Barclays*** - a pioneering electronic printing and publishing company - and his expertise enabled Tom and me to streamline our mail-order business.

Bruce eventually sold Barclays. Some years later, he was appointed by President George W. Bush, and approved by the U.S. Senate, as the 24th public printer of the United States. From 2004 to 2007, he worked in Washington, D.C., overseeing a staff of several thousand people who print all the documents produced by the executive office of the president, the Congress, the Supreme Court, and many governmental agencies. Later, he served as chairman of the National Institute for Health.

Bruce and his wife, Nora, still have a home in San Francisco, but spend most of their time in Nevada, where they own the former Howard Hughes estate on Lake Tahoe, near Incline Village. It's always been a joy to visit them there. In a recent conversation, however, Bruce told me that since he's turned 70, he and Nora have decided to place their Tahoe home on the market. He said their place "just isn't practical" for their retirement years. Even the guy in my life who would "charge windmills and who could get anything done" is now starting to adjust his sails - to think more in terms of comfort and practicality.

Steve Puglisi remains one of the truly gifted architects on the Central Coast, creating thoughtful and elegant designs for major developers. His architectural firm designed several impressive commercial buildings in San Luis Obispo and numerous residential estates in the area – many of them can be viewed at puglisidesigns.com.

Steve is also known for his volunteer work on the Avila Valley Sea Life Center. The center is located in a building that Steve designed that houses marine aquariums as well as exhibits detailing animal and plant life in the ocean and estuaries. The mission of this non-profit center is to educate children in a hands-on fashion and to encourage a long-term interest in science. Visitors enjoy up-close encounters with local ocean species and develop a better understanding of Avila's marine environment. Steve was an avid deep-sea fisherman for years and has hauled more than his share of tuna from the sea.

Postscripts

Jim Agee We were originally introduced by our wives in 2002. Lynette and Barb often travel to golf tournaments together, and so our first meeting was pretty much a blind date. As I have grown older, it seems more difficult to make close friends, but Jim and I hit it off and continue to meet on a regular basis at a café downtown where we discuss a wide variety of subjects. More than a year ago, Barb and Jim stayed in our guest quarters for several weeks (while their residence was being renovated) and it happened to be during the period of time I was writing the first draft of this book. It's no accident that I often mention Jim in the book, because (being the gracious guest) he offered to read my drafts and his observations were always tactful, and often challenging. Jim has worked in management at Phillips 66 for 33 years, and Barb has worked for the past three decades, managing a medical office. Both are contemplating retirement. Jim claims he'll spend more time driving his classic Corvette and has begun a bucket list. *[See page 384]*

Paul Brydon was one of my friends in high school and we worked together on the ASL governing council. He was also a star on the varsity basketball team, along with his identical twin brother, Wayne. Everyone in our class knew the Brydon twins because they were truly nice guys, smart, and both were about 6' 4" and looked like teen idols. Not a bad hand in life. Paul now works as chief operating officer at a large hospital in Southern California.

John Doyle guided California Cooperage as vice president of operations until the early '80s. He became president of Dell Industries in San Luis Obispo, and for the past 20 years has been the vice president of operations and finance for The Spice Hunter, a division of S.F. Sauer.

Dan Lloyd and I first met about 30 years ago, when he was running an engineering firm that he co-founded. We also saw each other at weekly three-hour evening meetings as members of a small men's group. The group was formed after a communications workshop we had all attended, and we met consistently for about five years. We discussed current events, books, movies and our personal lives. Dan is a consultant with a statewide range of clients in real estate development, and is currently the national area chairman for the National Association of Home Builders.

Bob Silva served as CFO for Warehouse Sound Company and later for California Cooperage. We worked together for the better part of the '70s and Bob was always the calm, analytical mind that kept Tom and me from running too far off the tracks. It also helped that Bob had a good sense of humor. He went on to be a member of the accounting firm of GBP&B, a CFO for Lindamood-Bell Learning Processes, and then CFO for Specialty Construction before his retirement. Bob and his wife, Cathy, live in San Luis Obispo and will be among a rare group of my friends who will be celebrating a 50th wedding anniversary in the not-too-distant future.

Doug Johnson moved to the Bay Area many years ago and we lost contact. Carol is retired and lives in San Luis Obispo – but I'm not sure what she is up to these days.

Others involved: Several other key people helped grow our company and the stereo business, including **Mike Klickstein, Bob Jonte, Randy McClusky and Bob Oberg** – all great guys I lost track of over the years. I also worked closely with **Sandy Johnson,** who was department head at Warehouse Sound Company, later became a supervisor for Par Excellence Personnel and retired a few years ago.

Vineyard in northern San Luis Obispo County

The Branch Family

Above: Cliff, Greg, Russ, Tony – mid-'80s
Left: Greg, Tony and Cliff, 1967

Tony Branch, my oldest brother, is 72 and lives with his partner, Ed McCann, near the beaches of St. Petersburg, Florida. Tony is retired but still teaches a course in business and American culture at Eckerd College. He was an instructor at Ohio State University while completing his Ph.D. in European and American history, and after that had a 30-year career as an academic administrator at Golden Gate University (GGU) in San Francisco. Tony worked there in a variety of roles, including vice president of academic affairs. He set up the GGU programs in Southeast Asia, and taught a number of classes overseas.

Tony was always a good student and received a Woodrow Wilson Foundation Dissertation Fellowship in graduate school, which allowed him to spend the better part of a year in Paris and London doing research for his dissertation. He later earned an MBA from the Drucker School at Claremont University, working at night and going to college during the day. His energy and commitment served him well when he assumed his administrative duties at GGU.

Tony and I often talk politics and he recently stayed with Lynette and me on Galveston Island. Tony was a great help and very supportive as I worked on the political and social essays in this book.

Uncle Nick, aunts Aggie and Fran, mid-'60s

Grandfather Russel T. Branch and his son (our father) share a drink, mid-'60s

Greg and crew sailing the South Pacific, late '90s

Greg Branch, my second-oldest brother, is 68 and lives on Camano Island in the state of Washington with his wife, Michele. He currently works as a senior mechanical engineer for Lund Engineering in Seattle. Lund contracts directly with Boeing to develop manufacturing technologies – from prototype development to production processes – for composite structures used in the 787 airliner. From an early age, Greg was fascinated with machinery and seemed destined to become an engineer. My mom's brother, Dr. Steven Kline, was the department head of the mechanical engineering department at Stanford and was an inspiration to Greg. After working in the private sector for many years, Greg returned to the University of Washington to earn a master's degree in engineering, and based on his research at UW he co-founded MicroGREEN technologies. Greg has won design awards from *Popular Science, Hydraulics and Pneumatics* magazine and *Product Design* magazine. He is about to retire – Michele retired a few years ago, after a 22-year career as an elementary school teacher.

My brother was always an avid sailor. He and a friend started the Monterey Peninsula Sailing Club in 1965. At the age of 21, Greg answered a newspaper ad and crewed on a 36-foot sloop, *as navigator,* from Monterey to Hawaii. This was quite a feat for a young man, especially because GPS and cell phones were still far from invention. The voyage in the small sailing boat took 21 days, and most of the time the crew was beyond sight of land. At one point, they were more than 1,000 miles from any shore.

Greg continued to sail throughout his adult life, always telling the family, "At 50, I'm going to sell my home, quit my job and sail around the world." No one knew if he was truly *serious.* When Greg turned 50, he called to say that he had sold his house. He had also quit his *excellent job* as engineering manager at a solid company. Most of his next two years were spent on the water. On one voyage, he skippered a 46-foot Downeaster from American Samoa to Seattle, via Hawaii. He has logged about 20,000 nautical miles, including a year-long cruise down to Puerto Vallarta, Mexico, and on to the South Pacific. Greg and his wife recently called to say hi, but we didn't seem to have a very good phone connection. "Where are you guys?" I asked. "We're anchored in a little cove in the San Juan Islands," Greg answered. "We're sailing this week."

Greg and Michelle at Port of Edmonds Marina, Washington, during a 12-day sail around Puget Sound

The Branch Family

Mariah and Russ, circa 1975

Russ at 10

Mariah and Russ, circa 1995

Mariah, 2013

Mariah and Russell Branch are Greg's children, who matured into terrific adults (in my unbiased opinion). It was a joy to work with Mariah for two months during the TwoVoters campaign. After her undergraduate studies, Mariah served in the Peace Corps, worked in foreign countries, and attended the University of Michigan, where she earned a master's degree in environmental economics. Mariah currently works for Sun Edison Solar Company as a business analyst.

Russell graduated from the University of California, Davis, with a degree in chemistry, and works testing compounds for a manufacturer in North Carolina. Russell and his wife, Wendi, live with their two children in North Carolina. Wendi works as a nurse, and she and Russ are expecting a baby girl sometime in 2014.

Tony at 17

Greg at 17

Betty with Tony, 1944

Grandpa Russ and Mariah,
circa 1990

Left to right: George Branch and sisters Kathryn (Khaki) and Elizabeth (Bibi) and older brother Russ (my father), '80s family reunion

Cliff, Mariah, Russ and Betty, circa 1998

Lynette's father Carl with his two athletes, Jill (left) and Lynette (right), circa 1972

Russ and Wendi
on their wedding day, 2007

Lynette, a star tennis player at 17, received a full-ride scholarship!

Russ, Wendi,
Noah, Benjamin, 2013

Chris Nichols

From Getaway Driver to Advertising Whiz

I did not know my cousin Chris *all that well* growing up – since he lived on the East Coast and I lived on the West Coast, but about the time we were teenagers, my family occasionally spent vacation time on the East Coast, enough time so I knew Chris was pretty cool. He could play the guitar and sing really well and he even had his own rock band. Chris was also a handsome devil, a good sailor, and he had that East Coast dry wit and a quick grin.

Frankly, I was a little jealous – *but it was impossible not to like the guy.*

Truth is, had we lived closer to each other, our parents may not have allowed us to hang out together. We always seemed to get into trouble – quickly – anytime our two teenage brains were in close proximity.

That's Mr. Cool, at left, with his guitar, in 1967.

At some point, Chris figured out that his chances of becoming a rock star were not great. By 23, he started freelancing – writing advertising jingles – and thus began his career in advertising.

Given his charm and wit, he ended up working for Hill-Holliday (a large Boston agency) and then became the in-house creative director for UNUM Life Insurance Company.

In 1998, Chris started his own advertising agency which he grew into a $20 million enterprise. Chris was the creative director of his company, NL Partners, a firm that handles clients such as L.L. Bean, Time Warner, Subway Restaurants (from Maine to Pennsylvania) and other regional clients.

Chris sold the company in 2013, and that's why you see him reading a magazine in a 46-foot Tartan sloop.

Growing up, Chris was lucky enough to have great parents, along with an older and younger sister (Debbie and Patty) to keep him in touch with reality.

Chris now resides with his wife, Kim, on Orr's Island, Maine, overlooking Harpswell Sound. Kim is sitting next to Chris – the old guy reading the magazine in the goofy-looking hat (above).

At a recent family reunion (on the West Coast) Chris stood up in front of all of our families and recounted the night we were arrested and thrown in jail, as teenagers, for throwing rocks in the town of Huntington, Long Island, after one of the rocks found its way through a large bank window. *[See page 61]*

My cousin's version of the story went like this: "There I was, driving safely, hands at ten and two on the wheel, minding my own business, and these miscreants in the back seat went crazy. Don't blame their hooliganism on me – *I was only driving the car."*

However, with further discussion, it became questionable whether Chis even had a valid driver's license at the time of the incident, and his older sister also pointed out that he did not have permission to use his father's car. *Minor details to an advertising whiz.*

My cousin has now gone full circle. He still plays guitar, is currently in two bands, and (I think) he still secretly hopes to become a rock star.

A Letter to My Grandfather

The Boomer Generation began in 1946 – after World War II.

Growing up, most of what I learned about WWII came from high school history classes or from John Wayne movies. My father, who was in the Merchant Marine, did not talk much about the war, but he made it a point to instill in his sons an appreciation and gratitude for the sacrifices made by our servicemen, especially those who were wounded or lost their lives on behalf of our country.

The "Greatest Generation" made it possible for boomers to grow up with freedom and, for the most part, prosperity.

In late 2012, my brothers came for a visit and one night we found ourselves reminiscing about our family. Lynette was listening and decided to search the internet for information about our grandfather and found the book shown here. When it arrived, it was still in the original box. When we opened the leatherbound book, we found my grandfather's business card attached to the inside cover. The book was titled: *A Report to the People*. It was published in 1946, and it documents Stone & Webster's worldwide engineering projects, as well as their role in the war effort.

The letter from the War Department, addressed to my grandfather, was reprinted on page 24 of the book, and it is self-explanatory.

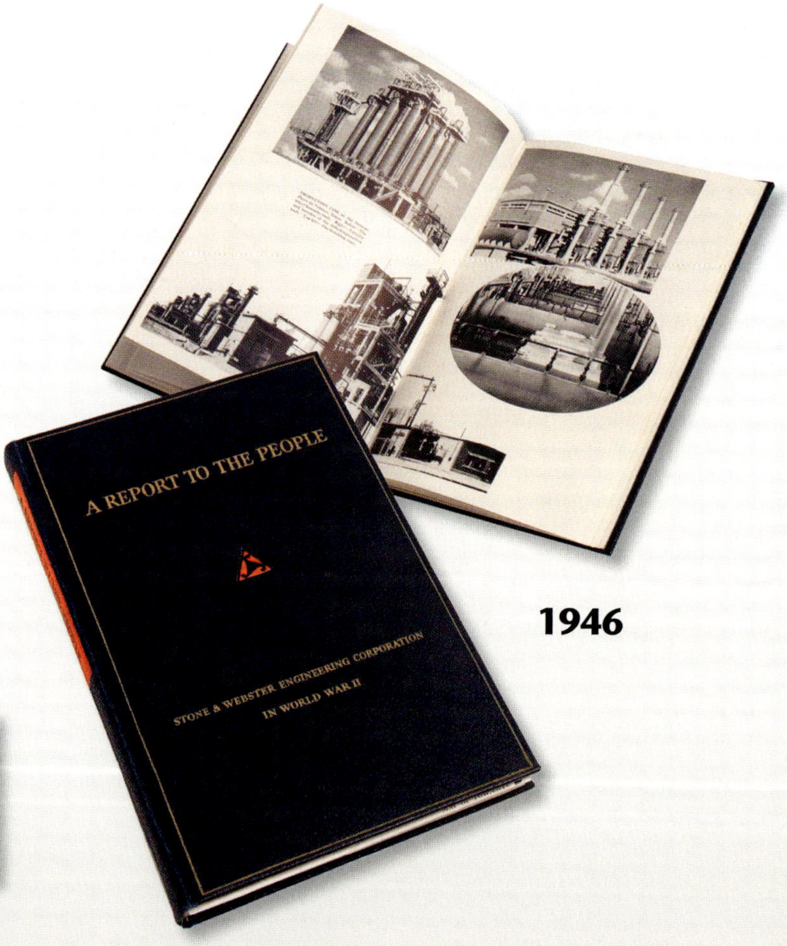

1946

WAR DEPARTMENT
P O BOX 2610
WASHINGTON D C

18 December 1945

Mr. R. T. Branch, President
Stone & Webster Engineering Co., Inc.
90 Broad Street
New York, N.Y.

Dear Mr. Branch:

This is our first Christmas at peace in five years. I wish to express my gratitude to you and through you to your employees and to your subcontractors and their employees.

The Manhattan Project played the vital part in the unexpected early ending of the war. By our united efforts victory was achieved much earlier than had been expected. Without our success many more American lives would have been lost in battle against the Japanese.

Cooperation by industry, labor, science, the Army and Navy and government as a whole was the true secret of our accomplishment. Only in America could so much have been achieved in so short a time. Only in America could there have been brought into action the intelligent cooperative efforts, of the tens of thousands, which were essential to the success of such a vast undertaking. Without American industry's unprecedented skill and efforts the Manhattan Project would not have succeeded.

Throughout the past three years I have made great demands on your company. No one outside the project can ever know how much we depended on you and the quality of your performance. Those of us who know will never forget.

To you, your subcontractors and all of your employees, a Merry Christmas and a Happy New Year.

Sincerely yours,

L R Groves

L. R. GROVES
Major General, USA

Sports and Friends

From the 1961
Carmel Valley newspaper.
I was 12.

"Cliff Branch, Pistons' first baseman, is shown hitting a first-inning home run. The Pistons went on to beat Hollister 10-1. The Pistons will travel to Greenfield for the multi-district championship."

Our team went on to win the championship – and it was the thrill of my young life. Another big thrill came only months later, courtesy of Pamela Gamble, a gorgeous teenage girl who lived a couple of miles down the road. She was much older – about 17. Her family picked me up once when I was hitchhiking and Pamela sat next to me in the car. She was the most beautiful girl I had ever seen. She talked to me, and when she looked into my eyes, she put a spell on me. I turned mute and all I could do was giggle. The next year, in 1962, Pamela was crowned Miss California – it was front page news and very exciting for Carmel Valley.

Pamela Gamble,
Miss California, in 1962.
She was 18.

Sports page photos from the Santa Barbara newspaper.

DP Varsity Tournament Champs. Dos Pueblos players make the all star team. Left to right: Paul Brydon, #41; Doug Hehnke (SS), Cliff Branch (1B), and Dennis Mangini (2B)

1998

1967

During my high school years, I don't think either one of my good friends Cheryl Higgen and Debbie (Alison) Windsor or other students came to baseball games. Football was the "glory sport," but I loved baseball and played in every league I could from ages 9 through 17.
Left: Cheryl and Debbie in 1967, and the three of us together about 30 years later.

Cliff and Tom at the Trout Farm in Tassajara Canyon, with dirt bikes, mid-'70s. At that time, Tom rode a Husqvarna and I rode a Yamaha 360. By 1974, Tom was driving a Porsche RSR race car, somehow "transformed" into a street legal vehicle – it was one of only 15 IROC cars built by Porsche that year. I was driving a Maserati Bora and a Ferrari. We had both developed an appetite for fast cars.

Men's Group: For several years during the mid-'80s, this motley crew met one night a week for a few hours to discuss our lives, books, movies and whatever else was on our minds. Bottom row (left to right): Mike Hartwell, Dr. Robert Simons, Steve Caminiti. Middle row: Steve Thayer, Cliff and Mark Johnson. Top row (left to right): John Spatafore, Buzz Hamlin, Dan Lloyd and Chuck Gorrill.

In the early '70s, Tom and I developed our first real estate project in the hills overlooking the SLO Country Club.

A, B and C are photos of my former residences, which were designed by Paul Smith.

D A typical Alta Mira view from one of the hot tubs

E The Avila Beach house on San Rafael Street

Commercial RE: See CalCoastCommercial.com

Scrapbook

Bassi Ranch
The 200-acre residential development is located in Avila Valley. The gated community consists of 25 homes with 100 acres of open space and 35 acres of vineyards.

Railroad Square
The former home of Warehouse Sound Company until the 1980s, when Jim Smith's law firm took over the building. Hamish Marshall beautifully restored the historic brick building after a fire gutted the structure in 2002.

California Cooperage
The original complex, located on Industrial Way, SLO, just a few blocks from The Graduate, a long-time local nightclub

Nels Hanson

Nels Hanson, a San Luis Obispo resident, is also an accomplished writer who has won multiple awards for his fiction. Nels also helped edit this book. I asked him if he had anything that might work in American Made. *He sent me the following excerpt from* Sleeping Child Lake, *a novel about Bill Ryder, a boomer in the late 1980s trying to find himself as he wanders the Pacific Northwest with an old friend, seeking a deep Montana lake sacred to generations of American Indians.*

Bill held the pickup steering wheel lightly as they drove east through the forest of redwoods and cedars. Looking at the passing ferns along the shoulder, he said to Tug, "This reminds me of Santa Cruz."

"Yeah," Tug said after a while. "It was a magical time."

The '60s, Bill thought. When everything was in tune – Woodstock, Flower Power, Make Love, Not War . . . .

But the Summer of Love had turned into a long winter and the Pepsi Generation had scattered, dropped their muskets sprouting daisies and dispersed – become lawyers, realtors, or car salesmen, taken up aerobics or cocaine, joined strange cults, found a pottery commune or a guru in Nepal.

Some even learned India's kundalini – bringing energy from their loins up the spine through the chakras past the heart to the head, opening the Third Eye for a better angle on a crazy world spinning through space.

Free spirits tried open marriage, or went into therapy to reenact the primal scream, or moved to Costa Rica to grow organic coffee.

Bill recalled an old story recounted by his surfer friends, who were driving their VW bus through Yucatan when they saw a puff of smoke up the hillside. A moment later the bus was divided perfectly in two. Bandits with sombreros and bandoleers and a little cannon on wheels rode down and robbed them to their underwear before disappearing into the jungle.

He glided the truck over a bridge in a shadowed curve and looked across the cab at Tug.

"In the '60s we knew what we wanted but we never found the road to the Emerald City," Bill said. "Our hearts were in the right place – maybe our heads were somewhere else. One day you wake up and realize what a long strange trip you're on."

– from *Sleeping Child Lake* by Nels Hanson

Photo and Art Credits

Vicki **and** ***Nels Hanson*** **are the primary editors of** ***American Made.***

Associated Press: Baez Summer of Love, 39; Martin Luther King Dream, 173, bottom right; American flag covered caskets, 175, C-RMBett, ©Bettmann/Corbis/AP Images, upper right; Muhammad Ali – 1971 press conference in London, ©Colorsport/Corbis, 175; Richard Nixon farewell, 177, top, right; Jim Hendrix, 177 bottom; Morrison Doors, 177 bottom; Janis Joplin performs, 177 bottom; Bush Mission Accomplished, ©J. Scott Applewhite, 294; Bush Lincoln, ©Denis Poroy, 294

Brian P. Lawler: 46, 200, 305 bottom, 331 top, middle

California Polytechnic State University, Kennedy Library Archives: 80, top, inset

CanStock Photos: Surface of sand csp3898736 ©Can Stock Photo Inc. /Paha_L, front and back covers background; Couple csp15357137 ©Can Stock Photo Inc./michaeljung 4; Blackboard csp0089291©Can Stock Photo Inc. /Carolina Smith, 10 background; Vintage photo frame csp4507108 ©Can Stock Photo Inc./robynmac, endpapers, 13,14, 60, 148; Vintage portrait csp0361274 ©Can Stock Photo Inc./sparkstudio, 14 bottom right; Joshua trees csp7139086 ©Can Stock Photo Inc./billperry, 17; Water in the beginning of the Grand Canyon csp4584993 ©Can Stock Photo Inc./tobkatrina, 21; Polaroid csp0404261 ©Can Stock Photo Inc./Peterfactors, 32; Golden trophies csp20143032 ©Can Stock Photo Inc./Peterfactors, 33 inset; Vintage flashlight csp1383788 ©Can Stock Photo Inc./RedDaxLuma, 35 bottom; Open book csp9741767 ©Can Stock Photo Inc./dvarg 50 background; Drums kit csp6412196 ©Can Stock Photo Inc./Nmorozova, 95 top; White Dice csp2479981 ©Can Stock Photo Inc./piai, 160 middle; Dock on a lake csp12477025 ©Can Stock Photo Inc./koi88, 188 background; Open bottle of beer csp6025872 ©Can Stock Photo Inc./galdzer, 188; Colorful peace signs csp440289 ©Can Stock Photo Inc./roxanabalint, 188; Web buttons set csp6605057 440289 ©Can Stock Photo Inc./PiLart; 192; Group csp5970848 ©Can Stock Photo Inc./mandygodbehear, 217; Coffee stains csp4964579 ©Can Stock Photo Inc./PicsFive, 269; Lens flare abstract csp9082783 ©Can Stock Photo Inc./Jalin, 272; Morro Bay Sunset csp17441016 ©Can Stock Photo Inc./aijohn784, 320-321; Daisy csp2895623 ©Can Stock Photo Inc./realrocking, 377 middle

Corbis: The Lone Ranger and Tonto, supervised by Silver, ©Bettmann/CORBIS, 160 left; The cast of *Father Knows Best,* ©Bettmann/CORBIS, 160 middle-left; John F. Kennedy in a U.S. Navy PT boat, ©CORBIS, 164 top left; Family sitting in model fallout shelter, ©Bettmann/CORBIS, 166 middle left; President Kennedy confers with brother Robert F. Kennedy, ©Bettmann/CORBIS, 173 middle left; Kennedys riding in Dallas motorcade, ©Bettmann/CORBIS, 174, top; King balcony, ©AP/CORBIS, 174, left middle; Peaceful protests during the Vietman War, ©Bob Adelman/ Corbis, 175 right middle; Walter Cronkite broadcasting, ©Bettmann/CORBIS, 175 bottom; John Sebastian-Woodstock-August 15, 1969, ©Jenry Diltz/Corbis, 176 top

Liz Scott Graham **was a co-producer and strong supporter helping to raise funds to produce the documentary** ***Botso – The Teacher from Tbilisi.*** **The inspirational film was produced over an eight-year period, has garnered awards from several film festivals and is due for national release in 2015. Proceeds of ticket sales go to support the San Luis Obispo Youth Symphony. To obtain a DVD, go to: Botsomovie.com**

***Terry J. San Filippo* and *Tyler Jenkins* are responsible for image acquisition, production and editing.**

Crown & Sceptre Yearbook: 64

David E. Garth: Copyright and Acknowldgements

Depositphotos: Wall Street ©Depositphotos.com/Ignacio Gonzalez Prado, 250

Dreamstime: Big Sur 20544030 ©Jeff Halback, 44 background; Redwood forest hiking path 1267567 ©Richard J. Thompson, 44 left inset; Waterfall 133093 ©Jenny Solomon, 44 right inset; Sand dollar 2762453 ©Photoboykane, 298

El Padre Yearbook: 293

Forrest L. Doud: Author, glasses, background, 2; Bubbles, 25-27; Golf balls, 34 background; Pebble Beach Golf Course, 34, inset; Sand and shovels, 40, background; Sandals and hat, 42 inset; Hippie beads, 43; Grand Central Station, 56; Broken glass, 60 background; Coins, 70; San Luis Obispo/Cal Poly, 78-79; California Cooperage buckle, 109; California Cooperage ad, 111; California Cooperage catalogs, 112; *All-American Cocaine Story*, 117; California Cooperage/Coleman, 124; Avila Bay Athletic Club, 136 top; Images of America, Avila Beach, 137 bottom; Professional office building, 140 bottom; Tape measure, 190; Video kids, 238; Sail, 308-309; American flag pin, 317; Row crops, 318-319; CES badges, 343; A *Fine Romance*, 344; *Autumn*, 345; Susan Branch *2014 Heart of the Home Calendar*, 345; TwoVoters.com, 352; Dick's helicopter, 354; Lucy, 354 inset; *A Report to the People*, 366; Aerials A, B, C, E, 370; Developments and businesses, left, aerial, middle, bottom, 371; Production staff, left, middle, 378; Production staff, top, bottom, 379; South San Luis Obispo County agriculture, 381; San Luis Obispo's Edna Valley, 382-383; Roldan family, 382; San Luis Obispo downtown, 384-385; Jim Agee, 384; Avila Beach Golf Course, pages 386-387; Avila Beach, 386; Lynette Branch, 386; Bikers on Bob Jones Trail, 386; Los Osos Valley seed farm, 388-389; Morro Bay Estuary, 390-391; Bikers, 391; Scenic Highway One, 392-393; Production staff, 392 inset; Hang gliding, 394; Kayakers, 394; Elephant seals, 394; Hearst Castle, 395

Gary Crabbe, Enlightened Images Photography: 359

Gene Francis: Front cover; Endpapers front; Title page; Palm Street, Contents; Kookie, 162; Homeward Bound, 162; Perfectionist, 163; The Chase, 163; GI Joe, 165; Ranger Neutron, 166; John's salute, 169; Big Show, 172; Supremes, 172; Elvis, 172; Robert Kennedy, 174; Beatles 1963, Beatles 1969, 176; Kent State, 177; AdMan, 179; Murdoch, bin Talal, Ailes, 275; O'Reilly, Limbaugh, Hannity, Rove, Beck, Coulter, Palin, Jones, Savage, Varney, Kudlow, Santelli, 276; Saigon air lift, 288; U.S. helicopters, 288; Young soldiers, 288; Endpapers, back; Back cover; Visit Gene's Gallery at genefrancis.net

Getty Images: *Perry Mason*, CBS Photo Archive, 160; *Superman*, Hulton Archive, 160; Cast from TV's *Leave It to Beaver*, R. Gates, 161; Silhouetted figures of workers watching thermonuclear, Los Alamos National Laboratory, 166;

***Forrest Doud* has spent many years covering the West Coast swing of the PGA Tour and has been taking photos professionally for the past 30 years. It's always been a pleasure to work with Forrest. Some months ago, I asked if he would shoot many of the local photographs seen throughout the book – including all of the shots seen in these last pages.**
ForrestDoud.com

Photo and Art Credits, continued

Bio-Mandela-France, AFP. 174, 301; Assault weapons with American flag, Karen Bleier/AFP/Getty Images, 244

Greg Gorman: Jessica Lange, Sally Field, Barbra Streisand, Goldie Hawn and Jane Fonda, 197

Joe Hall: 131, 345, 346, left and right, 347

HistoricImages: 368, upper right

iStock Photos: Running through pounding rain 3525363 ©Christine Glade, 36; Carmel meadow 16455808 ©BehindTheLense, 37, background; Jail cell at Alcatraz, 1912098 ©Jultae, 63; Fishing boats at the Monterey Bay 23189824 ©PacoRomero, 73; Old paper 22474788 ©Zocha_K, 129 background; Galveston beach 1046266 ©DHuss, 150; Urban teenagers 2439379 ©Izabela Habur, 192; Cost of healthcare 26005723 ©Maudib, 226; Latin church fathers 32483532 ©KenWiedemann, 232; Road through forest 12246438 ©vicm, 376-377

Las Pilitas Nursery: Lupins 8, 9 background

Los Altos Historical Museum: 14, bottom, 15, top

Luke Patrick Dempsey: 361

MPTVImages.com and Mark Shaw: Jacqueline and John F. Kennedy at Hyannis Port 1959, 164 top right

Mary Richards Luch: 74

NASA: 173

Nels Hanson: Excerpt from *Sleeping Child Lake*, 377

PARS International Corp.: *Time* magazine: "High on Cocaine," July 6, 1981, and "Fighting Cocaine's Grip," July 11, 1983, used by permission, 116, 119

Stefan Möding: California Highway 1 ©1996-2014, 9

Santa Barbara News-Press: 71

Shutterstock: Entering Carmel Valley sign 135623204 ©American Spirit, 37 inset; California coast at Big Sur 62918335 ©Jeremy Pettitt 42; One vintage tin camping mug 18076810 ©RoJo Images, 45; Highway sign 168076810 ©andrzej80, 28 inset; Avila Beach 185481254 ©Juancat, 130; Nice doctor with stethoscope 73307038 ©Rusian Guzov, 167; Different colored medicine 200982113 ©blackboard1965, 167; Classic car 1184558 ©Peter Clark, 171; Birth control pills 11026174 ©Jacob Kearns, 172 top; Coquette beauty 128665691 ©Accord, 180; Primary school teacher helping student in computer room 147597581 ©michaeljung, 220; Future, technology and people concept 211125667 ©Syda Productions, 223; Close-up blue smart watch 170488085 ©Alexey Boidin, 223; Man wearing glasses 225447976 ©Stefano Tintim, 223; Young man sitting at desk working 159888116 ©Andrey_Popov, 224; Two female researchers 88343182 ©lightpoet, 224; Kids using modern tablet computers lying on the floor 131428508 ©Ilike, 225; Parents holding baby feet 114431803 ©Zurijeta, 227; View of the healthcare.gov website in Caldwell, Idaho 166171757 ©txking, 228; Prescription medication 9098254 ©Rob Byron, 229; Happy mother with newborn baby 58142125 ©Mikhail Tchkheidze, 231; Seamless pattern with rockets, 148752635 ©tapilipa, 238-239 background; The Hollywood bowl amphitheater ID 89718916 ©Palette7, 243; Nightmare on Wall Street 24509713 ©justasc, 254; Cracked cement symbolizing broken trust between people or parties 214799962 ©Lane V. Erickson, 266; United States Capitol building for Congress with American flag flowing in breeze and columns in background 126373181©Lane V. Erickson, 281; Hands manipulate the radio-control for toy ID: 221567866 ©Bombaert Patrick, 340; Flying drone in the sky 130188164 ©Robert Mandel, page 340

The San Luis Obispo County Tribune: 306 middle, 307 middle

Sports Car Racing Association of the Monterey Peninsula: 48 inset

The Carmel Valley *Outlook*: 32

The C.J.J.S. Cormorant Yearbook: 52 top, bottom left, right

The C.J.J.S. Cormorant Yearbook: 40, 53 inset

The Image Yearbook: 68

The Image Yearbook: 65, 67

The Sunset Cypress Yearbook: 50, 51

Other Sources: California Cooperage; Ergo Computing, Inc.; Capitol Records; Super Sonic; Warehouse Sound Company; Vetter Corporation

Right: South San Luis Obispo County farming operation. A portion of the Pismo Beach sand dunes can be seen in the background, looking toward the Pacific Ocean.

Sarah Roldan *and her children Kai, Nakoa, Maile, and Leiloa admire the fruit at the Thursday evening downtown San Luis Obispo Farmers' Market. Held year 'round, the market is a draw for area residents and thousands of visitors to buy locally grown produce, nuts and flowers. Music, barbecue and fun abound.*

San Luis Obispo

Jim Agee – a good friend who patiently critiqued my rough drafts – is standing proud with his 1963 Corvette in front of the Fremont movie theater in downtown San Luis Obispo.

Morro Bay
Highway 1
Cal Poly
Highway 1
California Blvd.
Johnson Avenue
San Luis Obispo

Lynette Branch, playing on the Avila Beach golf course.

Avila Beach

Los Osos Valley

Morro Bay Estuary

Ashala Lawler was responsible for the graphic design of American Made. She and her husband, Brian, are involved with the San Luis Obispo Children's Museum, a remarkable facility that enables children and their families to explore, discover and learn through hands-on exhibits and programs.

Scenic Highway One

Hearst Castle

078001
The End
078001